Deleuze an

Aura of Expressionism

Gillian Howie
Lecturer in Philosophy
University of Liverpool

palgrave

First published 2002 by
PALGRAVE
Houndmills, Basingstoke, Hampshire RG21 6XS and
175 Fifth Avenue, New York, N.Y. 10010
Companies and representatives throughout the world.

PALGRAVE is the new global academic imprint of St Martin's Press LLC Scholarly and Reference Division and Palgrave Publishers Ltd (formerly Macmillan Press Ltd).

ISBN 0–333–63467–5

This book is printed on paper suitable for recycling and made from fully managed and sustained forest sources.

A catalogue record for this book is available from the British Library.

Library of Congress Cataloging-in-Publication Data

Howie, Gillian
Deleuze and Spinoza: aura of expressionism / Gillian Howie.
p. cm.
Includes bibliographical references and index.
ISBN 0–333–63467–5 (cloth)
1. Deleuze, Gilles. 2. Spinoza, Benedictus de, 1632–1677. 3. Expressionism. I. Title.

B2430.D454 H69 2002
194–dc21

2001058214

10 9 8 7 6 5 4 3 2 1
11 10 09 08 07 06 05 04 03 02

Printed and bound in Great Britain by
Antony Rowe Ltd. Chippenham, Wiltshire

For my Mother and Father.
Sadly missed.

Contents

Preface

I first encountered the work of Deleuze as a graduate student when I became interested in Foucault and the social definition of madness. This current work is of long gestation and expresses a number of the ideas that I began to formulate then in response to the emancipatory aspirations of The Anti-Oedipus. Although this is a critical study, the arguments are not *ad hominem*, and I do not attempt to discredit Deleuze merely by pointing out the origins of his philosophical speculations. But still it will please neither 'ironists' nor those who are fellow travellers with Deleuze, and self-defining Anglo-American philosophers will be disinterested in the arguments outlined. I hope, at least, to have added, to a philosophical armoury, ideas and arguments that can be marshalled against certain strands of (poststructuralist) postmodernism; which is indeed, I believe, merely the philosophical logic of modernity.

I would like to thank and acknowledge a number of people who have helped me in a variety of ways. Without the inspirational teaching and professionalism of Michael Webb and Cyril Skuse I would not have embarked on this particular journey. I am indebted to Susan James for her kind and patient supervision, as well as to Howard Robinson and Gyögy Gereby for their constructive and thoughtful comments at various stages of this manuscript. I would like to thank Drew Milne for introducing me to Adorno many years ago, Ashley Tauchert for her continual humour and good sense, the graduate students at Liverpool Philosophy Department, whose lively interest in Critical Theory kept my spirits high, and Simon Hughes for his support through these difficult few years.

GILLIAN HOWIE
Liverpool

Introduction

Rather disingenuously, Alex Callinicos once remarked that his only excuse for producing another work on postmodernism was a sense of personal satisfaction gained from alleviating, however temporally, the irritation he felt when confronted by the hubris and obsfucation of certain postmodern texts. More earnestly, but along the same lines, Christopher Norris introduced *The Truth about Postmodernism*, noting that large sections of the erstwhile left or left-liberal intelligentsia had been won over to consensus-based doctrines of meaning and truth that left them unable to articulate any kind of reasoned or principled opposition. Although the melancholic period of Thatcherism, the context for the above works, has since been superseded by Tony Blair's new times, and Anthony Giddens' third way, their language of change and modernisation might be considered to be a sanitised version of the familiar obfuscating pragmatism. As a prolegomena towards a critique of the discourse of globalisation, social exclusion and identity politics, this present work is a commentary on such obfuscation, the process of concealment common both to 'modernisers' and postmodernists. It is in effect a commentary on ideology.

In 1996, Alan Sokal created a stir in intellectual circles, consternation in some and amusement in others, when he published a hoax article in the journal *Social Text* parodying the style of postmodernism. He followed 'Transgressing the Boundries: Towards a Transformative Hermeneutics of Quantum Gravity' with 'a Physicist Experiments with Cultural Studies' in which he offered an explanation and justification for the earlier hoax. Meditating on their motives, the author, later

---

Note: in this volume, the work to which the page numbers in brackets refer is *Expressionism in Philosophy: Spinoza* (G. Deleuze, first published 1968).

writing with Jean Bricmont in *Intellectual Impostures*, confessed to feeling suspicious of a thoroughly fake intellectualism that has percolated down through significant postmodern texts to key intellectual constituencies. The hoax article consists of a series of quotations taken from works by Deleuze, Guattari, Derrida, Irigaray, Lacan, Latour, Lyotard, Serres and Virilo. On examining these influential works Bricmont and Sokal conclude that authors often speak with a self-assurance about science that far outstrips their competence. They conjecture that scientific language is now being used in cultural or literary fields of enquiry in order to exploit the prestige of natural sciences and to thereby seal a veneer, or suggest a hinterland of rigour or robust argument. No one, say Sokal and Bricmont, is prepared to call out that this particular emperor is naked.

The use, or rather the abuse, of scientific theories they discover, is accompanied by a more or less explicit rejection of the Enlightenment tradition, of discourses connected to any empirical test, and an extensive cognitive and cultural relativism that 'regards science as nothing more than a "narration" or a "myth"'.[1] Sokal and Bricmont find a peculiar mélange of intellectual positions where eulogies to materialism coexist with a general rejection of any concept, epistemological or metaphysical, relating to the mind-independent nature of the external world. One consistent belief, lending the appearance of cohesion to these disparate theories, is the belief in the break up of the principle of individuation tending to supervene on a more primary belief in a 'realm of material forces'.[2]

The very name of the continental philosopher Gilles Deleuze is often considered to be the credible and authoritative mark of this 'new' materialism, and, more importantly, a new (postmodern) ethics and perspectivism that is supposed to circumvent problems of transcendence associated with realism in ethics and epistemology. Rather than expounding a theory of critical realism, I have chosen to take one work by Deleuze and to explore the moments of dissonance between the appearance of the work and its essential systematic argument; the rift between the manifest argument and the latent inferential pattern, which forces the reader to reach conclusions quite distinct from those glittering through the text. It is in the gaps and silences, the premature closures and the question-begging moves where, I contend, we can detect the 'unthought' of Deleuze's thought. Once this 'unthought' is made manifest, the ideological logic of the (post) modern becomes obvious. The ensuing reading attempts to illuminate this logic found in one text as well as to indicate why there might be problems with

Deleuze's later work, and thus indebted postmodern philosophies, depending upon the system as elaborated here.

Deleuze has surely had one of the most profound effects on the cohort of 'continental' academics working within the geographic shores of the Anglo-Australian and Anglo-American tradition and no other philosopher, apart from Heidegger perhaps, would be so disparagingly classified as 'continental' by 'analytic' philosophers. Yet plaudits range from Foucault's description of this century as Deleuzian, to the claims that he has been the most consistently read and important philosopher since the sixties, with a stature in Paris equal to that of Foucault and Derrida[3] and the most tenacious thinker of otherness in contemporary philosophy.[4] Others describe him as the poet-laureate of immanence,[5] applaud his erudition and describe his writing on mathematics as 'the intense manifestation of a sovereign mind'.[6]

Deleuze was born in 1925 and attended the Lycée Carnot in Paris. He studied philosophy at the Sorbonne between 1944 and 1948 where he mixed with such as Michel Butor, Michel Tournier and François Châtelet. The principal pedagogic influences were Ferdinand Aliquié, a Descartes specialist and surrealist, Jean Hyppolite, the Hegel specialist and Georges Canguilhem. After his agrégation in 1948, he taught philosophy at a number of Lycées and from 1957 until 1960 he taught at the Sorbonne. He worked with the Centre National de Recherche Scientifique (CNRS) for four years and, after a period of five years at the University of Lyons, he was appointed a professor at Vincennes.[7]

Structuralist, poststructuralist and deconstructionist philosophy, specifically in postwar France, is only one aspect of, undoubtedly rich and fruitful in its contribution to, continental philosophy. Deleuze tends to be associated with poststructuralist postmodernism but his first publications were fairly traditional studies within the history of philosophy and his later work clearly demonstrates the influence of Austro-Hungarian philosophy, specifically Brentano, Meinong and Frege. More surprising than his sustained enquiry into the intentional object is his philosophical interest in the ideas of limit, series, function and calculus. *Spinoza et le problème de l'expression* was presented by Deleuze in 1967 as his minor doctoral thesis, the major thesis being *Différence et Répétition* and by then he had already completed studies on Hume (1953), Nietzsche (1962), Kant (1963) and Bergson (1966). *Différence and Répétition* was published, alongside *Logique du sens* in 1969. The dates are compelling. The historical works preceded the events of 1968 and others, such as the most famous *Anti-Oedipus*

(1972) and *Mille Plateaux* (1980) co-authored with Guattari, were published in a post-68 world.

Over simplifying matters, Foucault observed that in postwar France there were two traditions: a philosophy of sense experience and the subject and a philosophy of knowledge, rationality and the concept.[8] Sartre, he claimed, was the spokesperson of the former and Canguilhem of the latter. The philosopher of science, Canguilhem, passed his agrégation in philosophy alongside Aron, Nizan and Sartre at the Ecole Normale Supérieure. By the time he succeeded his former teacher Bachelard in the chair of philosophy at the Sorbonne in 1955, he had sharpened his method of historical analysis, initially apparent in his doctoral thesis on norms and the normal. As Foucault's supervisor he was obviously enormously influential but was neither a cultural nor an epistemic relativist. Following Bachelard's project, he distinguished between 'scientific ideologies' that may provide the foundation for a future advance and 'scientific concepts' which can be distinguished from common sense or intuitive knowledge but which can come to play a role in different, sometimes incommensurable theories. One purpose of his investigation was to avoid the sorts of confusions evident when concepts are taken out of context. This is not to concur with Foucault's description of Canguilhem's scientific method as a history of discontinuity but does explain why and how his historical approach may have influenced the young Foucault and, indeed, Deleuze.

From 1945, critiques of the modern world and the values of liberal democracy dominated French intellectual life. The works of Heidegger and Marx were central to these critiques. Heidegger and Marx were not such an odd-couple: Marx offered an analysis of bourgeois idealism and Heidegger assessed and explored the effects of the 'technical' world. 'In contemporary humanism, neo-Marxism, from Althusser to Bourdieu', write Ferry and Renaut, 'modern humanism was simply assimilated to bourgeois ideology'.[9] The collapse of Marxism as a political force within France has been much documented, but during this rather protracted 'death' the odd-couple became one, and Heidegger the single beneficiary of a space previously filled by Marxism.

Heidegger was adopted and used to criticise the totalitarianism of the East and to offer a critique of bureaucratic, repressive disciplinary consumerist society of the West. Indeed, Foucault's work on the normalising effects of Cartesian reason cannot be understood except in relation to Heidegger's history of being.[10] Although Deleuze's *oeuvre* has been understood as a move away from the three H's (Hegel, Husserl and

Heidegger), a critique of being and the concept of the subject in the name of a radical anti-humanism runs through.[11] In an interesting twist, modernism and humanism have become identified and associated with arrogance and (masculine) self-assurance. The argument runs that this self-confidence and, indeed, social or political power is secured by an epistemology central to which is the belief in neutral processes of justification that can be regulated by rigorous scientific method and directed, with penetrating insight, towards malleable and knowable nature. The classical episteme, of rationality, autonomy and representation, has thus been linked with the discursive practices of modernity and, specifically, Enlightenment philosophy as the philosophical discourse of modernity. But herein is the twist. This critique of modernity is carried out under a political banner, for the oppressed, the marginalised, the disciplined, but, due to its critique of representation and realism, is structurally incapable of taking up, except insincerely and seemingly in spite of itself, the promises that are also those of modernity.[12] Subsequently, the 'ends of man' debate became the critique of the subject which, in turn, has become a form of anti-humanism. But let us note, it is an anti-humanism which is at one with an extreme and 'virile' form of political individualism – the individual is to be freed from social constraints in order to discover his or her own *daimon*.

Before commencing his analysis of Heidegger, Bernstein writes that: 'the basic condition for all understanding requires one to test and risk one's convictions and pre-judgments in and through the encounter with what is radically 'other' and alien. To do this requires imagination and hermeneutical sensitivity in order to understand the 'other' in the strongest possible light. Critically engaged dialogue requires opening oneself to what the 'other' is saying. Such an opening does not entail agreement but rather the to-and-fro play of dialogue. Otherwise dialogue degenerates into a self-deceptive monologue'.[13] Bernstein thus raises the point that interpretation, analysis and commentary require the reader to recognise the 'other', be it text or author, in order to hear what is being said. With a different emphasis, although perhaps on the same intellectual terrain, Rorty argues that according to the ironist, the names of authors and philosophers stand not for anonymous channels of truth but as abbreviations for a certain final vocabulary, beliefs and desires typical of its users. The instrumental purpose of reading then becomes evident for Rorty as he declares that: 'What we want to know is whether to adopt those images – to re-create ourselves in these people's image. ... We ironists hope that, by this continual redescription, to make the best selves for ourselves that we can'.[14]

Deleuze's *Expressionism in Philosophy*, and his book of definitions, *Spinoza*: *Practical Philosophy*, are works on the history of philosophy but they are not mere exegesis. Undeterred by the niceties, or hermeneutical integrity, outlined by Bernstein, but certainly succumbing to the dangers of self-deceptive monologue, Deleuze's authorial voice appropriates or colonises that of Spinoza. We are presented not merely an expository work on Spinoza but Deleuze's assertion of a philosophical system:

> My way of getting out of it (the tradition) ... was, I really think, to conceive of the history of philosophy as a kind of buggery or, what comes to the same thing, immaculate conception. I imagined myself getting onto the back of an author, and giving him a child, which would be his and which would at the same time be a monster. It is very important that it should be his child because the author actually had to say everything that I made him say. But it also had to be a monster because it was necessary to go through all kinds of decenterings, slips, break-ins, secret emissions, which I really enjoyed.[15]

Expressionism is indeed an elaboration of a system. Although echoing Nietzsche's distaste for systems and systematisers, specifically Hegel and the dialectical method, Deleuze was inspired by Spinoza's rationalist system and uses it to develop an alternative to the Hegelian–Marxist philosophical enterprise.[16] Understanding *Expressionism* as the elaboration of a (rationalist) system is to take a position against the ironist or pragmatist interpretation of Deleuze's work. I contend that the concepts and ideas developed by Deleuze cannot be 'euphemised', they do not constitute a 'toolbox' – a reading encouraged by Deleuze – but gain their meaning in context. In order to make sense of the context, this work explores the arguments posed by Deleuze – and he not only poses various arguments but also addresses quite obscure scholastic points. Most importantly, though, I examine his arguments to see why it is that his conclusions lead to political consequences at odds with the political commitments manifested in this and later texts. I have approached the text, I hope, with Bernstein's recommendations as practical ideals. Because I have a certain faith in Deleuze's own philosophical integrity in places I have attempted to reconstruct his arguments. However, I also use this book to show a number of key philosophical problems with a project such as this: inconsistent claims regarding representation and behaviour, a tendency towards the elimination of mind at odds with the ethical theory and contradictory arguments concerning identity.

Of all his writings, I chose *Expressionism* for three main reasons. It is the key with which to unlock later works that are more explicitly concerned with ethics: the ethical implications of the 'new science' – a 'reworking and extension of the Nietzschean terrain'.[17] Secondly, the system provides the metaphysical backdrop for anti-dialectical arguments. Spinoza's thought–extension parallelism is considered as an alternative to subject–object dialectical interaction. Deleuze's search for an alternative to dialectics is partly motivated by his 'distaste' for the 'labour of the negative' and by examining his assessment of Spinoza's concept of substance we can give some content to these various claims relating to negation and affirmation, specifically in relation to the determination of finite things. Finally, it is with the description of the finite modifications of substance that we arrive at Deleuze's much vaunted notion of singularity – a re-elaboration of the philosophical study of Bergson.[18] Central to his project of 'difference' is the thought of the singularity. In this study we will note how Spinoza's modes are presented as singularities and that these singularities, which are material points of force, might be open to a mathematical translation as points in a series. Such willingness to translate modes into singularities and singularities into mathematical points lends credence to the idea that Deleuze occupies a place as a philosopher of modernity, taken in by the glamour of scientific explanation and the will to express the 'irrational' in pseudo-mathematical terms.[19]

It is this proclivity that is grist to the argument that the cleft between English- and French-speaking traditions of philosophy is more of image or style than substance. Not only do continental and Anglo-American philosophy have a common heritage but the philosophers also tend to orbit the same sorts of problems, in similar ways. Nowhere is the intricate weaving of ideas and origins of the two traditions more apparent than in the Austro-Hungarian roots of twentieth-century philosophy. The pivotal role of mathematics in postnaturalist thought can be seen both in the philosophical problems arising within the discipline and in the rejection of the naturalist conviction that scientific reasoning was based on experiential induction or observation. This 'arithmetisation of analysis', the definition of real numbers in terms of rational numbers, was a culmination of a movement that had begun with Cauchy early in the nineteenth century.[20] One of the aims, giving coherence to the movement, was the attempt to establish rigorous definitions of 'function', 'continuity' and 'limit'.[21]

The continental roots of analytic philosophy might be surprising to those who, following Ryle, consider there to be a distinction of species if not genera. Ryle is reported to have distinguished between the two by appropriating to the description of analytic philosophy logical studies which had on the continent 'unfortunately been left unfathered by most philosophy departments and cared for, if at all, only in a few departments'. Glendenning, commenting on this, raises the salient point, made by Russell and Wittgenstein's biographer Monk, that Russell 'actually learnt his logic from an Italian (Peano) and a whole lot of Germans (Cantor, Weierstrass, Dedekind and Frege)'.[22] Dummett notes that the root of both branches of philosohical analysis is Frege, although we can also add Lotze and Brentano.[23]

Norris argues that continental and analytic philosophers of science share an intellectual heritage and that there is coherence to the types of questions and problems addressed.[24] Although naïve realism is eschewed by most philosophers of science those typically called 'continental' have tended to focus on the historical situatedness of discourse and hypothesis formation, whereas those typically described as 'analytic' had concerned themselves with the logic of propositions and justification. This analysis of philosophical divergence is given some support by Mitchell who quotes, without full endorsement, Barnes: 'The English vice is to covet truth while ignoring history; the French vice is to be content with the past whilst forgetting philosophy'.[25] The analytic quasi-Kantian approach seemed to offer a critical standpoint outside the vagaries of figurative language. Subsequently however in post-Logical Positivist analytic philosophy referential theories of meaning and justification have largely been replaced by coherence theories of truth and justification and the processes of interpretation have been given quite a central rôle. Once the interpretative character of judgement is highlighted, questions relating to the causal process of belief acquisition and conditions of assertion came to the fore. In addition to this, by acknowledging the role of interpretation in the analysis of the success, or otherwise, of scientific hypotheses the relevance of the history of scientific enquiry became undeniable.

Abstract thought, presented in logical or mathematical notation, in analytic or some examples of continental philosophy, runs the risk of reifying and inverting the world of social experience. Sokal and Bricmont themselves were actually worried more by the grand claims made as to the social implications of mathematics and the natural sciences, a trait more discerned in continental than analytic philosophy, than the fact that many of the quotations were meaningless or erroneous. The reification of the subject of 'intensity', its fetishisation in such guises as 'singularity', singular (mathematical) points or *daimon* is no accident. It is a response to a particular social condition. The fetish of relations, emotions and responses perpetuates the myth of an abstract and free individual, struggling to find his or her singular destiny. This myth fairly grooves along in the rut of (post)modern bourgeois society. The cult of subjectivity, the continual self-referential critique of desire, of identity, of 'the subject', is a direct response to its eclipse.[26] The more authentic human experience and relationships disappear the more they are invoked – for exactly that reason. The post-modern, new ageist thirst for satisfaction, for the experience of uncoded or unlimited intensity; indeed, for fulfilment, is quenched on the philosophy of Gaia, of univocal Being, the One, the whole. It is a draught of sunny delight, a touch of the divine. And who could object? As Stephen Clark once wrote:

> In actual fact, philosophers as we now are *are* mostly, indeed, rhetoricians, and need extensive retraining if we wish to acquire an expertise in language, psychology, biology or physics. The old tutorial system was generally designed to teach the skills of rhetoric and plausible repartee. The new seminar system teaches, or purports to teach, committee skills – or else the art of bluffing and convenient silence.[27]

1
God

Commenting on the history of philosophy, Bertrand Russell wrote that it is a disappointing fact that after initiating modern philosophy with Descartes, and continuing with Malbranche, philosophy in France became content to imitate what had been begun elsewhere. The philosophical development in France before the Revolution, he claimed, was an outcome of Locke and Newton and afterwards was premised on idealism imported from Germany.[1] Following this trend, post '68 French philosophy leant heavily on German. philosophy and tended to identify the philosophical concept of the subject with a concept of the subject found in (rationalist) German philosophy, specifically Enlightenment philosophy. The Kantian concepts of subjectivity and justified belief were considered to underpin philosophically a more general discourse that was linked to the social or political processes of liberal modernity. Thus through a number of quite complicated philosophical moves humanism, defined in terms of the Cartesian–Kantian conception of subjectivity, was cleaved to modernity.

Anti-humanism, which originated in part from a climate of resistance to the processes of modernity, took on the challenge to deliver at least philosophical discourse from the enclave of modernist Cartesian and specifically Kantian subjectivity and, incidentally, German Romanticism was ploughed to unearth alternative philosophies. This was in the hope that such philosophical or theoretical labour would go some way in undercutting the authority of the discursive practices connected to the processes of colonisation, expansionism and global industrialisation. Due to the connection assumed between topics of truth, power and ethics, where deliverance was sought it was found in philosophical systems that offered an alternative vision of the connection. Preferably these systems would also provide solutions to the problems of representation, identity, will and consciousness.

Thus we find that at the same time as Deleuze published *Expressionism in Philosophy*, Guéroult published *God* and Matheron his *Individu et Communauté chez Spinoza*. The timing of these publications indicates a remarkable resurgence of interest in Spinoza at a specific historical point. Macherey suggests that all three insisted on Spinoza's anti-Cartesianism, making of him a radical critic of the illusions of subjectivity and consciousness and that, more importantly, the authors found within Spinoza's system a way to unite the concepts of power and necessity to counteract the teleological nature of humanism.[2]

However, as often with such cases, one loses the baby with the bathwater and we can observe that what appears to be a radical gesture in fact concedes the very principles at stake. We find Heidegger writing that: 'The essence of philosophy resides in this: that the free Extension takes serenity into itself and assimilates it. ... To arrive at serenity is to detach oneself from representative thought with a transcendental structure and to renounce the will brought back from the horizon'.[3] Such a derelict concept of the subject, one of an indifferent self with a failing will, is not uncommon in anti-humanism or post-Cartesian philosophy. The accommodation of the subject to its condition is a theme that Heidegger shares not only with Spinoza but also with the Stoics. If Macherey is pointing us in the right direction then it is less surprising to find these echoes of ancient philosophy and Stoic themes also present in *Expressionism*. Stoical influences prevail not only in the ethical naturalism of the later part of Deleuze's work but are also apparent in the natural theology of the first part. By natural theology we mean something quite specific. Aristotle had argued that if immaterial substances do not exist then philosophy is just physics. Although no doubt intended as *reductio ad absurdum*, the argument suggests that any belief in the non-existence of immaterial substances would entail the identification of theology with physics. The Stoics, having rejected substance dualism, were quite happy to endorse this conclusion and argued that a genuine theology is indeed part of physics.[4] I will be arguing that there is a fairly straightforward connection between Deleuze's take on natural theology and his ethical theory which demands of the finite subject that he or she must accommodate him or herself to the laws of their condition.

If European philosophy is the history of metaphysics or Platonism, as Heidegger would have it, then *Expressionism* can be read as an attempt to unveil a counter-tradition. In the boiling pot of philosophies in the work, Stoic materialism angles for space with neo-Platonic Plotinian philosophy. This is particularly curious as Plotinus viewed the rather forsaken third-century Stoic materialism as the one serious adversarial philosophical position. The principal point of contention for Plotinus concerned the Stoic concept of *archē*. In ordinary or pre-classical Greek, *archē* signified a beginning or starting point, the principle of ordering. This meaning was later extended because as *archē* was identified with the governing principle of the world it then also explained why the world was so ordered. Because the principle, as explanation for the arrangement, was identified with the principle, as cause of arrangement, it could be said that logic was collapsed with causes. The definition of God as both a simple and necessary existent in need of no further explanation lent itself to a Stoic interpretation. The materialist Stoics tended to identify God with the active principle of the organic continuum.

The most distinctive and implausible feature of Stoic natural theology is the attribution of reason to immanent material *archē* of the universe. The criticism featured most prominently by Plotinus concerns the identification of being with matter and thus this kind of conceptualisation of *archē*. In Stoicism the organising principle is depicted as God, soul, fire or *pneuma* and all physical events including the continuous stability of bodies through time are explained by the *logos* operating through the dynamic character of *pneuma*.[5] According to Plotinus, this identification of intellect or reason with matter is a major flaw in the argument. Indeed he goes further and also rejects the description of divine rationality as that which functions to match means and ends. This it would seem places Deleuze in an awkward position. Elsewhere, Deleuze, along with Guattari, comments approvingly on the Stoic insight into the *spermatikos logos* or generative principle, the immanent principle of cosmic organisation.[6] Such positive commentary tends to suggest that Deleuze believes Spinoza is able to offer a way to think about reasons and causes, first principles and immanent principles or laws of organisation, that would satisfy even the Plotinian reader. Conversely, the Stoic philosophical themes must be thrown into the boiling pot for some reason. I suggest that they are leant on to give (undue) weight to the linguistic theory and later to the particular form of ethical naturalism Deleuze finds inspiring.

Deleuze's insistence on systematic enquiry into being explains why his natural theology occupies a curious position between the Stoics and Plotinus. The arguments for a necessary, singular existent God, the identification of God with nature but the insistence on a non-reductive materialism bring us to Deleuze's critical appraisal of being and the identification of being with God. In various places in Deleuze's work, the terms 'immanence' and 'univocality' are bandied about and are supposed to describe both God and the principles of being. Deleuze, and later Guattari, assume that the fully worked out system delivers not just the *archē* or principle(s) of being but also the concept of immanent substance – which later became the body without organs.[7]

We expect, then, that Spinoza's *Ethics* will offer an alternative to the Cartesian–Kantian concept of the subject and the Categorical Imperative, a way of responding to the terrible spectacle of the modern legitimation crisis by rethinking the grounds of ethical theory. We will thus expect Deleuze's interpretation of Spinoza's *Ethics* to concentrate on its pantheism and to focus our attention on the ways in which we can transvalue our traditional moral notions. As importantly for Deleuze, Spinoza's arguments for pantheism are based on a theory of parallelism, a controversial theory we will look at in some depth later but nonetheless a theory which Deleuze takes to support a thesis distinct from the dialectical method and an alternative to Hegel's Infinity or Absolute.

With this chapter I intend two things. Firstly, I wish to reconstruct the arguments so that we may be clear as to the system that underlies oft-quoted Deleuzian phrases. Secondly, I hope to prove that it is impossible to cherry pick the ethical naturalism from this system and this means the inevitable inheritance of certain problems; the consequences of the flows and gaps, the rather woolly references and pot boiling characteristic of Deleuze's arguments even at this first stage.

The pantheism

The relationship between pantheism and monism is not strict. One could be a monist and not a pantheist; a materialist might take this position. One could argue that God is in everything but that there are many sorts of things. Or, one could argue that God is everything. For the sake of this argument I shall distinguish between monism where there is only one kind of thing and monism where there is only one individual. The former is the position of a normal materialist; however, it is this last position that will occupy us throughout this chapter, where monism and pantheism coincide.

Part one of *Expressionism* presents three sets of arguments intended to prove the necessary existence of God and to identify God with nature. Each argument is named a 'triad' which is a reference to a form of argument named a syllogism. According to Deleuze each 'triad' brings together three different things or concepts through the middle term; the middle term alters throughout the syllogisms. The first triad brings together the concepts of attribute, essence and substance. The second the concepts of perfection, infinity and the absolute. The final triad draws together the ideas of essence, with the thing of which it is the essence and the capacity of that thing to be affected. It is surprising to find the appearance of a dialectical argument but Deleuze does quite plainly state that each term, substance, attribute and essence, is a middle term relating the two others, in three syllogisms (28). Following the structure of his argument we shall begin with the first triad and concentrate on the relationship of attribute to essence.[8]

Before proceeding it may be worth clarifying the principal concepts: substance, attribute and mode. Substance, according to Spinoza, is that which is in itself and is conceived through itself. It is the source that requires no further ground. The concept of substance must not postulate anything outside of itself. 'The being of Being – or of substance as Spinoza calls it – is for him not a mere idea; it is the overwhelming, all-encompassing, infinitely rich intuition of God, which finds confirmation through thought and experience, whenever we look into their ground'.[9] An attribute is that which the intellect perceives of substance constituting its essence. What we know of substance we know through the attributes of Thought and Extension. An attribute 'explains' or 'expresses' the essence of substance. Each attribute is infinite in kind but not absolutely infinite. Modes are individual things; they are temporal and finite. A mode is an affection of substance, is in another thing through which it is also conceived. The meanings of these terms will be exemplified as we continue with Deleuze's argument. The main problem concerning Deleuze is the apparent incompatibility between three propositions stating the relationship between these three terms.

The monistic argument depends on the claim that 'there is a substance which has every attribute' as well as the proposition that 'two substances cannot share any attribute' and the assertion that 'no substance has more than one attribute'. Deleuze intends to show how these three propositions can work together. Indeed, he submits that the first nine propositions of the *Ethics* lead to the tenth; the assertion that although the attributes are really distinct they do not constitute plural substances. This is the clearest account in *Expressionism*, and perhaps in all Deleuze's works, of the thesis of (the anti-dialectical) parallelism. To establish the argument Deleuze needs to prove that the terms 'thought' and 'extension' relate to the *same* object. It is here that his arguments are at their most strained, relying on Stoic linguistic themes, Duns Scotus' theory of formal distinction and Frege's account of substitution. In many places Deleuze merely suggests the movement of the argument by alluding to philosophical names and systems. For this reason, and with Bernstein's comments on hermeneutical integrity in mind, I have attempted to reconstruct Deleuze's arguments. Surprisingly, I have found that Frege's account of substitution is integral to the project as it is only this which would really allow Deleuze to make the move that the infinity he is discussing, God, is not merely possible but actual.

Deleuze advances the idea that the proposition that 'although attributes are distinct they do not constitute plural substances' provides support for 1df6 in the *Ethics*, which is where Spinoza defines God as 'a being absolutely infinite, that is, a substance consisting of an infinity of attributes'. He argues that this definition is a real – rather than a nominal or stipulative – definition; it is the affirmation of the essence of something. With a spin on this, and to simplify; Deleuze argues that substance can be completely defined, that is, includes all its descriptions or reasons within itself and that the term 'substance' can be substituted by its complete description Because reasons are identifiable with causes he then concludes that substance or God is self-caused. In other words, from the argument concerning substitutability Deleuze moves to a theory of the logical possibility of Infinity and from that to the 'proof' of the actual existence of God or substance; the positive Infinity.

Although we find Deleuze posing arguments referring to the nature of being and beings, a sideswipe at Heidegger's *Introduction to Metaphysics*, for Hardt, the main focus for Deleuze in the first few sections is to establish that numerical distinction cannot pertain to substance. Although this might make him sound somewhat Aquinian, if successful it would enable him to argue that substance is unique, not one or singular. I would say that really the conclusion is established to act as a main premise in all arguments against pluralist interpretations of substance. By implication this would be a refutation of Cartesian dualism. The discussion is presented against a general meditation on the nature of distinction and for Hardt this consideration of distinction constitutes the underlying purpose of the opening section.

One substance

Deleuze begins with an abbreviated discussion on how thought and extension and the concept of substance function within Descartes' *oeuvre*, specifically how their relationship leads to or supports a dualist thesis, which, in turn, embeds a representative theory of knowledge. Against such representational epistemologies, we can take it that

Deleuze wishes to prove two things. First, he wants to prove that thought and extension are not the properties of numerous substances and secondly, that substance, or anything which can be considered 'in itself', must be unique or singular. The uniqueness and singularity of God is not supposed to be the same as the description 'one God'. The argument begins by focusing on the relationship between numerical and substantial distinction and Deleuze claims that numerical distinction cannot pertain to substance. Although as Jaspers suggests for the finite man, the statement 'God is one' remains in force, and we shall find ourselves occasionally using this formulation.

Deleuze's argument against dualist metaphysics, such as that expounded by Descartes, begins by him considering how the concept of (infinite) substance relates to number, that is, can there be more than one? It advances in the following way: number involves limit and therefore requires an external cause. Because substance is not limited (by an external cause (1d2 and 6)), numerical distinction cannot pertain to substance. The salient point is not that number itself is limited but that anything countable is limited. The above argument should be rephrased and begin with the claim that what is limited requires an external cause. Because that which can be counted is limited then that which can be counted must have an external cause. Substance, however, is infinite and so does not have an external cause, therefore substance cannot be counted, that is, numerical distinction cannot pertain to substance. The contentious and central claim is that substance does not have an external cause. This same clause is operating in the further argument that no two substances could share an attribute. Numerical distinction, according to Deleuze, requires an external cause to which it may be referred. Because substance cannot be referred to an external cause – due to the contradiction implied by such causal principles – we have to conclude that two or more substances cannot be distinguished *in numero* and that there cannot be two substances with the same attribute (32).[10] It is not altogether clear why it is the case that no two substances could share an attribute unless we take attribute to mean, or be identical to, a substance; but Deleuze specifically argues against this. Incidentally, because modes are limited by an external cause, numbers would be appropriate in their case (33).

Supporting both positions is the description of substance as self-caused. The argument is that by definition substance cannot be caused by anything else and, as it must be caused by something, it must be self-caused. There are three main arguments why substance cannot have an external cause. First, if it were caused by something else it would be limited and finite, but because by definition it is infinite and unlimited, it must be self-caused. Secondly, if the cause were external, substance would not be infinite because there would be something other than this substance. This 'other' thing would have to have properties or qualities lacked by this substance and, as we know, this substance lacks nothing, therefore there cannot be an external cause. Finally, the conception of this substance does not depend on the conception of another thing. If this substance were caused by another we would have to conceive this one through its external cause and not through itself. As substance is conceived through itself we can conclude that it does not have an external cause.

The point that substances can only be distinguished according to attribute as opposed to modes is premised on the unsubstantiated belief that modifications are dependent on the attributes. Even so, the argument does not demonstrate either that substances need to share all attributes or if they shared some they would be a limiting relationship.[11] The only way that this could be strengthened would be by arguing that substance is identical to the set of all possible attributes. So far Deleuze's argument is supposed to demonstrate that there is one substance *per* attribute, that the attribute is a formal cause or reason of substance and that substance is self-caused. We can now see that this is dependent on a point that will be the conclusion of the next group of arguments. Further, it does seem as though Deleuze is content to rest on the laurels of Spinoza's, or the Stoic, explanatory or causal rationalism where everything *must* have an explanation or cause. Otherwise, it would be perfectly permissible to say that the substance may be uncaused or caused by something other than a substance. Deleuze might respond by saying that if substance were caused by anything else it would be dependent on that thing and because substance is independent and yet must be caused by something, it has to be self-caused. We can see that this argument concerning causal dependency relies on the postulate that anything in a material causal relationship with another thing is conceptually dependent on that thing, in which case its reasons as well as its cause would be external. If we would allow that substance could be uncaused we would also be able to say that there could be many substances and that numerical distinction could pertain to substance.

One substance *per* attribute

The successful proof of the actual existence of God, or the positive infinity, relies on the conclusion, which is 1df6 of the *Ethics*, being a real definition.[12] This is the definition of God as 'a being absolutely infinite that is a substance consisting of an infinity of attributes'. Deleuze believes that if he satisfies two criteria, the identification by description of a singular thing and its full or complete description, he will then be able to affirm the thing as actual and infinite where infinite is defined as self-caused. Aside from the association of reasons with causes in Stoic philosophy, we also find textual support for this hypothesis in the *Ethics*. 1ax3 queries the proposition that an effect necessarily follows from a cause. According to 1ax4, knowledge of the effect depends on or involves knowledge of its cause and 1p6c adds that a substance cannot be produced by anything other than itself. Hence if a substance exists then it must be its own cause and consequently its existence must be deducible from its essence.[13] As a first step, Deleuze begins with the primary elements of the system, the *definiens* – the attributes – and by beginning here, he can also prove that Thought and Extension are not properties of numerous substances. The first triad is an argument to the effect that there can only be one substance per attribute.

An attribute, a primary element in the system, is not a substance. So, while it expresses an infinite and eternal essence it must attribute this to something else.[14] According to Deleuze this attribution occurs because an attribute does not have *necessary* existence. Throughout the *Ethics*, the 'must' of necessity means that the thing under question must be caused or explained. If a thing is necessary by virtue of its own essence, and essence is identified with its nature or definition, then for a thing to be necessary in a strong sense is for it to be self-explanatory, which means self-caused.[15] Only substance is properly speaking self-explanatory and so only substance is independent. But this still leaves us somewhat bewildered as to why the attribute expresses an essence and why that essence is of something else, a substance.

There are at least four *a priori* arguments supporting the claim that no attribute is itself a substance. The first is that if each attribute were a substance then there would be many substances and these would have to be in a limiting relationship. However, because substance is unlimited this means that an attribute cannot be a substance (37). This argument presumes not only that there is more than one attribute but also that conceptual and causal dependence are mutually entailing. The second argument is that if each attribute were a substance then there would be many substances and each would require an external cause. Because we define substance as that which is self-caused and self-explanatory, an attribute cannot be a substance (45). A third argument introduces the idea that an attribute is conceived *per se*. If attributes were substances then they would be in a limiting relationship. Now we know that a limiting relationship is a causal relationship and Deleuze, following Spinoza, adds that for one thing to cause another there must be something in common. But an attribute is conceived without the aid of another; it is conceived through itself, and therefore there is nothing in common and there can be no causal relationship and there must be only one substance (70). Another argument uses the idea of perfection and once again begins with the proposition that if attributes were substances, they would be in limiting relationships. Because an attribute is not in a limiting relationship we can say that an attribute is unlimited and perfect and therefore we can infer that all attributes are equally perfect and unlimited and that none is a substance. These four arguments depend amongst other things on it being the case that there is more than one attribute.

The proof for this is the *a posteriori* argument that because every object (of thought) is conceived either through the attribute of Thought or Extension there has to be more than one attribute. But if this argument shows anything, it is that we know there are *two* attributes. This is vital because there are supposed to be an infinity of attributes. Yet, if we only know two and are assuming that we are ignorant about the rest, then it is conceivable that we are likewise ignorant about a multitude of other ways in which substance 'expresses' itself. If it were true that substance expresses itself in other ways then an attribute might not be the formal cause or reason of substance. This quite clearly demonstrates that the argument, if it works at all, works first because Deleuze has a prior commitment to the ontological 'furniture' of the world, substance, attribute and mode, and that he has a belief in something he calls 'real definition' which, purportedly, excludes the possibility of error.

Well why identify attribute with essence at all? Deleuze draws on Spinoza's doctrine that essence is something which, when given, necessarily posits the thing and which, when taken away, destroys the thing. According to Spinoza, if a is conceived through b then b must be the cause or explanation of a and a and b are said to involve one another. Further, if the essence of something necessarily involves x then x is said to belong to its nature. If x belongs to its nature then it follows from its definition since 'the true definition neither involves nor expresses anything beyond the nature of the thing defined'. So we will discover that the notion of attribute as essence is quite central to the later proof, using the concept of real definition, that God is self-caused.

But we are not prohibited, it seems, from saying that each attribute is self-caused or self-defined and therefore substantial. This is indicated when Deleuze accepts that an attribute has necessary and actual existence but denies that it has 'existence in itself' (44) and this is supported by the claim that only substance exists through itself that is, necessarily (43). Deleuze also suggests that an attribute is an essence and because existence follows from essence an attribute, as essence, is the cause of the existence of something. We must infer that the something is something other than itself. So he concludes that all essences relate, or are attributable to, substance, because substance is the only being whose existence necessarily follows from essence.

Deleuze's later proof of the actual infinity, or the existence of God, depends on the above arguments and the description of an attribute as a cause, explanation or reason of substance. This description depends on Spinoza's claim that to conceive one thing through another means that the latter is the explanation or cause of the former. Let us assume that an attribute a is the essence of x. If a is the essence of x then we can say that x is conceived through a, but because substance is conceived through itself, we can conclude that a = x.[16] The conclusion would be that substance and attribute are identical, that there is nothing additional about either term. This would leave us with the conclusion that there is one substance per attribute or that an attribute is itself a substance.

Now for two reasons Deleuze needs to reject this thesis. He does not wish to accept that an attribute is a substance, as this would leave him with pluralism or dualism rather than monism. Secondly, the pantheism under discussion here depends on the fact that substance can be defined in terms of *all* the attributes. Yet he does wish to affirm something like it with reference to isolated attributes. The problem is that although he wishes to affirm only 'something like it' he offers no good reason why each attribute is not strictly identified with substance, except the bald assertion that 'substance is privileged to exist through itself: it is not the attribute that exists through itself'.

We can see that the argument that there is one substance per attribute relies on the assertion that the attribute attributes its essence as to something else, that is, it does not, itself, have necessary existence. Yet even if we concede this point we are left with two responses. Deleuze's argument relies on the fact that we actually conceive more than one attribute. We could reply that we only *know* one attribute, Thought, and this is known through itself, which means that it is self-caused and independent, and this means that there is only one substance – Mind. He will have to demonstrate more convincingly that the attribute of Thought is not the only attribute. Because if we do not accept the argument as given and maintain that the attribute of Thought is the only attribute then even on his own terms there would be nothing inconsistent with defining it as substantial and necessary. Alternatively, we might claim that because there is one substance per attribute and many attributes there must be many substances and this would mean that there is pluralism rather than monism.

Aside from the weak *a posteriori* argument, the above arguments rely on the principle of non-contradiction: because it would be a contradiction to assert more than one substance and because there is more than one attribute we are forced to conclude that an attribute cannot be a substance. We could in response reject the first premise and say that there is no actual contradiction. We could deny that if there were more than one substance, the substances would be in limiting, either conceptual or material, relationships. Or, we could simply refuse to accept the original definition of substance. All these perfectly plausible responses would stop Deleuze's argument in its tracks.

One substance for all attributes

Initially and somewhat surprisingly there appears to be some overlap between the proofs that there is one substance per attribute and one substance for all attributes. To clarify the steps in the argument I shall pursue Deleuze's own suggestion that we can follow the proofs in two ways: from attribute to essence to substance and from perfection to infinity to the absolute, the first two triads. The latter proof depends on two basic principles: the more reality a thing has, the more attributes it has and the more attributes a thing has the more existence it has.

The primary principle is that because each attribute is not itself a substance, each must attribute its essence to something else: an attribute is attributed to a substance. From here Deleuze moves to the proposition that all attributes are attributed to a *single* substance. Actually the proof is very short and it is that attributes must be attributed to the same substance because there can only be one substance. In a less truncated form, Deleuze argues that because each attribute is infinitely *perfect* and because none is a substance then each attributes its essence as to something else (42). This something else is substance. We know that there is only one substance (45), therefore each attributes its essence to the same substance (65). The claim is that an attribute is attributive because it does not have necessary existence.

This raises a whole host of problems and queries. The first concerns the relationship between the attributes. We have already suggested that in some sense the attribute can be described as a reason or cause of substance and also that substance is self-caused. It would seem that the logical implication is that substance, or God, must be *causa sui* under each attribute. If an attribute is an essential property of something then F(a) such that a is F in all possible worlds. Now there are two possibilities. If there are two essential properties (F, G) and if each is strictly identified with substance then there must be more than one substance such that (F(a) and G(b)). Alternatively there might be only one substance and two essential properties such that (a) is both F and G. Deleuze clearly admits that an attribute expresses *an* essence (13, 45, 50, 57) but also claims that an attribute expresses *the* essence of substance (13, 37, 50, 65). This really confuses the issue. Is it the case that a is the same in all cases? If it is, then is a *identical* to its essence? If so, then is it the case that F and G are identical?

Let us develop this second case. If a is both F and G, then F(a) and G(a) must be true in all possible worlds, God must be *causa sui* through each and, specifically this should not contravene the law of non-contradiction. That a is both F and G cannot mean F(a) and not F(a). This is interesting because if a is a substance which is identical to all its attributes, and if F is an attribute, then if F expresses the essence of substance, it must also express all the other attributes. If F expresses all the attributes then it expresses attributes other than itself and so other attributes would be involved with F and F cannot be conceived through itself. Yet the assertion that an attribute is considered *per se* is quite pivotal to the previous arguments.

To secure the claim that an attribute is conceived *per se*, Deleuze fleshes out the definition. He states that an attribute is something that is conceived without the aid of another thing, is really distinct and through 2d6 perfect. Because it is really distinct an attribute is without limitation and therefore involves no negation: it is positive (60) and without limit it is infinite. Deleuze has described an attribute as an infinite form of being, an unlimited and irreducible formal reason (49). But if we understand negation as limitation we encounter a circle, one that will be repeated. The attribute, according to Deleuze, is infinite because it involves no negation, it involves no negation because otherwise it would not be infinite. Or else we could say that an attribute is infinite because it is not limited (finite) which would appear to be a simple tautology or analytically true, until one starts to question the intuition.

Deleuze responds to this in two stages (i) the essence of substance is constituted by the attributes (ii) this essence is then reflected and multiplied in the attributes, each of which, in its kind, expresses the essence of substance. This is not a good answer. To be able to distinguish between attribute and *propria* (description), Deleuze states, one first needs to know what are the essential properties (57). But this is to beg the question as he also states that an essential property is identified through its description (*propria*). This, though, addresses a different point. Here we are concerned with whether or not an attribute can express the essence of substance, when the essence is identified as 'all attributes', and still be conceived *per se*. Finally, Deleuze admits that one attribute is denied of another but alleges that this negation does not imply an opposition or a privation. His reason for this is that the idea of real distinction forbids the definition of an attribute through its opposite (80).

The argument is either unusable or introduces negation into the general scheme. When we try to decipher what is meant by the claim that an attribute can express the essence of substance, when essence is itself identified with all the attributes, we seem to be left with two options. Either Deleuze must accept that each attribute expresses the essence of substance and that there are many substances (pluralism) or he must accept that there is only one attribute, for example the attribute of Thought (idealism). His answer is to convince us that an attribute is a verbal entity and that therefore such distinction between the attributes need introduce neither substantial multiplicity nor negation into being.

Pluralism or idealism?

The basic problem is that if an attribute is identified as constituting the essence of substance and if there is more than one attribute then substance must have a plurality of essences or there must be plural substances. The ontological argument in *Expressionism* depends on the fact of there being really distinct attributes. Spinoza's *Ethics* encounters the same problem. To say, as Spinoza does in 2p7s, that there is one substance, now considered under one attribute, now considered under another, appears to privilege the mental act of conception while emptying the concept 'substance' of all real content – for what could the concept 'being' or 'substance' designate? Indeed, we ought to ask at this point who or what is doing the conceiving? Subjectivists, or idealists, as an answer to the problem of pluralism, claim that attributes are inventions of the human intellect. We ascribe attributes to substance 'as if' they constituted its essence.[17] This subjectivist interpretation rests on defining *tanquam* in the phrase 'I understand that which the intellect perceived of substance as (*tanquam*) constituting (*constituens*) its essence' to mean 'as if constituting its essence'. An objectivist would reject this interpretation for four reasons. *Tanquam* can simply mean 'as'. Secondly, Spinoza implies that the intellect is successful in its comprehension and marks something actual. The third objection is that substance reveals and constitutes itself through the attributes. Hence, and finally, according to the theory of knowledge, a true idea is a true idea of something actual.[18] The argument between subjectivists and objectivists stems from textual ambiguity: the opaque relation between attribute and substance. Different definitions and propositions support the claims that attributes express the essence of substance, that attributes pertain to the essence of substance, that substance and attribute are identical and that attributes constitute the essence of substance. An objectivist interpretation would be inconsistent with the claim that attributes are 'merely' linguistic devices or a logical requirement of grammar.

As a response to the subjectivists, Deleuze argues that there is real distinction,[19] which seems to put him in the objectivist camp and to run the risk of pluralism. But, he says, it is quite possible to have distinct attributes that are not distinct substances, if we adopt a 'weakened sense' of real distinction. This would mean keeping the idea that attributes are conceived *per se* but rejecting the implication that this means a distinction among things which would imply a pluralist thesis. Hardt suggests that Deleuze was undisturbed by the subjectivist and objectivist argument and for this reason does not treat the issue in any depth. Yet, Hardt also suggests that the stakes are high because the ontological integrity of the system is paramount to Deleuze's overall project. I believe that Deleuze was well aware that if he were unable to clarify the relationship between attribute and substance then his whole project would fail.

Weak thesis of real distinction

The proposition now before us is that one substance has formally distinct attributes. For the time being the two attributes that concern us are Thought and Extension and the claim is that it is the same individual qualified by these attributes (F(a) and G(a) where F and G are Thought and Extension). Trying to avoid the pitfalls of dualism and reductionism, it seems as though Deleuze introduces a double aspect theory such that a is the sort of entity to which the predicates or properties of thought and extension are equally applicable. These references to the attributes though play a key role within the general argument. To satisfy the two criteria required before a proposition can count as a real definition, and so prove the actual existing nature of God, Deleuze needs to show that an attribute is a designating term and by offering a complete description, that there can only be one individual so designated.

I have to confess that I have struggled to clarify the argument Deleuze intends and have had to do some work to reconstruct the argument; both a response to the problem of pluralism and the foundation for the proof of the actual existence of God. Beyond doubt the central point is that there is a connection between the description of the attributes and the problem of real definition. Deleuze is looking for a convincing response to the problem of real definition so that he can prove the actual existence of God. And endeavouring to find a solution to this problem, Deleuze turns to two sources. The first is Duns Scotus and the second Stoic logic. The former affords Deleuze a notion of formal distinction, and the influence of this medieval theologian will be seen more fully when we set out the thesis of univocity. From the latter source Deleuze draws his inspiration that the notion of formal distinction can be tied into acts of expression. It has to be said that Deleuze tends to reference names as though demarcating systems or expressing arguments. This creates the affect of a scholarly work, well researched, brimming with interesting ideas and new angles. However as soon as the reader scratches the surface, the richly woven tapestry simply begins to disintegrate.

So what does Deleuze take from Scotus? According to Scotus, God's attributes are essential to him and they are inseparable from each other, that is, they are identical but not the same. Formal distinction occupies a point midway between rational or conceptual distinction and real distinction.[20] The principal criterion for formal distinction is that different formal definitions pertain to the thing in question. The argument, as presented by Cross, is that the general thesis depends upon the theory of univocity.[21] This theory, in short, is that definitions of some terms applied to God are exactly the same as the definitions of those terms when applied to creatures. Because these terms mean different things when applied to creatures, they must be different from one another and if they were not distinct in God they would not be distinct in creatures either. We can therefore conclude that God's attributes are formally distinct, that is, that separate definitions pertain. Although this might help us see why Deleuze believes that Scotian semantics is of any relevance to his own argument, he is left having to prove that attributes can be afforded separate definitions even though they are not different when considered as attributes, or properties, of the divine. Scotus argued that identity could be explained as the impossibility of real inseparability. Two objects, x and y, are inseparable if and only if, it is not possible for x to exist without y and it is not possible for y to exist without x.

There are three problems. Firstly, whichever way we look at this, the Scotian account of formal distinction only makes sense within an essentialist ontology, that is, a thing's identity is its form or nature. Surely Deleuze cannot merely assume this as his underlying ontology? Secondly, the medieval theologian devised this type of argument within a different environment where there was no need to prove the uniqueness or indivisibility of God as these propositions were all known to be true through biblical revelation. The principal ontological axiom is that there is one God who is indivisible. So where God is concerned the intriguing question is how an indivisible being can have essential properties that cannot actually be separated but which can be known distinctly. Also, of course, because God is not identifiable with, is over and above, any of the usual categories of the understanding, any claims as to God's properties are rather limited. Indeed, for Scotus, the idea of formal distinction when applied to God is only *metaphorical* because one essence is manifest in all the different properties. Thirdly, these ruminations concern a transcendent God. This raises two further points. Deleuze is emphatic that one of the properties or attributes of God is Extension. For Scotus this would be absurd. The definition of the property as Extension rather than beauty or goodness marks Deleuze's attempt to force some very strained Scotian ideas into his own ontological system.[22] Secondly, whereas some consider that Scotus promotes the idea that God is his essence and more, that there is divine surplus, God cannot be thought to be convertible with his properties, Deleuze will later need to prove that God or substance is convertible with *all* the attributes.

To contemporary readers it seems odd that Deleuze turns back to an ancient and fragmentary source to answer this central problem of convertibility within Spinoza's system but the appeal must be motivated by the belief that the Stoical concept of *lekta* can solve this riddle of essential properties. The allusions to attributes as divine names and as *logoi* suggest that Deleuze is using ideas from Stoic logic and we shall return to Deleuze's references to *logos*. Although there are certain problems with Bogue's account of Meinongian and Stoic philosophy, his point, highlighting the pertinence of *lekta* in the slightly later

Difference and Repetition, is well made and in *Expressionism* we find an early version.[23] There seems almost no good reason why Deleuze would find Stoic logic or theory of signs philosophically attractive. A thorough account of the actual philosophical relevance is problematic. Our access to this aspect of the philosophy of the Stoa is primarily through commentators, such as Sextus and Diogenes Laertius, who offer divergent accounts of the Stoic theory of signs and the Stoics themselves contested the meaning and existence of *lekta*.

Ebert notes that Sextus credits the Stoics, and perhaps the Peripatetics, with a theory of signs highlighting the functional character of signs in order to show, before going on to demolish the overall argument, how signs can be identified neither with things nor with events.[24] Sextus would have us believe the Stoics asserted that the function of a sign was to 'make evident' a consequent: blushing and swelling of the vessels and thirst are signs of diseases. The consequents in question are classified as things altogether non-evident, things naturally non-evident and things occasionally non-evident. Central to this theory of signs is the *lekton* defined as a proposition complete in itself and declarative as far as its being so depends on itself.[25] Yet this theory of signs is entirely absent in Diogenes Laertius' exposition of Stoic logic. One explanation for this is that Stoics concentrated on the logical relationship between the antecedent and consequent rather than on the evident or non-evident nature of the consequent. Indeed proof is defined as 'an argument (*logos*) inferring by means of what is better apprehended to something less well apprehended'.[26] In this case distinctions are drawn between the sign (sound), the significate (*lekton*) and the denotation (external object) and *lekta* are described as incorporeal, unlike the sign and the denotation.[27]

It is significant to this project that the *lekton* is that which subsists according to a rational presentation, and a rational presentation is one in which what is presented can be conveyed in speech.[28] As a *lekton* is that which is expressed we can tentatively see here a connection from Stoics through to Brentano, and his thesis of intentionality, and thus to Deleuze.[29] In this version, the *lekton* can either be deficient or complete. Incomplete *lekta* are divided into two classes, roughly subjects and predicates. A subject is a generic term for entities expressed by individual or class names. A predicate is a deficient *lekton* which combines with a subject (in the nominative case) to form a proposition.[30] A proposition is said to be a complete *lekton*, assertoric in itself.

Although much of what we know about Stoic logic and theory of meaning has been inherited in fragmentary forms and scraps of doctrine, we can see a number of similarities, between Stoic semantics and certain modern theories, particularly those of Carnap and Frege, and these are discussed by Mates.[31] Aside from Carnap's notion of explication, it is the distinction between intension–extension or sense–denotation that is relevant to this particular discussion. We have said that deficient *lekta* are signified by verbs lacking subjects and that these are different from *lekta* that lack reference.[32] It is difficult to see how the Stoics might take isolated predicates as referring expressions. I contend that Deleuze requires something like a Fregeian account, to help bridge the gap in Stoic theory concerning the principle of interchangeability, in order to prove that attributes and substance are convertible (47). He needs to prove this possibility of conversion to establish that the set of finite modes and infinite substance are not the same thing. In short, then, Deleuze is looking for a way to demonstrate how we can know that two expressions, with distinct senses, refer to the same object.[33]

Deleuze suggests that the distinction between the attributes is a distinction of reason, that the attribute is a form of being (46, 49), a dynamic and active form (45), an expression and a divine name or *logoi* (61). At the beginning of this chapter we noted that the Stoics explained physical events as *logos* operating through the dynamic character of *pneuma*. *Logos* is variously defined as creative, the force of the universe, material, is identified with fire and nature and the linguistic theory distinguished between interior *logos*, or thought, and exterior *logos*, speech.[34] In his analysis of Heidegger's commentary on Being, Rosen discusses the Socratic use of the term. *Logoi*, he says, are neither propositions nor statements about Ideas, any more than they are concepts or statements about Being. But because *logos* exhibits the ratio of intelligibility of beings it is something that is common to beings and to speech in so far as both exhibit the Idea.[35] Heaton picks up this point during his discussion of Deleuze's logic of sense where he points out that even propositions denoting impossible objects have sense.[36]

Deleuze describes attributes as names, verbs, reasons and says that they have expressive value as words. To help clarify all these different functions he uses the term *logoi* and draws two examples from the *Ethics*. The first is Spinoza's claim that 'by Israel I understand the third patriarch: I understand the same by Jacob'. The argument here is that attributes are distinct names or divine words, that names can be distinguished by their senses even when they designate the same object (44, 61). The second example is Spinoza's suggestion that a surface might be described as a plane or it might be described as white in relation to the person looking at it. The former description is the same as a description under the attribute of Extension, the latter under the attribute of Thought.[37]

First then, we have to decide whether or not an attribute is a name of substance or if it is a name of a concept or Idea. If it is the latter is an attribute a proper name? If it is the former then is it a name of a concept-word or a function? Finally we shall need to enquire into the ontological status of the concept itself. Without using something like Fregeian theory of sense and reference to plug the holes in the argument, I do not see how Deleuze could possibly argue how it can be known that the attributes are attributed to the same substance. Without this he cannot argue that there is only one substance. Nor can he argue that the equivalence of the attributes can be known and identified. Without this he would be unable to begin his argument that substance is self-caused or that God actually exists. I have reconstructed the argument to show how Deleuze might justify the various philosophical moves he makes.

Sense and reference

From Spinoza's *Compendium Grammatices Linguae Hebreae* Deleuze draws three elementary principles: (a) the a-temporal character of the infinitive; (b) the 'participal' character of the modes; (c) the determination of various kinds of infinitives, one of which expresses an action referred to a principal cause. This, I take it, is the ground for the claim that attributes express an essence, that is 'a nature in the infinitive' (57). If we combine this with the above statement, that attributes are names or words, we have 'attributes are names: verbs rather than adjectives. Each attribute is a verb, a primary infinitive proposition, an expression with a distinct sense' (104). This clearly sounds like nonsense but indicates the various ways Deleuze considers the term 'attribute' to function both as a property and a form of expression – a way of talking about substance.

Within Stoic taxonomy, a verb is said to signify a predicate, a *lekton*, but both common and proper names are said to signify properties and these do not occur in the list of *lekta*. The Kneales advance the thesis that the Stoics were concerned with units only in their grammatical theory and complete *lekta*, or functions otherwise.[38] But this does not really help us. If attributes are names then it seems that they are signifying either the properties of extension and thought or the complete *lekton* 'a is E'. Boundas states categorically that the infinitive as a verbal mode (to extend) guarantees the specificity of an event ('a is extended').[39] Frankly, I do not see how this is the case. Even if we can understand how an attribute may be 'verbal' it would still signify something like a predicate and we would need to know generally how to fix the 'a' in question. Thus the issue of function rises to the surface. Further, for the overall argument to be coherent, we have to be sure that a is the same in 'a is Extended' and 'a is Thinking'. In addition, we have not yet been convinced that the description of *lekta* as incorporeal overcomes the objectivist dilemma. I shall now explore the possibility that Frege may at least help with the first problem.[40]

If an attribute is a name of God then it must either be a proper name or a substitutable description. If it is the latter then it must be a definite description. This means that it can only designate one object. If it were to designate more than one the reference would not be clear. Let us take an example suggested by Frege in *On Sense and Reference:*

> Let a,b,c, be the lines connecting the vertices of a triangle with the mid-points of the opposite sides. The point of intersection of a and b is then the same point of intersection of b and c. So we could have different designations for the same point and these names ('point of intersection of a and b' 'point of intersection of b and c') likewise indicate the mode of presentation; and hence the statement contains actual knowledge.[41]

In this example, the names 'the intersection of a and b' and 'the intersection of b and c' are different designations of the same point. The point, or object designated, is given in *distinct* ways, the same point is designated by two expressions with distinct senses. This suggests that an identity statement can convey information. We have to draw a distinction between a proper name and a definite description, although both ordinary names and definite descriptions are referred to as proper names. In the sentence 'the Author of Waverley is Scott' the copula signifies a judgement of identity, that 'the author of Waverley' and 'Scott' are the same individual. A definite description not only designates something but also asserts something – a property or quality of the designated object and at the same time communicates something of the uniqueness of the object.

If we have two sentences and we wish to discover whether or not the two designate the same object, without prior knowledge, we must first, according to Frege, discern whether or not the whole sentences are identical in sense. There is some ambiguity. Frege appears both to say that only in the context of a sentence do words mean something (contextual principle) and that the sense of the sentential component is necessarily of constitutive significance for the sense of the sentence. By this he may mean that words have their sense in reference to the context of speech, in reference to sentential context. If, however, they were not in context, as objects of semantic observation, it would be absurd to deny them sense. We could then say that words have sense and reference only *in* sentential context but do not acquire them *through* it.[42]

Frege argues that the sense of the sentence is the thought that it expresses. In answer to the above question we can now say that two sentences designate the same object if they express the same thought. This, though, leaves us wondering two things: whether an adequate account of 'thought' can be provided and whether we can find criteria to enable us to identify the 'thought'. Frege suggests that there is equality of sense when two sentences are synonymous and designate the same object, if they are logically equivalent but that neither they, nor any of their parts, are logically determined.[43] Let us take two simple sentences '4 + 1' and '1 + 4'. Do these sentences have distinct senses because the mode of presentation differs, or the same sense because they both express the same thought '5'? Even before we can answer that, it seems we have a more pressing question. Are we equating 'the object designated', 5 or the value, with the 'thought'? If so, it seems that we are confusing the sense (concept) with the reference (object designated). One answer to this may be that the content of the judgement is a logical entity, or object. For example, a number is a non-actual, objective and belongs to the realm of reference and a thought, being complete, is an object.[44] We can now say that the two sentences carve up their content in different ways, differ in linguistic form, but have the same sense, the 'thought', which itself can be an object of reference. This, however, is the case with '4 + 1' = '1 + 4' because the expressions are complete and have definite value (5, true).

Thus far we have been considering the comparative senses of well formed phrases but now we must break down the sentence into its components. Frege analyses a well formed phrase into two main parts: function and argument. A function is a part of a complex expression, is incomplete and is considered as invariant relative to certain possible substitutions or arguments. The argument is defined as the variable element. We could have the expression F(a), where F is the functional expression and a is the argument. As concept expressions are incomplete their meaning cannot be determined except by considering the role they play in complex sentences or phrases.[45] Each function has an extension or value-range. The extension is less basic than the concept, so the concept takes logical precedence. The extension of the concept is not, for Frege, the traditional notion of classes or sets. The nature of a function is to correlate arguments with values and the correlation is called the value-range or extension of the concept.[46] The extension of a concept is thus always complete because it has a value-range. A value-range is defined as the value-range of truth functions. To take a simple example, we can consider 'is the capital' as a functional expression, 'a country' as an argument and 'city' as the value. The function of this expression correlates the argument with the value. The argument 'country' can be substituted for 'France', the value of the argument will be 'Paris' and the function would correlate the argument with the value 'true'. The extension of the concept 'is a capital' would be all truth values produced by the substitution of the argument and the corresponding value. Consequently, statements about concepts can be replaced by statements about corresponding truth values.

Again we see the difficult already encountered: is the extension of a concept equivalent to the objects which 'fall under' it?[47] But this would be to contravene the Fregean injunction against confusing function with object. One solution may be to recall Frege's argument in *Begriffsschrift* concludes that the same content can be determined in different ways. To each way of determining the content can be assigned a name, a name then associated with a different mode of determining content. For example the same point in a geometrical construction can be named in two ways: one intuitively and one which satisfies a particular geometrical description. The first reflects the fact that a name can stand for itself and the second reflects the fact that a name can stand for a content. The way in which an expression names a thing is determined by the simpler terms out of which the expression is composed: 'evening star' determines the thing it stands for as the thing (first) visible in the evening. In this case, an identity statement would be true because the thing named by two expressions – evening star, morning star – is the same thing.

However, *Sense and Reference* is concerned with an epistemological problem. The identity between the two appears to hold if and only if we *know* that the two designate the same thing. Frege pushed the analysis of the sign in order to determine how the signs themselves reflect the ways in which the object is given. If two sentences have the same sense then their equivalence can be known *a priori*, regardless of the linguistic form or content, and without recourse to an external object. How might two sentences have the same sense? Two sentences have the same sense if the thought expressed by one is the same as the thought expressed by the second, even if the first appears to concern functions and the second appears to concern value-ranges and even when the functions themselves are different.[48]

The candidates for name in a Fregean sense then are (i) proper names (ii) sentences (iii) descriptive phrases. All names have sense and reference because they are complete. A sentence is a completed expression because the argument is correlated to the value and refers to the true or false, is a name of a truth value. But Frege also indicates that functional expressions, or concept-words, are names which name functions and which refer to an object, a value-range.[49] But there is still some ambivalence. Frege defines an object as something complete and a function as incomplete. We are arguing here that a functional expression does refer to something after all – to a function (which is incomplete) and that this has an extension, a value-range (a logical object) which is not identical to the objects that might fall under the concept.

Given what Deleuze and Guattari have to say about Frege in *What is Philosophy?*, it is surprising to note that even apart from the direct references to Frege, there are a number of passages in *Expressionism* which support the interpretation that an attribute as a name refers us to a function. First, Deleuze stresses the point that although an attribute expresses the essence of substance, it is attributive, it attributes itself as to something else. If an attribute were a name of a substance then it would be a proper name, complete and impredicable. Deleuze, however, states that an attribute is predicable of both substance and modes and is not substitutable (49, 61). In the expression 'a is extended' 'is extended' would be the functional expression, standing for the function, 'a' would be the argument or variable element and 'attribute of extension' would be the name of the concept or function. The essence of the functional expression lies in the part of the expression over and above the variable element, the 'a' – in other words it has distinct sense (63). A function is not inert, it connects and correlate arguments with values. This would explain one reason for the identification of an attribute as a dynamic and active form (45).

If this interpretation works then we would need to identify the distinct sense of the functional expression. According to Frege, the extension of a concept is the value-range of the function. According to Deleuze, the extension of each concept is infinite. We know that when an extension of two concepts are equal we can also say that the functions are equal. Thus we have 'attribute F = attribute G ', which is the same as 'the extension of the concept F is the same as the extension of the concept G'. As Frege has it, it is only our subjective perception and our manner of speaking that distinguishes the statement about functions from that of value-ranges. This does not mean that the functions are the same as value-ranges only that the *thought* concerning the function is the same as the one concerning value-ranges. The 'thought' or sense is the *same* but expressed in a *different* way and this explains how functional expressions or predicates can be substituted *salva veritate*. This is one plank across the Stoic theory of sense. If two sentences have the same sense then their equivalence can be shown *a priori*, this equivalence is necessary and can be known without recourse to an external object. Thus the equivalence of all attributes could be known and identified as 'the infinity of all attributes'.

The idea that I have been pursuing is that although a concept-word or a functional expression does not refer to an object as such, because it is unsaturated, it requires an object for its completion. Once completed, the function will correlate the sentence either to the 'true' or to the 'false'. The predicate or concept-word here is always a verb. If an attribute is a name, in so far as it is an expression, then we need to know what the content of the expression is. Deleuze states that an attribute is 'an infinite form of being' which expresses 'unlimited quality' (46, 49). If an expression is a mode of determining content then his claim appears to be that the content is 'being' and that the mode of its determination is unlimited. Yet, if the expression is essentially incomplete then we are presented with the claim that an attribute names a functional expression, a description and not a definite description.

In summation, we have the assertion that F(a): where F stands for an attribute and a is the argument or variable – this must be the case otherwise F could not take both substance and mode as its arguments. In the sentence or expression 'substance is extended' 'is extended' is a functional expression referring to a function or concept. On this reading, each function or concept is named an attribute. Each has an extension, the extensions are equivalent and so, too, are the names. Due to this, the sense of the *thought* is the same for each attribute, although the mode of presentation differs. Because the attribute names a functional expression, it is unsaturated or incomplete: the (a) is a logical requirement. But even if we accept this, the claim is only that the names (of the functional expressions) are substitutable *salva veritate*. Deleuze requires more than this. For his argument to work he needs to demonstrate that the a remains the same throughout. Now we know that if a and b are identical then if F(a) is true then F(b) is also true. We also know that if F can be substituted for G and if F(a) then G(a). But we cannot say that a and b are identical merely because the predicates are shared. I have been arguing so far that by the phrase 'attributes express the same sense' we should take Deleuze to mean 'the thought' (functions and value-ranges are equal) and the phrase 'each attributes expresses a distinct sense' to mean 'the mode of presentation' differs. This still leaves us with the question 'what is the object that is designated by the completed or saturated expression?'

Repeating and underlying the connection between himself and Frege, Deleuze states that attributes are points of view on a single object. Just as 'the intersection of a and b' is a name of a definite description, identical to 'the intersection of b and c', an attribute is a name in so far as it is an expression (44). He then states that an attribute explains the nature of God. This explanatory value allows him to distinguish between words as names, and words which are mere descriptions or adjectives. *Propria*, which can be predicated of the attributes, include adjectives such as infinite, perfect, immutable and eternal (49) but these do not explain the nature of substance. An attribute is a name of a definite description because it communicates information relating to a single thing. But the problem is that as a functional expression, the expression is incomplete and indefinite and requires an object for its completion whereas in the analogy drawn from geometry the two expressions are already complete, yield a definite value and for this reason are substitutable. To put it slightly differently, 'the attribute of extension' names a concept or a function that is the reference of the incomplete expression 'is extended'.

As a response to this problem, Deleuze has three options. First, he might claim that the expression is already complete. This claim could be supported by the assertion that expressions, *qua* attributes, are ways of presenting the same content: being. The completed expression would thus be 'being is extended', 'is extended' would be predicated of being. Once we have a full list of descriptions we could argue that we have arrived at a complete, if complex, description. This solution would rely on the invariability of a in F(a); that there is an identity of being (63, 64). Otherwise, Deleuze might argue that all functional expressions can be substituted, the principle of equality, and that the content of 'the thought' remains the same whether one says 'is extended' or 'is thought'. The 'thought' is the designated logical object. This logical object is the object of the definition that could appear in different guises. This would make sense of various passages referring to the 'conversion' of the infinity of attributes to absolute infinity. Frege himself argued that to take a concept and its extension, and indeed the 'thought', as an object of investigation requires there to be a conversion. This would also explain two further assertions: that all attributes designate the same object, express the essence of substance and that substance has no existence outside its expressions. This would fit rather nicely with Frege's contention that a complete description fully describes the thing and that words have sense and reference only in sentential context but do not acquire them through it (41, 42). Alternatively, one could say that Deleuze exploits the distinction between definite and attributive description. The latter indicates what an individual would be while making no existential (actuality) claims but would imply that the expression is well formed and complete.

This final option is attractive because it avoids one major problem. So far I have argued that the expressions are equivalent because there is an equality principle operating: the extensions are equivalent. Another option would be to take the concept as unlimited. But there is an ambiguity; it would appear that the functional expression refers to a function that is unlimited or infinite. And this seems to take us back to the initial presentation of the problem. Now we must ask 'what are the extensions?'. Deleuze claims that the extension for each term is unlimited, is infinite. Immediately we can see that this requires quantification. It is just not the case that everything is extended – only extended things are extended. Also, though, Deleuze does not wish to identify the term with the class of things falling under it – the attribute of extension is not a class of extended things. Indeed he insists that an attribute is infinite because it has no parts (30). The argument for this is that substance is convertible with attributes and not modes, that the infinite cannot be defined in terms of an infinity of parts, otherwise there would be two different types of things and the infinite would not be infinite. With a no parts doctrine, however, it is more difficult to see how the extensions could be considered to be equivalent.

Perhaps one solution is to begin with the perfect nature of the attribute. If each attribute is unlimited (conceived *per se*) then it is infinite and perfect. Because there are infinite attributes and because there can be no interaction between these attributes, no form is inferior or superior to another. Thus, we can conclude, that all forms of being are equal. Alternatively we could argue that all attributes are qualities and corresponding to each infinite quality is an infinite quantity. Quantity is divided into intensive and extensive degrees and can be considered as an infinite series of finite parts. Each part of the quantified quantity is in an isomorphic relationship with a part of the corresponding series. Because one series can be mapped on to another we can say that the two are equal. This satisfies our demand for equality between two function-concepts and therefore we can say that there is one object designated.

Unfortunately, although these are attractive solutions they leave two problems. The first is that the attributes are supposed to be the conditions for ascribing absolute power to God and this precedes the quantification of the quality. If this really is the proposed solution then the general argument is quite useless and fundamentally question-begging. Secondly, the attributes are predicable of both mode and substance but substance is convertible with all attributes. This means that the statement 'substance is extended' is an identity statement: there is only one thing which is extended or 'is extended' has a value-range (substance, true). But we can see no good reason advanced not to say 'is extended' has value-range (modes, true).

To conclude this section, Deleuze seems to offer a solution to the Spinozistic problem of the relationship between attributes and substance; pluralism or idealism. Apparently he finds the key through Scotus' account of formal distinction and Stoic semantics. However, the arguments are poor and vague and leave the reader confused both as to what he means by the term 'attribute' and how he is supposed to have demonstrated that each attribute relates to the same substance. Ambiguity in this sense is not a clever aesthetic: it is a device to enable him to move from one insecure premise to another.

Explication

During this section I will assume that above arguments are secure. Now we shall turn our attention to how Deleuze proves that the possible object, the Infinite or God, actually exists. This argument comes in three sections: real versus nominal definition, real definition and God and the argument from power. I will be arguing that the most important and yet most contentious philosophical principle is the *Principle of Sufficient Reason*. Incidentally, the system itself, as we will see, is not open to diversity and plurality, it is closed and bound by rationalist principles and reasons are collapsed with causes.

In order to prove that God, substance, is self-caused, meaning existent and necessary, Deleuze had to avoid the problem of circular reasoning. If God is the cause of *adequate* ideas then the proof of God's existence, and the description of God's nature, can be based neither on the intellectual comprehension of the idea of God nor on the attributes. If the axioms in the proof of God's existence are to have truth value they should not be merely stipulative. The same methodological difficulty was recognised by Spinoza who, in correspondence with de Vries, drew a distinction between two types of definition.[50] He drew a distinction between a definition explaining a thing as it exists outside our understanding and a definition explaining a thing as it can be, or is, conceived by us. Only former definitions are, properly speaking, axiomatic or propositional and 'ought to be true'. In response to Tschirnhaus, Spinoza extended this, referring back to 1df6 and pointing out that a true idea will express efficient cause and that from it can be deduced all other properties. Returning to Spinoza, Deleuze states that whereas the first few definitions in the *Ethics* are nominal, 1df6 is a real definition. To recall, 1df6 runs like this: 'by God I understand a being absolutely infinite, that is, a substance consisting of infinite attributes, each of which expresses eternal and infinite essence'. It is a real definition because it is complete and the proof, contra Leibniz, demonstrates the necessary compatibility, indeed equivalence, of the descriptions (77). This, then, also demonstrates the logical possibility of the object defined.

'Explication' is a term much vaunted by Deleuze. Carnap defines the process of explication as the transformation of a more or less exact concept into an exact one, such that the former less exact concept is replaced by the latter more exact. The definition is then an abbreviation of a process of proof, which may well insert different argument premises or axioms. Showing that a term has a reference amounts to showing that it is epistemologically primitive or that what we have amounts to an appropriate definition of this term from primitive elements.[51] When this is made explicit, the epistemological foundations of the science, in which the terms are used, are exhibited. Each attribute is, for Deleuze, in this sense, primary. Because none is defined through another, each is conceptually independent. Each is a primitive element, the *explicatum*, serving to explicate, and thereby transform, the *explicandum* which is now newly determined. The definition, he states, explicates the nature of what is defined, the attributes not only express the nature of God but explicate it (16). An important feature of the definition is that it is supposed to be an 'unfolding of the object' through the primitive axioms. The axioms 'involve' the object itself. The Spinozistic question for Deleuze is 'how properties deduced independently might be taken together and various points of view extrinsic to a given definition brought within that which is defined' (21).

From the above comparison with Frege, I hope to have clarified a number of significant steps in Deleuze's argument. The term 'attribute' designates a logical object. The logical object is the attribute or the 'infinity of attributes'. 'Infinity of attributes' can be converted into the 'absolute infinity'. This concept of absolute infinity transforms the original concept. Because this logical object is designated by all primitive terms, there remains nothing external to the concept. Now we are back onto familiar territory. If one thing is conceived through another then the latter is said to be the cause or explanation of the former. If the set of definite descriptions is complete then that which is defined can have no appearance outside the expressions describing it. The definite descriptions or attributes can now be said to be the formal causes of substance and that the concept 'substance' is self-explanatory or God is self-caused. At the same time as the attributes working as an explanation of substance, the absolute infinity is said to be the sufficient reason of infinite perfection (74).

Idf6 of the *Ethics* is considered to be a 'real definition' because it proves the possibility of the object defined. Within the Scotist tradition the objective possibility of something is dependent on its logical possibility. 'Logical possibility' expresses the mode of composition produced by the intellect marking a lack of conflict among the concepts composed.[52] Deleuze proposes that in this case the definition should be taken as true (75). Well, what has he defined? In various passages he claims to have defined 'the nature of God', 'substance' and the 'One'. He has done this by asserting primitive elements or irreducible notions which have explanatory power; communicate something about the nature that is being defined. These irreducible notions determine their content in different ways but all designate the same (logical) object, the logical object is the infinite set of irreducible notions. This can be converted into an object of semantic investigation and named 'God' or substance, and so on. This would imply that 'God' is an abbreviation of the list of irreducible notions or complete descriptions. Thus to say that 'substance is extended' would be to pick out one description already constituting the definition 'substance', or the 'nature of God is extension' would be to explicate the original *explicandum*. Thus Deleuze moves from postulating the possibility of an object to the actuality of the object via the process of determining the description.

The Ontological Argument

Here is Frege, writing to Husserl:

> With a concept word it takes one more step to reach the object than with a proper name, and this last step may be missing – i.e., the concept may be empty – without the concept word ceasing to be scientifically useful. I have drawn the last step from concept to object horizontally in order to indicate that it takes place on the same level, that objects and concepts have the same objectivity. In literary use it is sufficient if everything has a sense, in scientific use there must also be *Bedeutungen*.[53]

Ontological arguments usually begin from the premise that the greatest being is conceivable and unless existence were contained in the concept then the concept would be incoherent. The argument can be outlined in this way: (i) it is logically possible that the greatest conceivable being exists; (ii) if it did not exist, its existence would be logically impossible, that is, if it is logically possible then it (actually) exists; (iii) therefore it actually exists.[54] The first premise asserts possibility in terms of logical coherence but the second adds that the first could not be logically coherent unless there was an actually existing being. McGrath points out that to say the second follows from the first is equivalent to saying that the internal coherence of the notion depends on whether the concept is exemplified, that is, on something external to the concept.

If we define God as 'necessarily existing' it seems that we require the concept of 'the infinite' to be synonymous with 'having a definition which includes existence'. In the *Fifth Meditation* Descartes states that 'existence can no more be taken from the divine essence than the magnitude of its three angles together (that is, their being equal to two right angles) can be taken away from the essence of a triangle'.[55] Spinoza's response (1p8) is that a 'definition of a triangle expresses nothing but the simple nature of the triangle, but not any certain number of triangles'. Elaborating this, he says that from the definition of 'human nature' nothing determinate can be discerned as to the actual existence or number of individuals. In order to ascertain the reasons (causes) for the existence of individuals, whose nature we can define, we must show why this number and not another and this ought to lead us to look for an external cause (reason). Obviously, this leans heavily on the *Principle of Sufficient Reason*: for each thing there must be assigned a cause or a reason, the actual existence of finite things must be explained by the existence of a thing which itself needs no further explanation. Deleuze illustrates the point with a similar mathematical analogy. The proof that 'the sum of the angles of a triangle consists in extending the base of a triangle' requires an external viewpoint: someone or thing to do the extending. But, he says, we can define a circle as the locus of points equidistant from a fixed point called the centre and the figure can also be described by the moving endpoint of any line whose other end is fixed. This still seems to leave room for the response that no endpoint moves by itself. To which Deleuze replies that such causes are fictitious or imaginary because we infer cause from effect.

The concept of perfection, we have seen, cannot form part of a definite description because neither explains nor communicates information concerning the designated object (73). Deleuze argues that traditional ontological arguments failed because philosophers tried to derive conclusions pertaining to existence from premises relating to perfections and found that they required an additional premise securing the connection between perfection and omnipotence.

The Cosmological Argument

The Cartesian argument can be outlined thus: an idea of a perfect thing could not be brought into being by an imperfect agency. Because doubt is inferior to knowledge, and because I doubt, I am imperfect. Therefore there must be a perfect being who is the origin of this idea. For Descartes, an idea has more or less objective reality depending on the metaphysical category of the object causing the idea. For every idea there must exist a causal object with as much formal reality as an idea has objective reality. From this one could argue that the idea of God has infinite objective reality and so its causal object must have infinite formal reality. In the *Fifth Meditation* Descartes makes it clear that the objective reality of an idea is a cognisance of a possible entity. When we have an idea of a true and immutable nature we cannot but affirm the formal reality of the cause.[56]

Deleuze quite rightly asks why should the cause of the idea of God contain formally all that the idea contains objectively? (86). In the introduction to *Expressionism* Deleuze clearly states that where the absolute is concerned we do not infer cause from effect because we know the nature of substance through the attributes. Because the attributes explain the nature of substance, which means they constitute the definition, they *are* formal causes. But, to avoid the pitfalls of the Cartesian argument, which requires there to be an external guarantor of clear and distinct ideas, he grounds this through a *Principle of Sufficient Reason*.

The argument is poorly formulated and goes something like this; I have an idea of God so I must assert an (idea of) infinite power of thinking as corresponding to this idea. Because the power of thinking is no greater than the power of existing, I must assert an infinite power of existing corresponding to the nature of God. There is another version of this argument. Let us assume that I have an idea of God. An idea is a modification of an attribute (the attribute of Thought), and an attribute expresses an infinite essence. Because essence can be identified with power, we can say that there is an infinite power of thinking. As the power of thinking is no greater than the power of existing we can conclude that there is an infinite power of existing (87, 91). Deleuze then argues that the power of thinking is the ground of the objective reality contained in the idea of God and the power of existing the ground of the formal reality of God. But to achieve this conclusion he inserts the claim that the more perfections something has the more power it has. Then he argues that because God has infinite perfections, God must have infinite power of existence, and that therefore God is omnipotent (92), and so God exists. Deleuze will tighten up his response to Descartes when he presents his argument for the parallelism.

The Actual Infinity: the Argument from Power

One could still argue that a real definition only pertains to a possible object. There is no independent reason to accept that what is conceivable or logically possible is actual, actualised or even actualisable. In fact, Spinoza suggests that there are possibilities not actualised but which, nevertheless, retain a certain reality as ideas in God. This invites us to doubt whether it is the case that all possible things are necessarily instantiated. In other words, just because Deleuze, for the sake of argument, has proved that the concept of God is *logically* possible, he has not demonstrated that such things are also actual. Recognising this, he claims that he has proved the 'non-impossibility of God' (79). His argument depends on us accepting that impossibility and internal contradiction are the same thing. The primary elements in the definition of God cannot contradict one another therefore the definition is a definition of a possible object.

The principle of possibility has a long philosophic history. Deleuze's argument seems to be that the essence of something that can be conceived as not-existing does not involve existence. From the conceivability of non-existence, non-existence is possible and so essence does not involve existence. On the other hand, because it is not possible to conceive of God as not-existing, and what is not conceivable is not possible, it is not possible that God does not exist. This is because to conceive anything involves conceiving through an existing attribute. Thus the impossibility of the conception entails, rather than a negative fact, a positive one: the actuality of the absolutely infinite or God. But if this is the argument it begs the question of the relationship between attribute and substance.

Deleuze now offers two arguments, one *a posteriori* and the other *a priori*, for the existence of God, both linking the concept of cause with power. I shall take the *a priori* argument first. It is a reformulation of the following argument: the more reality or perfection that belongs to a nature of something, the more power it has and the more forces tend towards its existence. Now, God is infinitely perfect which means that God has infinite power of existing and therefore God exists. Deleuze revamps this argument. Existence, possible or necessary, is a power. We have already proved that the absolute infinite is logically possible and necessary, so the absolute has infinite power of existing, therefore the absolute exists (89). Because, by definition, the absolute is identical to the infinite of infinite attributes, the attributes 'are the conditions for the attribution to absolute substance of an absolutely infinite power of existing and acting, identical with its formal essence' (90).

Deleuze picks up Spinoza's own *a posteriori* argument and argues that the essence of things, produced by God, does not involve actual existence.[57] Mastrius, a Scotist, argued that one must postulate 'real possibility' to explain how creatures have eternal essences. An entity has its possibility from itself in that its existence does not involve a contradiction but also through another, that is God. It is dependent on God because it is God who conceived that possibility. Thus it is God who 'thinks up the logic and the relations between concepts determined by logic'.[58] The existence of the concept thus depends, where a finite being is concerned, on God. Deleuze presents us with something a little more convoluted. The capacity to exist (possible existence corresponding to the essence of a thing), is a power. Now a finite being already exists necessarily (by virtue of an external cause which determines its existence). If an absolutely infinite thing did not exist necessarily, it would have less power than the finite being, which is absurd. Yet the necessary existence of the absolutely infinite cannot obtain by virtue of an external cause; so it is through itself that an absolutely infinite being exists. This argument asserts that a finite being has power in-itself but is also caused to exist. The causation here is a material causation and necessity is a strong claim of determinism. We can thus see a switch in meaning from the necessity of a finite being, materially caused or determined, to the necessity of an infinite being, that is, self explanatory and so self-caused. A similar argument is that the (logical possibility of a) finite thing exists, and because existence can be identified with power, and finite beings do not exist and are not preserved by their own power, the existence of a finite thing must, therefore, depend on God. Because this finite thing exists, God exists (90).

In *The Meditations*, Descartes suggests that necessary existence is entailed by other specific perfections, specifically the perfection of omnipotence. In his *First Reply to the Objections*, he argues that necessary existence is contained in the idea of a being of pre-eminent power not by fiction of the understanding but because it belongs to the true and immutable nature of such a being to exist. Kenny's response to this is that it is not evident, by the light of nature, that whatever can exist by its own power does exist, unless it is first evident that everything wants to exist.[59] Not only is there a problem of evidence but, as Wilson argues, one must distinguish an actual being desiring to exist, from the ascription to a possible entity, *qua* possible entity, the desire to become actual. There is a difference, she argues, between claiming that an existing entity has the power to exist by its own force and the claim that a possible entity has the power to make itself actual.[60] These criticisms are as devastating to the Deleuzian argument.

Conclusion

There has been a revival of interest in cosmobiology and Deleuze's own philosophical thought has been described by Ansell Pearson in *Germinal Life* as 'biophilosophy'.[61] Although this can be contested, as Deleuze is interested more in the idea of 'becoming' than evolution, there are undeniably parallels between Deleuze's pantheism and theories associated with cosmobiology. Cosmobiology is a thesis observable in Plato and is the view that the cosmos is a living animal, ensouled and possessing mind. The theory associated with Zeno and arguments delivered as proof for cosmobiology are directly inherited from the Platonic system.[62] The Stoics embellished Heraclitus' belief that *logos*, as the indwelling cause of all things, is part of nature, not something imposed on it by human convention. They also shared belief that *logos* pervades nature so that everything natural possesses some properties inhering in *logos*. This means that when describing the world the categories of description naturally cohere with the intended object. Lloyd concludes that 'features of description therefore were features of nature, so that their categories were like Aristotle's, facts of nature'.[63]

At the beginning, I noted a disagreement between Plotinus and the Stoics with reference to the nature of *archē*, which they seemed to have identified with God.[64] The Stoics offer a version of the argument from design. God is inferred on the grounds that individual phenomena are not otherwise explicable.[65] But this critically rests on a contestable method and the assumption that there is only one possible account: rational activity. Plotinus argues that a true *archē*, that which explains, must itself not be in need of the same sort of explanation it provides. All composites do require an *archē* and if *archē* is considered to be composite, *pneuma* and *logos*, then further explanation is demanded. Cotta, a Sceptic, adds to this that the Stoics confused nature with rationality. Plotinus argues for the need to posit a higher principle than *nous* as a first principle and so introduces the concept of the One as unique, simple and distinct.

It is insufficient to refer to a philosophical history as though one were offering proofs or arguments. If Deleuze's biophilosophy, or transcendental empiricism, is a version of cosmobiology then he will encounter criticisms similar to those first advanced by Plotinus and the Sceptics. For the moment, let us just note two things. Deleuze does not wish to eliminate all immaterial things from his ontology, hence the parallelism, but he does collapse reason with causes, hence his explanatory or causal rationalism. It would seem as though Deleuze posits the *Principle of Sufficient Reason* as the only principle that could account for or explain the system but as a principle it remains outside. Indeed, this seems to be a neo-Plotinian One – perhaps the only consistent position to take.

We have discussed general responses to Deleuze's argument. For instance, we could say that there is nothing inconceivable about there existing only finite beings; indeed, we could comfortably describe the infinite as the totality or complete set of finite beings. If Deleuze were to respond that this would be to forget that finite modes have an external cause, we could reply by just denying that this is the case, rejecting the assumptions concerning substance or objecting to the definition of cause. The definition of self-causedness as self-explanatory introduces the equivocation between logical consistency and material causation. There is otherwise no problem with saying that only finite beings exist in relation to other finite beings. If finite beings are necessary at all, it is because they are determined by other finite beings and this suffices. We cannot argue from the actual existence of this finite being to the infinite attribute and then to the absolute infinite without the metaphysical arguments already in place.

The assertion that an attribute is conceived *per se*, that it is irreducible, is absolutely pivotal. Yet it implies that the act of conception is fundamental or that the attribute of Thought is the only attribute – that all distinctions depend on conceptual analysis and therefore on the attribute of Thought. Even if we accept more than one attribute, Deleuze has not convinced us that the attributes are conceptually independent. Beyond merely asserting a definition of the attribute, the proof is two-fold. First, through the description of an attribute, its *propria*, we can identify which words are attributive (infinite and unlimited). Second, the *propria* do not explain substance, only descriptions proper, or attributes, communicate information relating to the nature of God. The attributes constitute the nature of God, taken together they are the complete description or definition of a single entity. We can identify an attribute as the description proper because it is unlimited, conceptually independent or infinite. But, if we define something according to its description, and if the description operates differently in differing contexts, as does the adjective 'finite', then we require sure ground for distinguishing these senses so that identification can occur. It would be, at best, circular to argue that one sense relates to substance and one to attribute; unless we could respond that in all cases the concept 'infinite' strictly means 'that which is conceptually independent' and this is not the case. Yet it is to these arguments that Deleuze refers when he maintains that attributes are 'affirmations' and that being is absolutely positive. Therefore, it is these arguments, along with those of the third triad, which underwrite Deleuze's proposition in *Nietzsche and Philosophy* that being is affirmation.[66]

More damning, even than this, is that as Delahunty argues, instead of proving that there are plural substances rather than one, Spinoza, and here the same is true of Deleuze, has not even proved that there is one.[67] Much is said about Deleuze's expressionism – for instance that he unveils the expressive and univocal nature of being – but the argument for a weakened sense of real distinction, formal distinction, is without real content. We cannot describe the attribute as a thing of reason, or an expression, without clarifying the object of reference. He is forced either into an idealist position or considering the refutation of the realist position, his own cosmology must collapse. We will see that Deleuze struggles to say anything meaningful about the finite modes as extended (bodies) or as thoughts (minds).

2
From the Infinite to the Finite

During the previous chapter I explored the problematic relationship between substance and attributes as presented in the *Ethics* and looked at Deleuze's response to the contradictory objectivist and subjectivist interpretations of the relationship. I investigated how the notion of formal distinction might be adapted from medieval philosophy but concluded that Deleuze could not give us a satisfactory answer as to how we might know that the attributes refer to, or are attributed to, the *same* substance. Because these attributes are in fact the properties of thought and extension there is already a suspicion that the realist or materialist waters are being irretrievably muddied. After assessing his arguments for the identification of God with attributes, I concluded that the account of formal distinction, his 'weakened sense of real distinction', fits well into his own project but fails to deliver a proper solution to the ontological problem of the existence of God.

In this chapter I pick up the suspicion that Deleuze fudges an answer to how the properties of thought and extension relate to substance. Ansell Pearson advises us that the principle of univocity should help us to clarify this relationship; indeed, he says that this principle cannot be avoided in any appreciation of, or encounter with, Deleuze. If that is the case then it would extremely unfortunate if the principle merely appeared to help him solve the problem of how substance relates either to infinite or finite modifications of attributes.[1]

When we say 'being is univocal', this is not a well-formed phrase because the term actually implies a property predicable of two things. The properties in this instance are the attributes Thought and Extension and the things in question are substance and modes. This means that for being, or the attributes, to be univocal it, or they, must be a property predicable of both substances and modes. Deleuze must be asserting that F(a) is true in cases where F is an essential property and a is either substance or mode. However, we have already said that for Deleuze an identity holds between attributes and substance which does not hold between substance and modes. This must raise a doubt that the properties, or attributes, can be predicated of both substances and modes. Magnifying this doubt is the fact that modes are not supposed to share essences, so that while the attributes are the essential properties of God they are not the essences of modes. We must then infer that when we say 'a is extended' either the 'is' or the concept must be functioning differently. In other words, we cannot say 'a is extending' means 'being in such and such a way, for example, extending' when substance and modes are not co-extensive.

Deleuze believes that the notion of immanent causation will help him to untangle these philosophical knots. A Scotian account of a univocal term includes the idea that the term has sufficient unity to serve as a middle term of a syllogism. Wherever two extremes are united by a middle term that is one in this way, we may thus conclude that there is a union of the two extremes themselves.[2] Deleuze once again attempts to adapt medieval semantics and rather creatively tries to show how attributes are such middle terms, bringing together substance and mode. This 'bringing together' is what Deleuze means by immanent causation. Throughout this section I shall be showing that the arguments are tenuous and that Deleuze is unable to show how the infinite, Natura naturans, can produce or cause the finite world of things, Natura naturata. This ought to begin to firm up our initial suspicion that Deleuze muddies materialist or realist waters into the belief that Deleuze's materialism is without substance.

The Problem of Derivation

In 1p16, Spinoza states that from the necessity of the divine nature there must follow infinitely many things in infinitely many modes. Expanding this in the demonstration, he adds that from a given definition certain things necessarily follow. The 'follow from' indicates a logical necessity: it would be a contradiction to deny the existence of infinite things. This implies that by virtue of the original definition, we can conclude that there are infinite things. The first point to be made is that although these infinite things follow from the divine nature in a logically necessary way, they are not logically necessary in the same sense as God or substance itself. Yovel refers to this as a 'degradation'.

The second point is that the 'follow from' does not indicate mere logical necessity but also (material) causality: God produces or causes infinite things. There are two problems. One concerns the claim that God can cause infinite things and the other relates to the apparent conflation between logical and causal necessity.

When Deleuze discusses the relationship of the infinite to the finite we cannot miss the Stoic undercurrents. Unable to parrot Diogenes, that nature is a craftsmanlike fire proceeding methodologically to bring things about, Deleuze affirms the logical point that it would be a formal contradiction to assert God's nature and then to deny the existence of infinite things. In the Introduction to *Expressionism* Deleuze states that God produces an infinity of things *because* his essence is infinite (14): God's essence is omnipotence, if God did not produce an infinity of things then God would not be omnipotent, God is omnipotent etc. An assertion of formal contradiction rests on the principle that there is no state of affairs 'p' such that both: it was in God's power to bring it about that p and: God did not bring it about. The 'follow from' relationship, for Deleuze, is then originally a logical point, 'where cause relates to its effect as a premise does to a conclusion that follows from it'.[3] In a similar vein, Deleuze also says that 'we can consider modes in infinite variety as properties jointly deduced from the definition of substance' (22). 'God ... produces an infinity of things which result from its properties as a definition' and 'modes are assimilated to logically necessary properties that follow from the essence of God'. This logical relationship is also a physical relationship, the relationship of cause to effect, and because the type of causality we are concerned with is supposed to be immanent causality, there is for Deleuze, contra Yovel, no degradation in being (172). Because there is no degradation Hardt for one is happy to assent to Deleuze's proposition that there is no hierarchy in being.[4]

Natura naturans

In the metaphysical systems of both Deleuze and Spinoza we find three sets of basic qualities, supposed to distinguish infinite from finite things. The first set includes the qualities of being-in-itself and the quality of being-in-another. The second set contains the qualities of being self-caused and being caused by another (which is immanently caused by itself). The final set contains the qualities of being conceived through itself and being conceived through another.[5] Substance and modes have polar properties. A finite mode is in-another which is, in turn, in-itself, it is not self-caused and is conceived through another. Substance, on the other hand, is in-itself, is self-caused and is conceived through itself. However, substance is supposed to be all there is. So it seems that either the finite thing is a modification of substance or else it has no ontological status. Substance, although it is convertible with the attributes, is not 'the same thing' as finite things. Modes are modifications of substance and substance cannot be strictly identified with those modifications. However, substance can, in some sense, be identified with the finite modes, otherwise the system would not be pantheistic and it is also the case that modes are not merely accidents. So, from this, if modes are necessary, in a logical or a material sense, then there seems little reason not to identify substance as the 'aggregation of finite things'.

Natura naturans is a Spinozistic term, Bennett translates it as 'naturing Nature' to retain the suggestion of activity, and it also identifies substance and attributes as 'things' distinct from modifications or finite things. The principal distinction is that substance is the only thing properly speaking that is necessary. It is 'the principle and result of metaphysical necessity'. By this Deleuze means that only substance has necessary existence. This is established, perhaps even presumed, by the arguments outlined in the previous chapter and the main idea we are to take from the first part of *Expressionism* is that we are to argue from the supposition of one attribute to the existence of substance: the first two triads. The argument can be spelled out in this way. First, we assume an infinite attribute, then we infer an infinity of attributes. Each attribute is attributed to something other than itself. All these attributes are logically compatible with each other and so the something else, to which they are all attributed, could be the same for all attributes. Furthermore, this something else is the same as all the attributes and this logically entails an existing or actual substance.

This argument depends on converting substance with an infinity of attributes and it fails because Deleuze is unable to convince us of the existence of more than one attribute. The conclusion, unpalatable to Deleuze, leads to idealism. The argument also relies on it being true that an attribute is not a substance and so it must fail. The *a priori* arguments, all of which drew on the principle of non-contradiction supporting this proposition, relied on a suppressed premise.[6] The argument also relies on us accepting that each attribute is attributed as to something else, a logical subject, and that it is only substance which is impredicable and independent. This too falls because we can just refuse to accept the definition of substance. Finally, the general argument, combining the two triads, depends on the definition of an attribute as distinct, that is, unlimited by another attribute. The main support for this was gained from the claim that an attribute has to be unlimited, has to express an unlimited quality, otherwise it would not be infinite. Incidentally, the argument that an attribute can be perceived *per se* was inconclusive and even if satisfactory is insufficient to prove logical compatibility.

Natura naturata

The term Natura naturata implies dependency, so Bennett translates it as 'natured Nature'. Infinite things are said to follow from, but are not identical to, the divine nature. Before we appraise exactly what this 'follow from' means, we need to scrutinise the sorts of things that are being said to be 'following from' the divine nature. Within the Spinozistic lexicon we have already encountered the terms 'substance', 'mode' and 'attribute'. Let us flesh this out a little. To each (infinite and eternal) attribute is supposed to be linked an infinite modification of that attribute. The immediate and infinite mode of the attribute of Extension is 'motion and rest'. The immediate and infinite mode of the attribute of Thought is 'the infinite intellect'. According to Spinoza these modes are infinite and necessary (1p23). Corresponding to the immediate infinite modes of the attributes are mediate infinite modes. These mediate modes are 'the total series of finite modes': individual modes or bodies. These individual modes or bodies vary in infinite ways without substance undergoing alteration. This means that the infinite series of minds/ideas is the mediate mode of the immediate mode of Thought. The infinite series of bodies is the mediate mode of the immediate mode of the attribute of Extension. The infinite series of bodies and the corresponding infinite series of minds/ideas form the face of nature or the surface of the world.[7]

Then we have finite modes. Finite modes are described as transitory differentiations of substance, differentiated according to the universal laws, which are the immediate modes of the attributes. For example, a body is a transitory mode, differentiated according to the laws of motion and rest – the immediate mode of the attribute of Extension. A finite mode is distinguished from other finite modes according to how it acts and reacts. Finite modes are also bound, or limited, by one another. Particular bodies come into existence and pass away as distributions of motion and rest alter, although the total amount of energy in the system is said to remain constant. Every finite mode is caused by an antecedent mode, and that antecedent mode is itself a causal product. It seems fair to infer that each mode is necessary due to material causation and, because cause is a law of nature, each mode is caused by the derived law.

Repeating Spinoza's general taxonomy, Deleuze states that an immediate mode is the first expression of an attribute, which is then expressed in a mediate infinite mode and finally in finite modes (105). The immediate infinite mode in the case of Thought is the infinite intellect and the immediate infinite mode of the attribute of Extension is motion and rest (SPP 92). The mediate infinite mode is called the *facies totius universi*: the relations that govern the determination of the modes as existing. For the attribute of Extension these are 'the relations of motions and rest that govern the determination of the modes as existing'. For the attribute of Thought these are 'the ideal relations governing the determination of ideas as ideas of existing modes'. There is an ambiguity here. Deleuze categorically states that the infinite modes *contain* in them laws, or principles of the laws, according to which corresponding finite modes are determined or altered. Elsewhere, however, he states that the mediate mode is *constituted* by actual finite modes.

Follow from

At this stage the principal problem for Deleuze is that he has to find a solution to the relationship between attributes and their modes. According to Spinoza, all attributes of God are eternal (1p19) and all things following from the absolute nature of any attribute must exist forever and infinitely, or they are eternal and infinite through the same attribute. The attributes then are eternal, which means timeless, and so all things following from any attribute of God must exist forever and infinitely. Infinite, when describing an attribute, means 'it is logically true that God is, and always has been, extended'. Given 1p20, a mode following from an attribute must be infinite. But the immediate modes are laws of nature, such as motion and rest. Infinite when applied to these modes of the attributes must mean something different, more like 'of endless duration'. It is only by accepting this shift in meaning that we can begin to clarify how an eternal truth can produce infinite alterations: how Natura naturans could possibily produce Natura naturata.

In a parallel fashion, when Spinoza claims that God is necessary he means 'a self-caused being such that essence implies existence'. With neither the infinite nor the finite mode is this the case because both are ontologically dependent. This is why Yovel argues that necessity is *transmitted* through a process of logical derivation. Yet even this transmitted sense of necessity is plausible if and only if there is strict entailment, that is, that one can derive these and only these laws of motion and rest from the attribute of Extension. If we accept that these laws 'cause' finite modifications and that these laws are themselves necessary, in a transmitted sense, then all things would derive, in a logical sense, from God.

We find this problem of necessity in the world of finite things as well. The finite modes can only be in causal relationships with other finite modes. Similar to the above point concerning derivation, the argument that finite modes 'follow from' infinite modes would be consistent with the nature of modal causality, if it were the case that this and only this sequence or series of finite differentiations were itself necessary. Garrett argues that if we can demonstrate that this and only this series of finite modes is compatible with these laws of nature then the series of finite modes would be necessary in a strong sense. It would only be this 'stronger sense' that could satisfy two important Spinozistic assertions. One is that in nature there is nothing that is contingent. The 'strong sense' delivers this by proving that there is only one possible world (1p29). The second is that finite modes do not follow from the absolute nature of an attribute. Garrett's proof runs like this: Spinoza holds that everything exists unless prevented from doing so (1p11d), and that substance's power to exist varies with reality and perfection (1p11s). He also holds that everything expresses some degree or other of reality and perfection (1p16d), and that substance with less than the greatest possible number of attributes is a contradiction, on the grounds that greater number is correlated with greater reality (1p9). From this he concludes that Spinoza would regard the following as a contradiction: 'substance whose attributes express less that the greatest possible reality and perfection through the series of finite modes'. This series of finite modes must therefore express the highest degree of reality and perfection. The mediate mode of the attribute, the infinite series of finite modifications, would then be necessary as the only possible sequence or series of finite modes. We could then say that this series of finite modes 'follows from' the absolute nature of the attribute.

There appears to be a straightforward logic of derivation operating vertically. From our definition of substance we deduce the attributes, from the attributes we deduce the immediate modes and from these the finite modes. We can now say that the finite mode is governed, produced or constituted by the immediate mode and move back up our chain of derivation. Their (logical) necessity seems to derive from, or in Yovel's terms, is transmitted from, the attributes and ultimately from substance itself. At the point when this logical chain ends with finite modes, we enter time or duration: the horizontal axis. Then finite modes effect other finite modes causally: 'horizontal causality realises the vertical line by translating its inner logical character into external mechanisms'.[8]

If Deleuze could either prove that there is no transmitted necessity or that there is no shift in meaning of critical terms then he would be more able to convince us that the infinite can produce finite things. The attributes, according to Deleuze, are each infinite in kind. We have already indicated that the term does not suggest an infinite series of parts but implies rather that an attribute is conceived *per se*, is unlimited. According to Spinoza, a mode following from an attribute must also be infinite. According to Deleuze, an immediate infinite mode is infinite or unlimited 'by virtue of its cause'. He defines the immediate modes as the infinite intellect and motion and rest, and links these with the laws or principles governing the determination of finite modes within each attribute. I can give little content to Deleuze's claim, except to point to the relationship of involvement that might be implied.

Spinoza, and for the sake of argument Deleuze, maintain that these three statements are equivalent: the knowledge of b depends on and involves the knowledge of a, the concept of b depends on and involves the concept a, b is understood through a. The term 'involves' is always ambiguous but could be said to mean 'the cause is conceptually included in the effect'. The argument might then be that where cause is conceptually included in the effect, the cause is somehow transmitted through the effect. There are immediately two problems with this. First, there is equivocation with the meaning of the term 'concept': is 'concept' strictly identified with attribute or does it name an attribute? With our three equivalent statements it seems that Deleuze and Spinoza presume that the two, to all intents and purposes, mean the same. Second, more prosaically, we can be sceptical about the claim that where the cause or concept is infinite or unlimited that this can, in any meaningful way, be transmitted to the effect or dependent concept. The argument is really bogus when, by infinite we originally meant something which is conceived *per se* and by mode we meant something which is conceived through another, an attribute.

Similarly, we can see Deleuze stumbling over the problem of necessity. Recall the Spinozistic assertion that necessity, where God is concerned, means self-causation: that essence implies existence. With neither the finite nor infinite mode is this the case. This is because both are ontologically dependent. Deleuze describes an order to the production where the immediate modes occur at the second level. This may be an assertion of ontological priority, a way to argue that the effect is as necessary as the cause because the effect depends on the cause – an order of being as well as an order of logic. Ontological priority can be asserted though if and only if two things stand in an ordering relation and each stands in that order by a feature essential to it. Two formulation of this are: x is ontologically prior to y if and only if y could not exist unless x did and x is ontologically prior to y means that the existence of x is a necessary condition of the existence of y but the existence of y is not a necessary condition of x.

Deleuze presumes that the immediate modes are derived from the attribute. He reminds us of an initial distinction between sense and reference, attributes and substance, then suggests that at the second level of production the immediate modes *designate* the attributes and *express* modifications. He states that modes are 'participial' propositions which *derive* from primary infinitive ones (105). It is no wonder Deleuze places the term in scare quotes. A participle is a verbal adjective qualifying a noun but retaining some properties of the verb, such as '(x) is going'. The modes are either 'intellect' and 'motion and rest' or the series of finite modes. The sense in which the mode 'motion and rest' could participate in the attribute of Extension is not at all clear and it is not obvious how he envisages the parallel with a verb such as 'to go' to work. Unless he is assuming that the derivation is a matter of logic, and that these and only these modes could be derived from the attribute, these laws of motion and rest from Extension. He certainly considers the 'participal' propositions to be necessary. Surely, though, for this to be the case, it ought to be argued not only that these and only these laws can be derived but also that these and only these attributes could be the condition for these laws. But, it is by collapsing the logical relation into a conceptual relation of dependency that Deleuze warrants his claim that because immediate modes are conceptually dependent on the attribute, they are derived from that attribute. Even at this stage the flaws in the argument for immanence are transparent.

When Deleuze argues that the mediate mode is constituted, or formed by, the actual infinite of finite modes, I take him to mean that the laws or principles of nature can be identified with the immediate mode of an attribute and that the mediate mode can be expressed in terms of the field of a relation (motion and rest, ideal relations). This is the set of things belonging either to its domain or to its range. The determination of the domain or range of this field occurs through the conceptual dependence, involvement, of finite modes. Recall that, for Deleuze, the mediate mode is the actual infinity of the essence of finite modes. As with Spinoza, we have the claim that a particular finite mode is necessary in the sense that it is caused by an antecedent and that the antecedent is itself a causal product. Deleuze argues that God could not have produced anything else or produced things in a different order, except by having a different nature (104). I take this to be a form of Garrett's argument that the mediate mode, the infinite series of finite modifications, is necessary as the only *possible* sequence or series. That the argument hangs on two principal claims, substance's power to exist varies with reality and perfection and that everything expresses some degree or other of reality and perfection, leads neatly to Deleuze's assertion that the power of substance is the sufficient reason of the quantity of reality. It also, therefore, falls for reasons previously outlined. To summarise, then, I think we can say that so far Deleuze has not proffered any solution to the thoroughly Spinozistic problem of deriving the finite from the infinite.

Immanence

Deleuze makes two, apparently contradictory, statements. The first is that a finite mode is not subject to a dual causality: a vertical relation between God as cause of the essence of the mode and a horizontal material causality (SPP 54). The second is that existence is necessarily determined, both from the standpoint of relations as eternal truth or laws and from the standpoint of extrinsic determination or particular causes (SPP 94).[9] He tries to resolve this tension by advancing the idea that God should be understood as *immanent cause*. Finite modes are thus dependent on God, due to the nature of their essences, and are caused by universal laws of nature, themselves derived from the attributes. As already stated, if we accept that these laws 'cause' infinite modifications and that the laws are themselves necessary, in a transmitted sense, then because God is the 'immanent' cause of all things, all things logically derive from God. The idea that God is immanent cause explains how God is the first term of reference for any finite mode and how the logical relationship of derivation is transformed into a material causal one. To explain why the logical relationship is transformed at all, Deleuze states that God necessarily understands his own nature. Deleuze believes that what is logically possible is actualisable. This would mean that God is able to do whatever is implied by his definition.

Before embarking on a discussion of these propositions, let us remember that for the Stoics substance and quality are categories and that everything in the world is a material object or substance. Substance and 'qualified' are both terms which can categorise anything that exists. Since matter is continuous, particularity refers to the shape or form marking one stretch from another but each owes its individuality to *pneuma*. Hence, each qualified substance has an individuating quality and this is part of what is means to be qualified. However, we arrive at common nouns only by the process of generalisation and proper nouns can refer only to this individuating quality. We will find that in his attempt to make sense of this idea of individuating quality Deleuze commits a mistake such that he assumes that the individuating quality is singular and variously instantiated as singular qualities. This is due to the earlier ambiguity concerning the object designated by the attribute as name.

The proof that God is an immanent rather than transcendent cause is an amalgam of three basic propositions. The first is that God can and must cause infinite finite things to exist. The second is that quality is the sufficient reason of quantity. The final proposition is that attributes are forms common to both infinite substance and finite modes.

God understands himself

Searching for an answer to 'why does God produce Natura naturata', Deleuze wishes for a deep explanation. What he comes up with will, in effect, tie up his causal rationalism with what Bennett describes as explanatory rationalism. He has already established, to his own satisfaction at least, that it is logically necessary that an infinity of things follow from God's nature. In the sixth chapter of *Expressionism*, Deleuze picks up this point and advances the view that God understands the science of his own nature. Carefully defining 'understanding' in terms of definitional analyticity, Deleuze repeats the claim that to understand something means to know the properties that follow from the definition. The argument at first glance seems to be unsound. God can deduce that from his own definition there follows an infinity of things. Given the parallelism, to each idea corresponds a thing, to think an infinity of things means that there is an infinity of things. This argument would be clearly fallacious as it presumes the parallelism and also uses without argument the idea that God can be an object of his own understanding.

To explain how the logical relationship of derivation is transformed into a causal one, without committing these errors, Deleuze attempts to show that God necessarily *understands* the necessity of his own nature and necessarily produces accordingly. To do this he will argue that in its *possibility* the idea of God is grounded in *Natura naturata*, to which it belongs, but also that, in its *necessity*, it is grounded in *Natura naturans* (123). So first he draws a distinction between necessity and possibility. Let us take the argument relating to necessity first. It appears to be two-fold. First, he reminds us of two propositions. A principle of equality holds between the attributes (parallelism) and that the attributes are the conditions for ascribing absolute power of existing and acting to God. He refers to this as God's formal essence. Secondly, he claims that, given the parallelism, each formally distinct attribute *must* be represented by an idea (120) and that each formally distinct attribute is objectively distinguished from the others in the idea of God. Hence we once again arrive at the pluralism (infinite attributes, infinite ideas (of) attributes) and monism (one object, one idea). So the argument is that there is an idea of the essence of God and to the formal essence of God corresponds an objective essence. Because essence is identical to power, there is a power of thinking and knowing corresponding to the power of existing and acting. Hence, we can conclude, that there is an infinite power of thinking and knowing. The deduction of 'infinite' here is unclear.

This takes us to a discussion of possibility. According to Deleuze, we arrive at the conclusion that the formal essence of God is existing and acting after first asserting an infinity of attributes. We arrive at the conclusion that the objective essence of God is thinking and knowing by asserting only the attribute of Thought. His point is this. We identified the infinity of attributes and this was the condition for asserting the absolute power of existing and acting. Now, to the formal essence corresponds an objective essence, such that there is an idea of the infinity of attributes, and because the idea is a modification, it belongs to Natura naturata. Then he makes a distinction between the formal being and objective being of an idea. All ideas, or objective essences, are formed in the attributes of thought, they have formal being as well as objective being. The idea of God has thus both formal and objective being. It has formal being as a modification of the attribute and objective being as the idea of God. The former, and here Deleuze follows Spinoza's terminology, is designated as the infinite understanding. Without formal being, there could be no objective being: 'objective being would be nothing without this formal being ... it would only be potential without this potentiality every being actualised'.

By definition, the absolute is identical to the infinity of infinite attributes and the attributes are the conditions for the attribution to absolute substance of an absolutely infinite power of existing and acting identical with its formal essence. Corresponding to this formal essence is objective essence, the idea of all attributes. The attribute of Thought is the necessary and sufficient condition for the attribution to absolute substance of an infinite power of thinking and knowing. The idea (God) is a modification of an attribute and therefore belongs to Natura naturata. Hence, for there to be the objective essence, the formal being of the objective, the move from Natura naturans to Natura naturata must have already been made. The power of thinking and knowing belongs to God's absolute nature but would remain unrealised if God did not form the idea, modify the attribute, through which he knows or thinks himself.

There are many difficulties with these arguments. Deleuze can argue that it is necessarily true that to the nature of God corresponds an idea only because he has first acceded to the truth of the parallelist thesis. According to the parallelist thesis it would be a contradiction to assert the existence of something and to deny the existence of the idea of the same thing. Second, the conclusion of the argument, that there is infinite power of thinking and knowing, is then used to justify the assertion that the idea of God is the cause of all other ideas, and that power of thinking is the sufficient reason of the series of ideas (120). This principle is required for the parallelism as it blocks causal interaction between the attributes. Third, when Deleuze implies that through his idea, God knows himself, he is referring to this series of ideas. Then, by invoking the parallelism, he once again presumes that for each idea corresponds an object in a different attribute. Fourth, thus, if God forms an idea of himself it means that the 'follow from' relation *must* be realised. Fifth, this can only be true if the idea of God contains the thought or idea of infinite attributes and infinite things following from them. My last point here is that the attribute of Thought can only be described as the necessary and sufficient condition for the power of thinking and knowing if and only if there is a power of thinking and knowing. Also, it might be the case that this power is a necessary, but not sufficient condition, if other attributes must provide the content.[10]

Essence: quantity and quality

It is unsurprising to discover that there is considerable debate, within Spinozist scholarship, as to the definition of the term 'essence' and over the nature of the essences of finite modes.[11] Haserot, quoting 1p8 and

1p17s, suggests that an essence of a finite thing is something which is eternal, that several individuals can share and is the sort of thing that if it were to be removed, the individual itself would be removed. Haserot draws together a number of key points, for example, that essences are not dependent on mind, that they are not known or perceived through the senses, that they are, nonetheless, objects of real knowledge, that many individuals can 'share' an essence. He concludes that Spinoza's account of essences demonstrates his Platonism.[12] Balz suggests that one should view an essence as a logical entity, synonymous with idea, something which can be explicated, or verbally expressed, as a definition. Knowledge of essences would then be a science of ideal forms.[13] Yovel advances the hypothesis that an essence of a finite thing should be identified with the place that the finite thing occupies – the metaphysical or logical point which belongs to its exclusively in the overall map of being. The essence of a finite thing would then be its ontological dependence on substance and its specific point, its determination through co-ordinates and other points on that map. I shall be arguing that Deleuze refutes the descriptions of essence offered by Haserot and Balz.

One aspect of Deleuze's reading of Spinoza is his assurance that the system delivers singular finite things. These things are to retain their singularity even when in material relationships to each other and even though they are ontologically dependent on substance. Singularity is a function of essence and Deleuze, using something like an identity of indiscernibles argument, wishes to prove that each essence is not merely distinct but also a *res physica*. Distinguishing between two notions of difference, difference in degree from difference in kind, he argues that concepts of quality and quantity have become confused. The idea of a quantifiable continuum constituted as or by physical points forms the basis for the philosophy of mathematics, appearing in later work such as *The Fold* or *Difference and Repetition*. Because Deleuze obviously had this sort of application in mind, one could approach these issues through the work of Lautman, Cauchy, Cantor, even Leibniz.[14] However, prior to such application is the argument that the quality can be quantified and that the resultant quantity is a *positive*, singular point: an essence. Macherey points out that Deleuze gives the impression that he is following as closely as possible the reasoning of Spinoza's text but that his presentation is in fact based on a concept that simply does not appear in the *Ethics*.[15] The assimilation of the distinction of *in se* and *in alio*, attribute and mode, to quality and quantity marks the opening gambit. To understand Deleuze's argument I believe it instructive to examine the relationship between quantity and quality outlined by Hegel in the *Logic*. Deleuze, I contend, uses various Hegelian insights but attempts to do so without the overall dialectical framework.

In the Hegelian system, quantity is designated as the category appropriate for pure being. It is indifferent. The concept 'magnitude', however, marks determinate quantity. This can be described mathematically, as 'that which can be increased or diminished without changing or altering form'. With the proviso that we are not to identify that which can be described mathematically with that which can be known, he concedes that the notion of quantity has a place as a logical stage of the Idea.[16] Hegel then draws our attention to the fact that quantity may be viewed either as a continuous magnitude or as a discrete magnitude: continuous being the one or the unit, the self-same point of the many ones. Quantum is the determinate being of quantity. The difference is that when we consider the notion of quantity, the distinction between the discrete and the continuous is only implicit whereas with quantum the distinction is actual and reaches its development in number.

A further distinction is made between intensive magnitude, or degree, and extensive magnitude. Hegel suggests that the concepts 'continuity' and 'discreteness' generally apply to quantity. The terms 'extensive' and 'intensive' apply to quantity when it is limited and determined. He then argues that *intensive* magnitude or degree is distinct from *extensive* magnitude. The example he uses may help to illustrate the distinction. A certain degree of temperature is an intensive magnitude and has a simple sensation corresponding to it. But, if we were to look at the thermometer we would find that this degree has a certain expansion of the column of mercury corresponding to it. The same is supposed to be true of the world of mind. The terms 'intensive' and 'extensive' refer to quantitative limits only, to quanta. The difference, at first sight, appears to designate a difference between what Locke might call primary qualities or powers and secondary qualities. However, the distinction is really one of a comparative emphasis between plurality and unity. When we consider an intensive quantity we prioritise unity and when we consider extensive magnitude, we prioritise plurality. As we have seen, the limit of the intensive magnitude is its degree. The suggestion is that extensive magnitude, plurality, is absorbed into intensive magnitude. Degree, in the *Encyclopaedia*, is the highest stage of quantity.

Hegel then argues that each quantum may be independent and immediate but when two are brought together their value is only through this relation. The relation between two quanta may remain the same even when the quanta are substituted for different quanta. When the ratio alters then the quanta must follow suit. He says that in place of 2:4 we can put 3:6 without changing ratio, as the exponent 2 remains the same throughout.[17] This exponent is also a quantum and any quantum can be figured as a ratio between two quanta. Additionally, in order to maintain the exponent if an increase or diminution of one occurs then the other will need to alter as well. If we take the ratio as a result of mathematical operation then either of the related quanta may increase, as long as it is accompanied by a diminution of the other term and within the limit that no term can increase beyond the exponent. This takes us to the ratio of powers, where Hegel posits a special relationship between a number and its square, a number and its exponent. This constitutes the dialectic of quantity and is not a mere return to quality but qualitative quantity or measure.

Hegel now proposes the case for determinate negation. When we take measure as our starting category, there comes a point when an increase, or diminution, will effect a qualitative change. The example offered by Hegel is that of water converting into ice. Another could be the vibration of a sound wave. If the quantity exceeds a certain measure, the quality is held in abeyance and the place occupied by the first quality is satisfied by a second. Each quantum can only be defined in relation to another quantum. The reason for this is that no reason can be found why one quantum should have this magnitude rather than another, except that one stops where another begins. The next step is important for our exegesis. The argument is that the move from the category of quantity to quality to qualitative quantity is the movement of determinate negation. The category of measure takes us to an understanding of the 'essence' of being: the transient nature of the unity of quality and quantity. 'In the passage of the different into different, the different does not vanish: the different terms remain in their relation. ... In Being everything is immediate, in essence everything is relative'.

Let us extract from this exegesis the points of relevance. First is Hegel's dual description of quantity as a continuum and as discrete. We can cease at any point on the continuum and discover a finite quantity. The second point interesting us is his characterisation of the 'differentiation relation', joining and separating parts.[18] We should note that that which is discrete is discrete by virtue of there being a continuous magnitude, otherwise there would be no limit. While quantity may be indifferent to its limit it is not indifferent to *having* a limit. The problem for Hegel, purportedly resolved in the passage on ratio and powers, is how to explain *why* one quantum might be assigned the particular limit it has, without incurring problems of infinite regress.

There is one major difference between Deleuze and Hegel with regards the general argument. According to Hegel, the notion 'quantity' designates indeterminate being: being without limit. The distinction between the discrete and the continuous remains merely implicit and it is only made explicit through the stage identified with magnitude.[19] We have already seen that Deleuze identifies the terms attribute and quality and then states that there is an ontological unity. This would mean that there is a single being, designated by all attributes, and that all attributes, taken together, designate one being or substance. The implication is that all qualities are identical to one (quantity): all forms of being identical to being. The term quality is thus not introduced at the level of measure or the quantum. Substance (quantity) is completely qualified (infinite attributes – one substance). By definition, an attribute is unlimited which means that it is conceived *per se*. Deleuze can therefore declare that the determination of being does not occur through a process of determinate negation.

There are three stages in Deleuze's argument, matching the Hegelian moves but without the thesis of determinate negation. The first, as we have just seen, is pure quality. The argument begins with the unlimited attribute conceived *per se* attributing itself to one substance. This stage for Hegel is the first stage of the Idea, which moves on to quantity then to qualitative quantity, or measure. The next stage for Deleuze sets the foundation for the quantification of the quality and is the thesis that substance expresses itself to itself and that the power of thinking is equal to the power of existing or acting. The final stage is quantitative. Deleuze states that to each attribute or quality corresponds infinite quantity. The notion that quantity corresponds to quality is elliptical. He also writes that each quality has intensive modal quantity. Quantity has two forms: intensive, in the essence of modes and extensive, when the modes pass into existence.

For Deleuze, an attribute as quality is indivisible but under certain conditions this quality as quantity is divisible. When we consider the quality in terms of quantity, at first the distinction between the discrete and the continuous remains only implicit. Let us, for the sake of argument, accept that an essence of a mode can be identified as a part or degree of power. According to Deleuze, these degrees of intensity, the parts of power, are intrinsic determinations of the quality. They form an infinite series, a total system, and an actually infinite whole (194).[20] When considered in this way, they must be thought as inseparable. Nonetheless, each must also be thought as discrete. The Scotian example, suggested by Deleuze, is that when we consider the colour white, its whiteness is 'constituted' by degrees of intensity. These degrees of intensity are the instrinsic determinations of the whiteness.[21] Deleuze offers a deductive argument for why we should consider this inseparable whole as divisible into singular degrees or parts. The argument seems to be that when we make distinctions between actually existing things we presuppose that to each existing thing corresponds a distinct essence. From this we can infer that modal essences are actually distinct or singular. Extrinsic determination presupposes a prior intrinsic one (196).

Here we can see Deleuze reflecting Hegel's stage of quantum, where the distinction between the continuous and the discrete becomes actual. There is both intensive and extensive magnitude. An infinite quantitative series is formed from each which is divisible into actual singular parts or degrees. I will pursue the 'correspondence' relation in a later chapter. For now it is instructive to note that the relation between essence and extrinsic determination is not reciprocal, the essence is necessarily actual even when the extrinsic determination is absent, that is, when the body has not been brought into the horizontal axis. Only when we consider the mode as an extrinsic part of the attribute, when the mode is existing, can we make an extrinsic distinction between mode and attribute (196). At this stage, the concept of number is appropriate if inadequate. It is inadequate because the mode is still not substantial, even though it is an extrinsic part of the attribute. The essence of a mode, intensive quantum, finds its limit in its degree. The 'body' of a mode is extrinsically determined which means that it is limited by other bodies. Distinction, or individuation, as in Hegel's logic, occurs at the level of quantitative differentiation. Here is one chief difference. Hegel, due to his principle that each quantum is defined in relation, encounters the problem of infinite regress when he is forced to ask 'why this limit and not another?'. Deleuze has two solutions to this. The first is that the whole series, its order and its composition, is necessary. God is the Sufficient Reason, or possibility, of this series (137). Secondly, where finite modes are concerned, essence does not include existence and so God is the cause.

It is clear Deleuze would reject Haserot's suggestion that an essence can be shared by various bodies and would also disagree with Balz that an essence is a logical entity.[22] Instead, for Deleuze, an essence is a *res physica*, a physical things, a part of power. Well, how does he establish this? He begins by reminding us that attributes are not in themselves powers but are the conditions for ascribing absolute power to one substance. This allowed him to say that God is omnipotent. Now, corresponding to this divine power are attributes as dynamic qualities. To each attribute, as dynamic quality, are linked two quantities, which are both continuous and divisible. Now he can claim that God's power is divided up and explicated in the attributes according to the essences contained in the attribute (92).

This implies that the existence of the essence precedes the attribution of power. However, he later states that the finite essence is to be strictly identified as a degree of divine power (183). The solution to this puzzle seems to be that an essence is a quantity of reality (94) and that to each quantum corresponds a degree of God's power (SPP 65). God's essence divides itself according to the quantity corresponding to that mode (183). Because God is omnipotent there are infinite finite essences. The point is, of course, that it is only by positing the attributes that we arrive at a real definition of God and thus conclude that God is self-caused and omnipotent. Without this initial move, we would be unable to argue that modes, as modifications of attributes, have a power identical to essence. Once again the argument form begs the question. The entire edifice of Deleuze's ethical naturalism is built on this argument.

Conceding the position that this argument ought to take in the general argument structure, there are further problems. There are two basic claims: a mode's essence is an irreducible degree of power and God explicates his power according to the essences contained in the attributes. If we could argue that the attribute could be divided into infinite parts then we could make some sense of this motion of 'irreducible degrees'. Aside from this contravening Spinoza's 'no parts doctrine', it is worth remembering that an attribute is infinite not because it has infinite parts but because it can be conceived *per se*. Acknowledging this 'no parts doctrine', Deleuze comments that an attribute is divisible 'modally but not really' (119). He argues that every attribute is a quality and is divisible into intensive and extensive quantity. Intensive quantity is an infinite series of degrees, infinite by virtue of its cause. Because such degrees cannot be distinguished, individuation occurs when the mode gains its extensive part. With this, Deleuze believes he has established the principle that a mode's essence can be identified with power because the 'intrinsic modes, contained together as a whole in an attribute, are the intensive parts of the attribute itself. And they are *thereby* parts of God's power' (198).

In conclusion, Deleuze is arguing that the essence of a mode is a power not merely caused by, but as a part of divine power. If this is allowed, then he can argue that as God is omnipotent and as all power is actual, if there is a God then there must be infinite finite essences, God produces an infinity of things by existing (94). We only need to add to this supposition that actuality does not have to come into existence, 'for by its very nature as independent the potency is eternally in act, and as such exists eternally. For its existence is not added to it: it *is* its actuality'.[23] But if we do endorse this conclusion we would be asserting that God is both Natura naturans and Natura naturata: the principles and laws of causal derivation and infinite finite things or that God, substance, is convertible with attributes and with modifications. However one frames these arguments it becomes glaringly obvious that aside from transgressing Spinoza's own no-parts doctrine, the Deleuzian quantification of quality is without reasoned support. If this falls then so too does the principle that God is the Sufficient Reason of the series of parts or degrees of powers and thus the mathematisation of the world of finite things itself fades from interest.[24]

Causation

We have noted that Deleuze distinguishes between the infinite self-caused substance and the finite caused modes. The previous arguments were supposed to show that infinite finite things must follow from God and here he has to prove that God is an immanent rather than transcendent cause of these finite things. It is with the second and third chapters in *Expressionism* that the Deleuzian slant on formal distinction shows its teeth and the principle of univocity gives way to the principle of immanent cause, through the Scotian definition of an attribute as a common form. There are three separate claims that might help us to understand what Deleuze means by immanent causation. First, we should recall the distinction between properties properly ascribed to substance and those to modes. Helpful too is the list of three equivalent statements: knowledge of b depends on and involves knowledge of a, concept of b depends on and involves concept a, b is understood through a. To this we should add a final point. To know something is to know it by its cause. We have already seen that this last proposition was the significant principle blocking the move to pluralism: if a is conceived through b, b must be the cause or explanation of a and a and b are said to involve one another.

Deleuze argues that God is the cause of all things, in the same sense as he is the cause of himself. He then attempts to prove how God is an immanent and not transitive cause of things. If Spinoza borrowed from Aristotle a distinction between immanent and transitive causation, then Deleuze is no less, and no more, justified in doing the same. The former signifies internal cause, where the reason for action is internal to the thing and the action realised through the thing's own power or perfection of its essence. Transitive causality, on the other hand, suggests the production of effects by virtue of external causes through the agency of other elements.[25] Typically, an instance of causation would be where A causes changes b in B such that A and B are distinct entities.[26] The formulation for immanent causation would be that A (mode determines God) causes b in B (mode determines God). This would be immanent cause because God is (in) both cause and effect. The claim that God causes finite things in the same sense as he causes himself introduces an equivocation. The efficient cause of a finite mode is another antecedent mode. God can be efficient cause, in the same sense as *causa sui*, only if he is identical to that finite mode. If God is identical to finite mode x then he is also identical to finite mode y where x and y are not identical and where God is not to be identified with all finite modes.[27] There are two candidates for causation: God and finite modes. As Taylor says, when we introduce finite individuals into the system, transitive causality makes its appearance and the immanentism, which was to be the central conception of the Spinozist system, is ruined.

Once again let us reconstruct Deleuze's argument. From the assertion of one infinite attribute we concluded that there is an infinity of infinite attributes. This infinity is said to entail the Absolute due to the fact it is convertible with it. This Absolute is self-caused (formal cause). This Absolute has infinite power of existing and acting through its perfections. Infinite things follow from God and because perfection is proportional to reality, and the power of existing to capacity, we can conclude that God produces infinite things through the attributes (efficient cause). Thus, we can say, in favour of immanentism that God produces as he exists, efficient causality is asserted in the same sense as self-causality (165).

But if this is the reconstructed argument then Deleuze needs to explain in what sense is God both cause and effect? Let us recall three further Spinozist axioms and one injunction. Things that have nothing in common with each other, also cannot be understood through each other, the concept of one does not involve the concept of the other (1ax5). If things have nothing in common between them, one of them cannot be the cause of another (1p3). The idea of a mode necessarily involves the concept of its attribute, which is the infinite and eternal essence of God. The injunction designates the rule of convertibility. First, then, God and finite modes must have something in common.

Where a mode is concerned, existence does not follow from essence and, as we previously saw, for Deleuze the mode has no power of its own except insofar as it is part of a whole, part of a power of a being that does exist through itself (91). Let us abstract from the general argument here. When considering substance, Deleuze posited an attribute as an essence of substance. He argued that the infinity of attributes is equivalent to the essence of substance. By claiming that each attribute is infinite (that is unlimited and perfect), he could argue that substance has infinite power of existing and acting identical to its essence.[28] Similarly, he wishes to convince us that a mode has a power of existence identical to its essence (89). I can discern three separate arguments. The more perfections something has the more power it has. Because a mode is always all it can be (perfect), it has power. Essence is identical to power and power is always power in act (93). All actions require an external cause and because material causation depends on the attribute, we can say modes depend on attributes. Attributes are formal causes of modes. The final point is the participation argument. God is omnipotent, infinite things follow from God's essence, God's power is infinite and infinitely divided up in the attributes according to the essences contained in the attributes.

The mediating effect of the attributes is thus seen in these different ways. The attributes are the conditions for ascribing to God omnipotence, the power subsequently divided up across the attribute. It is because of this initial positing of power that Deleuze can argue attributes contain the essences of modes, that is, infinite degrees of irreducible power 'according to which God's power is explicated'. Finally, the mode is conceptually dependent on the attribute, is caused by the attributes and acts according to the laws of cause and effect which, as laws of motion, are modifications of the attribute. I believe that this explains Deleuze's conclusion that 'the identity of power and essence is to be asserted equally (under the same conditions) of modes and substance. These conditions are the attributes' (92).

If, then, modes and substances 'share' the attributes as common 'forms of being', does this answer the problem of immanentism? Deleuze emphasises the rule of convertibility, which, in fact, is a reminder that where substance and attributes are concerned, the 'is' of identity, is an 'is' of predication, where modes and attributes are concerned. Thus, he says that attributes constitute the essence of God and do not constitute the essences of modes. But, then, one could ask whether the conceptual dependency is also an analytic truth: a finite body is, *by definition*, extended. His solution to this is that an attribute can be conceived without a mode while a mode cannot be conceived without its attribute.[29] In addition, the cause (substance) is more perfect than its effect (finite mode), has more reality and is omnipotent. This mode, of course, although as perfect as it can be, is limited. This is not only because it is conceived through another (the attribute) but also because it is in a material causal relation with other modes. There is one central equivocation though. On one hand, the finite mode differs from substance in that essence does not include existence. On the other hand, the finite mode is a part of God's power. The principle of participation implies an identity thesis. However, there are three things which keep the finite mode distinct from the infinite. The actions of a finite mode can be explained according to its own essence and the essence, according to which God's power is explicated, is an original, irreducible, degree of power. There is also the definitional point that the attributes (essences of God) can be conceived without the modes although this is undermined by the potency-in-act theory.

Wishing to draw a distinction between emanation and immanentism, Deleuze hopes this will suffice. Unlike immanentism, where emanation is concerned the 'cause remains in itself, the effect it produces is not in it and does not remain in it' (171). In his concluding remarks on immanent causation, Deleuze maintains that by definition an immanent cause retains its effect within it – in it, of course, as in something else, but still being and remaining in it (172). He proceeds with the suggestion that 'it is the same being that remains in itself in the cause and in which the effect remains as in another thing' (172). He reminds us that being is equal in-itself and argues that this proves being is equally present in all beings. Clarification of this occurs with the reminder that 'being in' is not the same as 'being contained in'. When we consider the infinite total series of the essences, we are thinking of the attribute as a unity or singular 'thing' and the essences are not conceivable as distinct from the attribute. When, however, the mode exists, when it enters into material relations with other modes, then and only then, is extrinsic distinction between mode and attribute possible.[30] But, here, Deleuze argues that extrinsic determination is a matter of duration[31] and seems to beg the eternal-durational question in a very Spinozistic fashion. In addition, he relies on the deduction from finite body to essence as detailed above (196).

It would seem that Deleuze wishes to suggest that the infinite is a common basis of existence of all things and is the 'indwelling power expressed by all things'. The argument fails for various reasons. The equality of attributes thesis is unconvincing. The identification of essence and power is a metaphysical thesis without obvious or reasonable support. The identification of efficient with formal causation is a conclusion of the shaky argument that substance is a principal of metaphysical necessity. As a final point here, the definition of an essence of a finite mode as an irreducible degree of power, according to which God's power is explicated, requires a much clearer explanation.[32] Deleuze could be relying on the quality of powers thesis (power of existing and acting is equal to the power of thinking) to provide the reasoned support for the quantification of the qualities and thus, indirectly, the distinction of essences and their identity with the infinite.[33] A final option would be to take the quantification of the quality through the argument from perfection as it relates to the attribute itself. But this would be an unfortunate step because, while it appears to answer problems from the *Ontological Argument* and to solve the problem of causation, it fails for many fairly obvious reasons.[34]

Conclusion

We have seen that Deleuze separates the infinite from the finite and asserts their non-identity. Yet he also wishes to argue against transcendent theologies and so he provides an argument such that finite things must follow from the infinite and that the 'follow from' relationship must be one of immanent causality. Because the logical derivation is supposed to be causal, we traced Deleuze's arguments for immanent causation. In order to secure the thesis Deleuze had to prove (i) that cause and effect share something (ii) that the effect remains in the cause while not being identical to it. The cause and effect are said to have the attributes in common and here we see the pertinence of Scotus' principle of univocity. Indeed, the attributes are causes, material, efficient and formal, of substance and modes but not in the same way. By collapsing reason with causes we mystify the assertions of derivation and material causality. Deleuze lays this to rest with the assertion that the attributes are the common condition for identifying essence and power. He assumes that he has achieved the latter with the distinction between intrinsic and extrinsic determination of the quantification of the quality. The thesis of quantification is invoked then to prove that it would be a contradiction to assert the logical without the causal relationship; the real definition without the actual production, both occurring through the attributes 'as causes' but we are to think of extrinsic determination in a weakened sense.

3
The Weak Identity Thesis

So far we have been considering Deleuze's version of Spinoza's monism, where the One is divided into two: Natura naturans and Natura naturata[1] and I have suggested that we should be unhappy about his account of the relationship. He is, I have argued, unable to convince us that finite modes can or do 'follow from' the infinite. For this and other reasons the ontological status of these finite modes remains thoroughly questionable. Now Hegel argued the same point against Spinoza. His concern for the individual mode was a response to his belief that Spinoza was also unable to explain the 'follow from' relationship. Unsurprisingly Hegel attributed this failure to the lack of interaction between Thought and Extension, which for him is the only convincing explanation of individual determination. Without wishing to agree prematurely to this explanation, I do concede that I believe the outcome to be the same in Deleuze's work as it is in Spinoza's. There is, indeed, a blotting out of the principle of individuality, of subjectivity.

We have already seen that there is no good reason to ascribe to the finite mode any ontological status. This, I believe, is one of the three ways in which the principle of subjectivity is blotted out in *Expressionism*. This chapter is an exploration of the second way. In her discussion of feminist philosophy of mind, Kaufman notes that Bradotti and Grosz underscore the difficulties associated with dualistic mind and body philosophies and use Deleuze's idea of 'thinking through the body' to obviate these problems.[2] I, on the other hand, shall be arguing that Deleuze's account of the mind–body relationship leads to an extreme form of materialism, even eliminativism at odds with fundamental feminist principles.[3] While eliminativism is obviously not his intention, it is a result of the logic of the argument for the parallelism. I shall also be arguing that for the same reasons he gives an anaemic story of mental events and cannot accommodate the role of representation in his account of ideas. This, I suggest in the next chapter, leads Deleuze to a number of confusions in his theory of knowledge acquisition. For those who wish to relinquish talk of mental events this may seem to be in Deleuze's favour but this would be to note and accept that Deleuze is himself driven into contradiction. His ethical theory, the 'positivity' of specificity, is dependent upon the very things he eliminates.

The general theory of parallelism

Before proceeding with our general account it is important to realise that Deleuze has leant heavily on the parallelist thesis. Of first importance is that Deleuze used the principle – that where there is an idea the idea is of something actual – to ground his claim that attributes are real, even if only in a weakened sense. This was an essential step in his overall position of substance monism or univocity: one substance – plural attributes. He also invoked an 'equality principle' and claimed that this holds for all attributes. It was with thanks to this equality principle that he was able to establish various premises in his *Ontological Argument*. For sure, although all attributes are conceived *per se* they are defined as equal mainly because it can be said that where there is an idea of a thing there is a thing and *vice versa*. This equality principle allowed Deleuze to argue that the idea of God is sound and therefore possible. It was also by asserting the equality principle that Deleuze was able to draw various inferences concerning the nature of power. For instance, he argued that each formally distinct attribute is objectively distinguished in the idea of God and that it would be a contradiction to assert the existence of some thing and to deny the existence of the idea of the same thing. From this he was able to establish the point that the attributes are the conditions for the attribution to absolute substance of an absolutely infinite power of existing and acting, identical with its formal essence. Thus we can say that for either or both of these important arguments to work, Deleuze must evidence, or at least make some sense of, the parallelist thesis. If he relies on any premise used in either argument, without independent argument, to prove the parallelist thesis then he will be seen to beg the question. Additionally, if he relies on conclusions drawn from, or relying upon, these two arguments to support his parallelist thesis then he will also be seen to beg the question. Without independent support the whole thesis is mere supposition. We would be led to endorse Delahunty's assertion that the thesis of parallelism is not a rigorously demonstrated theorem but an article of faith, or rather it is a creed in miniature.[4]

With reference to our discussion, then, we are asking Deleuze to explain what he means by 'parallelism' and to offer us convincing arguments for it, arguments that do not themselves rely on previously made arguments. So what is the parallelist thesis? There are two main versions of it. Before embarking on a description of these two versions let us recall that our ontological furniture includes substance, attributes, immediate infinite modes, corresponding to the attributes, mediate infinite modes[5] and finite modes which are ideas and bodies. The parallelist thesis takes as its starting point the claim that the order and connection of ideas is the same as the order and connection of things. For every item x we must assume that there will be a corresponding idea (of) x and x and (its) idea will be in the same order.[6] Spinoza's proof, a reformulation of 1a4, leads to the conclusion that for the infinite sequence of events or items there is an infinite sequence of ideas, that one sequence can be mapped onto the other and that for every idea (x) there is an x, where there is an x followed by a y there will be an idea (x) followed by an idea (y) and where an x has been caused by a y, the idea (x) will 'include' the idea (y).[7] From this we can see that the parallelist thesis presents us with a claim of correspondence and of causal isomorphism but strictly not of causal interaction. It also seems that we are talking about there being a parallel series of irreducible things, ideas and bodies, and so an ontological dualism. Let us call this a bare parallelism.[8] If ideas were to represent, be about, bodies in some way we would have to call the parallelism representational. Objectivists, those who maintain a real distinction between attributes, tend to stress this 'dual series' version of parallelism.

The second version of the parallelist thesis takes as its starting point Spinoza's assertion that it is the same thing that is being expressed, now under the attribute of Extension and now under the attribute of Thought.[9] For this to be true it seems that there is need for us to introduce a different sort of thing into our ontological map. This third thing could then be described either under the attribute of Extension or under that of Thought. The description of the third thing would itself be called a mode of the attribute. Modes of the attribute of Extension and of the attribute of Thought would constitute a parallel series. This would be a form of semantic parallelism: two descriptions and one thing being described. However, Spinoza and Deleuze insist that the finite modifications are 'thinglike', are at the very least causally efficacious and distinct. If we call the first version parallelism proper, this second version is best referred to as an 'identity thesis' because it is the same thing that is being described under the attribute of Thought and attribute of Extension. Because semantic parallelism concentrates on the dual series of descriptions, necessarily modifications of Thought, it tends to lead back to a subjectivist position. Subjectivists, those who focus on the attributes as forms of description, attempt to make sense of the identity thesis.

These different versions arise from the attempt to marry the claims that attributes are only rationally distinct from substance, substance monism, with the parallelist view proper, that there is real diversity between the attributes. Descriptions of the finite modes, and the relationship between them, will have to respond to any decision as to the ontological status of the attributes. Given that Deleuze advocates a 'weakened sense of real distinction' it will be instructive to see how he determines the relationship between the modes and I shall be arguing that he advances a 'weakened identity thesis'. For the sake of simplicity, I shall break Deleuze's argument down into three main argumentative steps: for an identity of order, correspondence and being.

Identity of order

There are two general arguments advanced for this first stage. Deleuze commences the parallelist thesis by reminding us that God produces things in all attributes at once, that he produces them in the same order and *so* there is a correspondence between them (110).[10] An assertion, though, is hardly an argument. At this stage he seems to be relying on the equality of attributes thesis: because attributes can be substituted *salva veritatae* there can be nothing in one attribute that is not in another. The second line of argument is also familiar. Deleuze begins by reminding us that God produces as he understands his own nature. There is, he says, an order in which God necessarily produces things (105). The relationship of attribute to immediate mode to mediate mode to finite mode is not merely one of logical derivation but also of cause and effect. From this Deleuze extracts the point that finite modes, in different attributes, are in the same order (106). This is obviously nonsense. For there to be even a glimmer of a chance of it being true the derivation would have to be necessary and we have already shown how such an assumption would be utterly fallacious.

That aside, there is clearly no guarantee that the actual series of finite modes match, in some sense, the modes of other attributes. In response to this problem, Deleuze proposes that if we were to conceive the modes as part of a unit then we would also have to conceive a correspondence between them (106). This would mean that there could not be a change in one without a parallel change in the other. Unless he can provide an independent guarantee that the modes *do* form a unit then this is no argument.

If we were to explain necessity in terms of some best of all possible worlds, there is room to argue that the necessary sequence of modes in attribute of Thought is entirely different from that of Extension. But before we even entertain this argument we must note that the link between (strict) necessity and best of all possible worlds depended on the parallelist thesis and that both were steps in the general argument that 'God produces as he understands his own nature'. Given the tenuous nature of the argument it seems implausible that Deleuze would argue that the ban on causal interaction between modes of differing attributes derives from the fact that there is an identity of order of production (106). Implausible but true. The important move is the claim that due to the identity of order, modes must be conceived through their own attribute. I will pick up this point later.

Identity of connection

Deleuze takes it as proven that there is an identity of order and that this is the same thing as an identity of correspondence between modes of different attributes. From this we are supposed to infer that there is nothing 'in one attribute' that is not 'in the other' (110).[11] Distinguishing between the idea of 'order' and the idea of 'connection', Deleuze asks a similar question to the one we have been pursuing. We were asking 'what guarantee can we have that the modes in each series can be mapped onto modes in other series?' By these arguments for an identity of connection, Deleuze is looking for an answer to 'what guarantee can we have that there is this isonomy?[12] He reminds us that the attributes are, in principle, equal. He follows this with the claim that attributes, or modes, taken together form parts of a whole. The only sense I can make of this is a two-stage argument: attributes are conceived *per se* (equality principle), the attributes can be substituted *salva veritatae*, for this to be the case there must be an isomorphic relationship. Because there are infinite attributes and infinite modifications of those attributes and because God's power of thinking is equal to his power of acting, then there must be a corresponding idea for every mode.[13] This would be circular; all he is entitled to claim – unless he can offer independent support for the second premise – is that there are: infinite attributes, infinite modifications, a corresponding idea for every mode. Then the conclusion would be that God's power of thinking is equal to his power of acting. But this would be to beg his own question. For this reason he tries to answer some of the problems relating to the parallelism by drawing on the arguments he links together as 'principle of equality of powers'.

Deleuze writes that epistemological parallelism (representational parallelism) 'follows from' the equality of powers. We will see below how Deleuze uses the equality of powers arguments to ground the distinction between the objective and formal features of an idea. This is a critical step to his overall thesis. Deleuze secured the assertion that there is an identity of order by implying that this is true because the idea and the mode are the same thing. When Deleuze writes that there is an isomorphic relationship between finite modes of the attribute of Extension and those of the attribute of Thought, he means that for every body there is an idea relating to that body: a basic isonomy. In order not to smuggle into the discussion a claim about representation, I shall follow Bennett and place one part in parenthesis. For every mountain there is idea which has as its content (mountain) and for every fish there is an idea which has its content (fish). If the event is actual (a penguin catches a fish) then there must be an idea isomorphic with the event. This would mean that when the penguin waddles forward there is an idea (penguin waddling forward), when the penguin breaks a hole in the ice there is an idea (breaking hole in water). If the fish dies *because of* the physical effects of the penguin catching it (x causes y) then it must also hold that I(x) causes I(y).[14] The 'must' here is a restatement of the parallelism.

A claim to isonomy runs the risk of incurring heavy philosophical penalties, firstly because there is supposed to be an infinity of attributes. We have two separate 'things'; idea (I) which, in some sense, has its content the event (x) and the event itself x. If the mode in the attribute of Thought and the mode in the attribute of Extension (I(x) x) is an individual and x is a modification with a matching modification, y, in a third attribute, what is the relationship between I(x) x and I(y) y? Secondly, what is the relationship between all these individuals and the ideas of all these individuals? Finally, how we can say that I(x) x is an individual, that for every x there will be a y, and so an I (y) and that

that this does not mean that I(x) y, especially when, given the identity thesis, x=y? This final point raises the question of whether or not it is possible to retain the distinctness of the attributes when each individual is necessarily conceived through the attribute of Thought. So it is by answering this fully that Deleuze will reveal what he actually means by 'weakened sense of real distinction'. A satisfactory answer would also allow him to say that even if we use the premise, that each attribute is conceived through itself, as a necessary step in our *Ontological Argument* this would not incur the penalties of Idealism. The premise that thinking/existing are equal powers would be inferred from the premise that ideas have formal and representational 'being'. Just as he would be able to say that we can conceive the modification x in one attribute and we can conceive the modification y in a second attribute and that by doing so we have not blurred the distinctness of the individual idea-attribute modification.

Bodies and modes

One problematic aspect of the relationship of modes in differing attributes is the initial characterisation of the mode itself, that is, what are these 'things' in isomorphic relationships? Deleuze truncates this problem by considering it to be the same as the problem concerning the relationship between the physics of bodies and the theory of essences (206). He believes that he can present us with a scheme which first clarifies the nature of the body and which can then account for the relationship of the body (mode) and idea (of that body). He must convince us that his scheme is tenable because without it the physics is inconsistent and the parallelism fails.

Deleuze inherited a quandary.[15] On the one hand substance cannot be divided into parts.[16] Yet, on the other, substance is extended and there are modifications of the attribute of Extension. To be consistent the modifications cannot be thought of as parts, as independent things or substances. The fairly traditional way to understand this problematic relationship between substances and 'substances' is as thing (substance) to its properties (modifications). While this 'predicative' relationship goes some way to explaining how substance might be related to, although not identical with, finite modes, it does not properly address the nature of the finite mode. To describe the finite mode as a property seems to deny it the very 'substance' that is at issue.[17]

To speak metaphysically, the term 'extension' is usually considered co-extensive with 'being spatially extended'. So, if we speak of one thing that is extended then we must mean either that there is one thing that occupies space or that the thing is itself space. If we identify substance with space then any division of space would be space as a region rather than a substantial part as such and any 'thing', as modification, would be a region or sub-region. The problem is that we seem to want to talk about 'stuff' that fills these regions.[18] If substance is co-extensive with extended[19] and if extended is co-extensive with space then a finite modification of extension is a modification, a 'thickening' or a 'colouring', of a region of space. Bennett proposes this analogy: 'A blush is adjectival on a face because the existence of the blush is the face's being red; and a pebble is adjectival upon space because the existence of the pebble is space's being thus and so. ... Space contains regions that are G'. This exposition of the nature of substance as extended is called a 'field metaphysic'. Bennett believes that a field metaphysic allows us to cut out talk of matter because matter is redundant in the overall ontological scheme. This would mean a thick red book would be a thickening and reddening of a region of space.

The field metaphysic interpretation of the *Ethics* has come under a certain amount of criticism. For example, Curley notes three objections. The first is that we are being asked to consider our talk of 'bodies' as supervenient, in some sense, on 'thickenings' of spatial regions. When we would normally talk about a body moving we are being asked to translate this into a number of space/time spirals or strings. In order to refer to 'this' body then we appear to assume that the position of the perceiver is necessary for the identification of these strings or this string as a body in movement. But this would be to make indexicals a prerequisite for all identifications and Spinoza himself rules out the use of indexicals from his theory of knowledge. Hence we are left without any way to identify strings as particular bodies. Following from this, the very description of thickenings and colourings of regions of space seems to be a misnomer as these are qualities that can only be properly attributable to actual bodies. Secondly, the field metaphysic makes little concession to the role of the infinite mode of motion and rest because regions of space cannot move. Now, when Spinoza lays the foundations for his epistemology he identifies the common notion, the 'building block' of his epistemological framework, with ideas of those features all bodies share: namely being in motion or at rest.[20] While this does not, in itself, mean that the metaphysic must be abandoned it does mean that either it should be abandoned or a new epistemology found. If the axioms of the system itself depend on the epistemology having some purchase then he has undermined his own argument. Finally, the field metaphysic defines substance in terms of the whole of nature and there is a tension between conceding that there is change in nature and that God remains immutable.

One possible way out from this is to argue that the motion of a body can be translated into a mathematical physics.[21] If we do this, argues Shipper, we could say that the physics of 'matter' can be accounted for in a quantum world where perfect randomness in fact implies a lawfulness. Indeed, we could turn to differential equations to explain how systems change over time. Differential equations could be said to represent reality as a continuum which changes smoothly from place to place and time to time.[22] If we were to say that the 'individual' is a unique place–time string then, by virtue of some sort of identity of indiscernibles, we might be able to side-step the problem of indexicals – the problem of making proper sense of statements that pick out particulars and say something about them in particular.[23] Deleuze could be said to go some way with this as he claims that movement affects Extension before there are any extrinsic modal parts (235).[24]

Alternatively, one could reconstruct the metaphysical argument. The field metaphysic is an attempt to make sense of the dual claim that matter is everywhere the same and that parts are distinguished only modally but not really. We could instead say that matter is divisible insofar as it is, for example, water but cannot be divided insofar as it is matter.[25] In line with this, we could also say that while the parts or things are not self-subsistent or independent they are parts in a 'weakened sense'.[26] This second interpretation gains credence because it helps us to make sense not only of the central role assumed for the immediate mode of motion and rest but also of Deleuze's description of the simplest bodies (*corpora simplicissima*) and of their interaction with one another, such that when they interact in specified ways these simple bodies form complex bodies.[27]

The individual

Deleuze recasts this problem of substantial parts as a problem of physical individuation. First we need to go back to an earlier passage concerning the quantification of the qualities. The argument goes like this: (i) every attribute is a quality; (ii) every quality is divisible into intensive and extensive quantity; (iii) intensive quantity is a series of degrees or intensities of power; (iv) extensive quantity divides into an infinity of simple bodies; (v) the simple bodies are distinguished from one another and related through movement and rest (205).

From this it would seem that Deleuze contravenes the 'no parts' doctrine by arguing that there are simple bodies. But these *corpora simplicissima*, or extensive parts, are not substantial, nor are they monadic or atomic. Deleuze offers three supporting reasons for why simple bodies are not atomic and so not substantial. The first is that if there were atoms then there could be a void. This argument is lifted straight from Spinoza and is one reason why Bennett credits Spinoza with offering an anti-atomic field metaphysic. The second is that an infinity of atoms could not correspond to something limited and the third is that atoms could not form greater or lesser infinities (204). Deleuze admits that these reasons are 'negative'. Indeed they suppose the definition that Deleuze wishes them to be supporting reasons for. According to Deleuze the extensive part is a limited infinity, with a minimum and maximum. This will be critical for his description of the behaviour of bodies but is not important here. Each simple body is already an infinity of parts and an individual is a composition of simple bodies or infinities.

Deleuze describes the simple bodies in terms of infinities because to do so allows him to introduce the term simple bodies and to get his account of complex individuals off the ground. But once this is achieved the complex bodies make talk of simple (atomic) bodies quite redundant. It also allows him to bolster Spinoza's account of individuation, where the individual body can be defined in terms of the ratio of movement and rest internal to itself.[28] This would mean that bodies are nothing more than infinitely divisible portions of the infinite expanse of matter, individuated by ratios of motion and rest. To put it otherwise, I contend that Deleuze defines the simple body in terms we would more properly associate with the complex body and what we would normally call the complex body is merely the coming together of a number of these simple bodies. However, each individual must have a corresponding essence. If the simple bodies were individuals then each simple body would have its own essence.

Deleuze makes five separate, and occasionally inconsistent, claims. First he says that simple bodies in this or that determinate relation form greater or lesser infinite wholes corresponding to this or that degree of power (modal essence). He also says that as they come together extensive parts correspond to certain modal essences *and thus* constitute the very existence of that mode. Thirdly, he suggests that simple parts have neither an essence nor existence of their own (207) and that there is no one-to-one correspondence between extensive part and modal essence. But he also submits that however small the intensity there is always a corresponding degree of power (205). The problem is that Deleuze offers a definition: a mode exists if it actually possess a great number of extensive parts corresponding to an essence of degree of power. But a definition is not an explanation. We need two things to be explained. First, what is the 'stuff' that composes the simple or complex body? Secondly, how does this 'correspondence' relationship occur?

I can find no real answer to the former question and can only suggest three responses that Deleuze could make. The first is only the blocking retort that any answer becomes involved in an infinite regress: of what is this simple body composed?; other simple bodies, and so on. The second would be an identification of the quantification of the quality with the composition of 'stuff' or 'matter' or energy. This would mean that through his argument from power, discussed earlier, Deleuze can deliver us with a specifiable constitution of the universe. This would be sophistry. We have already noted at least three flaws in the general quantification argument. Alternatively, along Bennett's lines, we could say that Deleuze identifies the term 'extensive part' with that which has time and place (213). But this would need to be rephrased as an identification of 'extensive part' with 'time and place': the 'that' being a misleading placeholder. While this neatly allows for a distinction between the intensive and extensive, it incurs some heavy cost – not least inconsistencies concerning the status of the immediate mode of motion and rest.[29]

In response to the second question Deleuze suggests that the simple body is subject to 'outside' determination of movement and rest and that the complex body is itself defined by a certain relation of motion and rest.[30] He says that it is *through* this relation that an infinite whole corresponds to a certain modal essence. This appears to be a statement of definitional analyticity: if there are internal relations of motion and rest then there will be a corresponding essence – the definition of 'existing complex body'. He tries to rescue this from tautology by adding that 'when an infinity of extensive parts enter into a given relation; it continues to exist as long as this relation holds' (208). Now what he seems to be saying is that there are intensive parts/degrees of powers or modal essences. These map onto the internal dynamics of some groupings of extensive parts.

To summarise so far, the necessary condition of individuation is that there are extensive parts and the sufficient condition is that the internal dynamics of extensive parts (temporarily) coheres with a modal essence. This relationship between intensive and extensive parts is neither isomorphic nor causal: the intensive part does not cause the extensive parts to come together in determined ways. The determination occurs according to the laws of the immediate mode of motion and rest where only extensive modes can effect other extensive modes (209). Thus Deleuze tries to secure a principle of individuation for finite things, while making sure that each thing within the system is itself necessary; in the sense that each thing is subject to material causal laws and not in the sense that existence is implied by essence, even though the essence itself relies upon God as cause. While it is tempting to describe Deleuze's metaphysics as akin to a field metaphysic, I think we have to be content with the attempt to present an account of a 'weakened sense of real distinction' where things are modally and not substantially individuated. The notion of 'weakened' distinction trades off the ambiguous definitions 'intensive' and 'extensive' in that we are being asked to accept that on one hand the definition is meaningful but on the other the argument that intensive quantity can only be considered as 'extensive' through a process of abstraction (197). We are also being asked to accept the poorly specified 'coherence' relationship between the essence, intensive quantity, and body, extensive quantity.

Ideas and modes

In our discussion so far we have been assuming that ideas and bodies form a parallel series and have been examining the nature of bodies, the finite modes of the attribute of Extension. What, though, are the entities called 'ideas'? For Curley 'idea' is equivalent to 'proposition'. This could allow us to say that the series of ideas is a series of propositions concerning facts about the physical world. Bennett responds to this by underlining the psychological component. Simply put, Spinoza was not at all clear whether idea meant a logical entity, a representation or belief, or the entertaining of a belief or idea. Holding aside this problem of mentalism, to which we shall return, it is not easy to decide whether ideas correspond to events or to things or to properties as it is quite possible that states, or properties or nouns are to be elided in some way. To add to this, it is quite perplexing to consider the problematic relationship of ideas to past and even future events or things, ideas to non-existent objects (golden mountain) and ideas to impossible objects (round square). Adding even further complexity, let us remember that Thought and Extension are only two of the infinite attributes. For any finite mode there must be a parallel idea and for every idea (mode) mode unit there must be infinite isomorphic units.

This last point was made by a contemporary of Spinoza; Tschirnhaus. He assumed that the terms 'idea' and 'mind' can be used interchangeably and then asked three things. If idea is equivalent to mind, is it the case that every unit I(x)x is animated with a soul or mind? If for every mode x there are infinite parallel modes in all other attributes, then what is the relationship between x and the other ideas? Following from this, is it the case that all the ideas of the infinite modes cohere and form a unity? A single mind?[31] Deleuze agrees that from an epistemological perspective it does indeed seem that not only does the idea (x)x unit form an individual and that the idea is the soul of that individual but also that there is an infinity of such individuals (114). In fact he merely repeats Spinoza's response to Tschirnhaus. First, it is true that for an idea of a given mode there is an infinity of idea (mode) mode units. Second, because each mode must be conceived within its attribute, and explained by other modifications of that attribute, these units remain distinct individuals. Third, because of this, there can be no unity holding across the attributes.

Deleuze must offer a way of thinking about the idea such that the idea and its content remains distinct from other ideas and their contents, without, at the same time, being forced into a position where the tightness of the relationship either implies a causal relationship between them or a blurring of their distinctness. He does two things. First, in a thoroughly Spinozistic fashion, he uses the Cartesian distinction between the objective and formal reality of an idea. Second, he manages to link this to the argument from power. Descartes argues that there are two ways in which an object of thought is said to exist: objectively and formally.[32] *Formaliter*, according to Bennett, refers us to the inherent features of the thing. The term *objectivè* refers us to the features which are represented or depicted, 'those features... possessed not by it as a psychological episode but rather by its meaning and content'.[33] The example used by Bennett is his thought '(of) Spinoza's death'. When writing *Spinoza*, the thought was characterised *formaliter* by the date 1982 and *objectivè* by the date 1677. According to Descartes, a mode of a finite mind has finite formal reality but as an idea of an infinitely perfect being it has infinite objective reality, that is, its object is infinitely real. As we have already seen, this is a necessary step in his *Cosmological Argument*, especially when taken with the assertion that 'for every idea there must exist a cause with as much formal reality as the idea has objective reality'. This would mean that the cause would have infinite formal reality even though as an idea in a finite mind it only has finite formal reality.

What does Deleuze do with this? Well, one of his principal aims is to prove that a 'materialist' reading of Spinoza is possible. To do this he must show, among other things, that the 'fullness' of the attribute of Thought does not make the system top heavy. These are the steps in his argument. The attribute of Thought, just as the attribute of Extension, exists. Because attributes are equal (irreducible), each is necessary to the proof of God's existence (120). Let us assume that God exists. We can now say that 'all attributes are equal relative to this power of existing and acting'. Because each attribute expresses the formal essence of God, each attribute 'has' formal being. Now, to each attribute corresponds an idea (of that) attribute. These infinite ideas, corresponding to the infinite attributes, constitute the idea of God. This single idea of God is 'contained objectively' in the attribute of Thought.[34] In summation, the attributes are equal *vis* formal being even though there is at least one idea in the attribute of Thought that represents, or corresponds to, all other attributes. We can now also say that ideas in the attribute of Thought have both formal and objective being: they 'exist' and they represent or correspond to something.

This allows Deleuze to say that when we consider ideas in terms of their formal being we can say that God causes them, even though they are 'about' modes of other attributes. Thus he salvages the block on causal interaction by asserting that just because the I (x) and x form a unit, the idea is somehow about x, x does not cause the idea. He has also now inserted the argument that the idea of God is unified and this will feed into his claims concerning the identity of being. For now I wish to raise just one objection. Deleuze seems to be saying that ideas have formal being *because* they are modifications of the attribute of Thought and that the attribute of Thought has formal existence *because* it expresses God's formal essence.[35] If this is the case then he is taking too much liberty with the argument structure. The attributes 'express' God's formal essence, or are formal causes, because they explain his nature. This means two things. First, we might consider attributes to be (definite) descriptions of God. Second, the positing of attributes, an *a posteriori* argument, is a necessary step in the proof of God's existence. The reconsideration of the proof of God's existence and argument from power became the argument that God's definition is instantiated and God can be known as the real cause of the attributes (substance is self-caused and the cause of all that follows from it).

It seems to be illegitimate to move from the description of an attribute as a formal cause to the description of an attribute as *having* formal being when we mean two quite different things. If we rely on the argument that the (conceived) attributes are irreducible, and given that the argument assumes a distinction between *objectivè* and *formaliter*, we cannot then use the distinction to argue that the attributes are conceptually independent and to claim that this does not prioritise the attribute of Thought. Neither do these arguments move us any closer to a clear understanding of what Deleuze means by the formal being of an attribute or a 'weakened sense' of real distinction. That said, Deleuze uses the distinction between *objectivè* and *formaliter* being to answer a number of the problems outlined above concerning the existence of ideas of impossible or non-existent objects and to give an initial account of mentalism.

The easiest one to take first is the existence of ideas of non-existent objects. Spinoza suggests that there is a correspondence between the ideas of singular things, which do not exist, and the formal essence of singular things contained in God's attributes.[36] The suggestion is that there is a distinction in ways of existing or being. A thing can be or exist insofar as its essence is contained in an attribute and an idea referring to this essence is contained in the attribute of Thought. A thing can also be or be said to exist when it has duration. Each idea must have formal being *qua* attribute of Thought and objective being *qua* content. It seems as though Deleuze is inclined to argue that ideas of non-existents have formal being regardless of whether or not the object of the content of the idea has joined its extensive parts. This would imply that for non-existents there is a correspondence between idea (x) and x where x is caused by an essence in the attribute of Extension. This lays the foundation for Deleuze's later work where he presumes that an idea can have content without referential purchase or the object being spatially extended. I shall explore this more fully in the discussion concerning epistemology. For now I would like to note that the later position requires the parallelism to be a sound thesis, which it is not, and ignores the problem of representational content which is, in fact, only of the brain state and not of the (external) object at all. The assumption that an essence can cause a modification of the brain and so an idea, must stretch the notion of causality and necessity too far. Within the Deleuzian and Spinozistic system there is nothing that is not strictly necessary and without a strong sense of necessity the system itself would break apart. For the moment, Deleuze is curious to see whether the idea of an idea can secure him an idea as object of thought.

Representation and cognition

Earlier I indicated that we were simplifying the relationship between the idea and its mode and that this would cause us problems. The primary problem is that the relationship appears to be a simple representational one, the idea represents or is about the mode, but, in fact, this is not the actual implication. If the idea has as its content a bodily state or cerebral event this is not at all the same thing as an idea about something else, for example, whatever the cerebral event relates to, or is about. The pertinence of this becomes clear when we consider an actual thought, say, a thought relating to the General Election. When I think about a forthcoming election then there is a physical or brain event. But can we actually say that the thought has as its *content* the brain event? Deleuze, once again following Spinoza quite faithfully, introduces a further representative element. He advances that ideas can be *indirectly* of something else. If y causes x (brain state) and I(x) then the idea must 'involve' y as well as x. Bearing in mind the strict parallelism all this permits is the claim that the bodily modification partly depended on y and not that the idea represents, or that the mind can perceive, y. Later we will consider the implications of Deleuze's account of representation to issues relating to the mind and body and epistemology. For now, let us note that Deleuze seems to have no qualms about introducing a representational element into the relationship of the idea to its content, I (x). He talks about modes of thought and things they *represent* (113) and of ideas and of a unity of an individual formed by that mode and the idea that *represents* solely this mode (114).

The question of the 'aboutness', or the representational quality, of an idea raises a second problem. With Spinoza's account of ideas it is clear that ideas, as 'objective presences in mind', cannot be explained in terms of some special relation between an object and an entity that is the mind. In Spinoza's account the mind is itself secondary to these objective presences and can, in fact, be reduced to a collection of ideas.[37] If we were to attempt to answer the question 'what then is the difference between x and I (x)', we would have to say that the difference is not primarily a 'presence' to mind but a form that x takes. Drawing a parallel between Spinoza and Sartre, Aquila argues that accordingly consciousness just is an awareness of the object, the ideational presentation of x just is awareness of x. So it is not the presence to a mind but presencing itself; if that makes any sense. The equivocation was pointed out by Descartes in his preface to *Meditations* where he was at pains to separate the idea taken materially as an act of thought or understanding from an idea taken in terms of what it is representing. Aquila clarifies this relationship for us by suggesting that, for Descartes, the act of thought, or an idea regarded 'materially', is nothing but the very process by which the 'form' constituting an idea's objective reality comes to be present in the mind.[38] The question is then whether this added cognitive element is being equated with the form itself or with the process of formation? Deleuze seems to address these two problems, representation and cognition, with one argument occurring in three stages. First, the attribute of Thought is the sole, necessary and sufficient, condition for the 'power of thinking'. The supporting arguments for this can be both *a posteriori* (I have a thought, etc.) and those that we can glean from the general argument from power. Second, 'contained' in the attribute of Thought is the idea of God, which includes ideas of attributes. This idea of God is identified with the infinite understanding: the immediate mode of the attribute (122). If a strict parallelism were to hold, it ought to be the case that for every I(x) there is an I (I(x)). Indeed, Spinoza argues that for every thing there is an idea of that thing and he extends this to the claim that if I(x) exists then so too does I (I(x)). Deleuze likewise posits that for every 'thing' with being is an idea of that thing, ideas have formal being therefore there are ideas of ideas *ad infinitum* (125).[39] The central and utterly contentious claim following from this is that herein lies the 'capacity of ideas to reflect on themselves'. 'For an idea and an idea of that idea may be distinguished insofar as we consider one in its formal being, in relation to the power of existing, and the other in its objective being, in its relation to the power of thinking'. Two things occur to me. The first is that the definition of the idea of God as the infinite *understanding* only addresses the problem of awareness by fiat. Secondly, even if there is a necessary abstraction of the form of I(x) such that I (I(x)) this would take us no nearer to understanding the nature of comprehension or cognition. The process of abstraction is not enough to guarantee the 'subject' or mentalistic component that is missing from, but demanded by, the account.

Deleuze describes the relationship between the idea of the idea and the idea, as logical and as a *spiritual automaton* (153). While this might refer back to Leibniz, it also summons a classical description of efficient cause as 'spontaneous' meaning without rational deliberation.[40] Let us accept that an idea has formal being and that the attribute of Thought is the necessary and sufficient condition of the power of thinking. From these two claims Deleuze deduces the fact that an idea *has* determinate power of thinking and knowing (130). The only possible basis for this would be to accept that there is power of thinking and that this power can be, must be, 'distributed' across the attribute, that is, intensive quantity. As difficult as this may be to swallow, even tougher is the next assertion that this means that an idea 'has' the power of understanding, that is, the idea of an idea considered in its form independently from content (131). Before moving on, I would like to insert here the point that up until now intensive quantity has been considered as an essence and not as an activity. From here onwards, Deleuze adopts Spinoza's position that it is by virtue of the idea of mind I (I (?))[41] that the mind perceives not only the states of its body but its own perceptions of those. The idea of the idea would then be the 'form', or with this reading the awareness, of 'simple presence': reflective awareness but not deliberation. One final point. For both Spinoza and Deleuze the relation of mode to its idea is the same as that between the idea and the idea of the mode. If the relation between idea and mode is one of identity, that is, the idea is nothing but its object, then idea and idea (mode) mode must also be identical. This tends to collapse the idea of the idea back into the idea (mode) and thus into the mode itself. Even the distinction of reason between ideas as *objectivè* and *formaliter* cannot rescue this, as Deleuze believes. And it is on this foundation that he builds his theory of self-knowledge.

Identity of Being

It is not merely his theory of self-consciousness that is built on this distinction but also his solution to the problem of parallelism (126). When arguing that there is an identity of order between modes Deleuze was forced to lean on the claim of mode identity. It thus seems that the theory of parallelism, two mapable and isonomic modal chains, depends on the thesis of identity and so the thesis of identity cannot be deduced from the parallelism.[42] For this reason, it seems that Deleuze is proposing a form of parallelism that we have previously defined as semantic. This would mean that the narrative he gives of the relationship between modes of different attributes does not presume that there are two ontologically irreducible 'thing-like' modal sequences.

Just as the epistemological parallelism, the arguments for identity of connection, is supposed to 'follow from' the equality of powers so the ontological parallelism is supposed to 'follow from' the equality of attributes. Now, 'identity of being' may indicate one of two positions. It could mean that an individual I(x) x is one thing and two descriptions: in the attribute of Thought and the attribute of Extension. This would be the position favoured by subjectivists. It is complicated by the idea that each description is itself called a modification of an attribute and as a modification has a corresponding idea. We would have to draw a fairly firm and careful distinction between the mode that is being described and the descriptions as modifications. Indeed, we seem to have not just three things but many things now in our ontology. Alternatively, the contention may be that I(x) = x: bare numerical, or mode, identity. On first reading it seems that Deleuze advances the thesis of numerical identity. He says, for example, that modes of differing attributes are one and the same modification, they are the same thing (109). Similarly he claims that epistemological parallelism directs us to simple unity (114).

Epistemological parallelism refers to the thought of two modes in some sort of relationship. Going down the route of numerical identity we would be saying that just as thinking substance *is* extended substance, a mode of Extension *is* a mode of Thought. This would mean that if my mind is a mode and my body is a mode and if my mind is my body then they are the same mode. Apart from the fact that we have not yet established the thesis that my mind is my body this also seems to rely on us forgetting that ideas and bodies are distinct modes. Indeed, the numerical identity thesis also runs up against one further damaging criticism, made by Delahunty against this sort of interpretation of Spinoza. He writes that, 'if a mode of Thought, x, simply is the corresponding mode of Extension, y, then, if x is the cause of mental mode z, it seems to follow that y is also the cause of z; and if y is the cause of extended mode z, then so must x be'.[43] Although it should be pointed out that this is not the same problem as that already encountered, namely the conception of modes of distinct attributes and the, arguably, entailed idealism. Nevertheless, unless we can find a satisfactory retort then these criticisms seem to impale Deleuze's *Expressionism* on the same spike of inconsistency as Spinoza's *Ethics*. But, as Della Rocca points out, this objection hangs on the role of causation.

If we wished to push the numerical thesis then we would need to argue that there is only an apparent conflict between a numerical identity thesis and Deleuze's denial of causal interaction between the attributes. How might we do that? Arguing the same point with reference to Spinoza, Della Rocca suggests that what we need to do is to rethink our position on the transparency of (transitive) causal events. We have encountered the point in a different context. According to Deleuze, if x is the cause of y then y is explained or conceived through x. Thus if x and z are identical, but belong to different attributes, then the causal ban is transgressed: Delahunty's point above. To which Della Rocca replies that all we need say is that the concept of x involves the concept of y when x and y are of the same attribute but do not involve the same concept when of different attributes. This would stay faithful to the premise that only modes of the same attribute are in transitive causal relations. The question is 'how is it, if modes from different attributes can be substituted with one another, that there is no causal interaction?' To respond to this by saying 'there is no causal interaction between them so they must be conceived separately' rather begs the question. That aside, if the numerical identity thesis only works through the assertion of opaqueness then one further problem arises: we could not say with any certainty that the modal chain of Thought maps onto the modal chain of Extension in such a way that the isonomy is retained. Thus the numerical identity thesis could not be used to explain the parallelism.

The equality of powers argument was used to support the distinction drawn between the objective and formal features of an idea. As stated above it is due to this distinction that Deleuze believes that he has proven how we can say that I(x) x is an individual, that for every x there will be a y, and so an I(y) and that that this does not mean that I(x) y, even if x=y. He concedes Delahunty's point that two modes of different attributes act on one another to the extent that they form parts of a whole. But quickly adapts this and argues that all this reiterates is the parallelism. Even though he also returns to 2p7 in order to construe transitive causation as support for the block on causal interaction between the attributes, we must adduce that he has not seen the fullness of the problem of substitution given an assumption of identity (115).

Deleuze though appears happy with this position and alleges that he can provide a better argument for parallelism than that supplied by Spinoza. In answer to Tschirnhaus, Spinoza is purported to have presented the idea–object pairs as merely multiplied throughout the infinite attributes – leaving, as Deleuze claims, an irreducible plurality of idea–object pairs (127). What is Deleuze's solution to the problem of the relation between infinite idea (x) x units? *Because* attributes constitute one and the same substance, he says, modes that differ in attribute form one and the same modification. How can we understand this assertion? What initially appeared to be an argument for numerical identity now seems to be something quite different. Although he talks about irreducible plurality of pairs, units and even individuals, his solution to the Tschirnhaus problem relies on the undeveloped principle of 'ontological unity': that the two modes express some third single thing.

Epistemological parallelism is defined as the theory that the same individual is expressed by a given mode and the corresponding idea: numerical or modal identity. Ontological parallelism is defined as the theory that one and the same modification is expressed by all such modal individuals in infinite attributes (114). The final part in the overall argument for parallelism, what Deleuze names the 'expressive model', is supposed to supplement Spinoza's account and thereby iron out certain inconsistencies. In order to work it must be possible to maintain a numerical identity thesis for modes and at the same time to suggest that each individual I(x) x relates to another 'thing'. In other words, Deleuze will try to mesh the two interpretations of ontological parallelism. He will use one argument for the identity of being to make sense of the epistemological parallelism (idea and body are the same thing) and use the other to make sense of the relationship between these individuals: one thing various expressions.

Deleuze presents us with two pathways to this thesis of ontological parallelism. Initially he asserts that the relation between (substance–attribute–essence) and (attribute–mode–modification) is identical (110). The second pathway begins with the pronouncement that God communicates something of substantial unity to the modes. There are two ways onto this second pathway. The first is with the distinction between form of being and 'formal' being. The second is with the idea of God. Let us initially explore the first pathway. Before doing so, we need to recall the different senses of the term 'essence'. We discovered many aspects to the meaning of the term. One of these drew on the claim that an essence of something is that which being given the thing is necessarily posited and that which being taken away the thing is removed, without which it can neither be nor be conceived. This we said could relate to the attributes in so far as it is only through the attributes that substance can be conceived. Thus it would make sense to say of an attribute that it is an essence of substance. We also identified the term 'essence' with 'being' and suggested that an attribute can be considered to be a form of being, a dynamic quality, that the infinity of attributes is equivalent to all forms of being. In this way we made sense of Deleuze's assertion that attributes express the essence (being) of substance. A third aspect was clarified in the identification of the term with the notion of power. Thus we tried to make sense of Deleuze's claim that attributes are the conditions for attributing to God the power of existing and acting.

For a congruence to hold we need to be able to match the relationship between substance and attribute with that of attribute and mode and with attribute and essence with mode and modification. Can we say that the mode is the only way through which the modification is conceived? Only by provoking two damaging retorts. Firstly, the mode is itself conceived through the attribute. Incidentally, because the attribute is not itself conceived through substance the analogy already breaks down. Secondly, the *a posteriori* argument is supposed to evidence for us the existence of finite modes. There is no such independent support for the supposition of modifications. Hence to claim that the modification has no existence outside its expression would do no more than merely repeat the dubious metaphysical postulation. One way to rescue the analogy at this stage would be to reply that just as substance is known through the attributes the attributes are only known through the modes. However, I have already proved that the *a posteriori* argument is itself flawed and the overall *Ontological Argument* required the *a priori* proof encountered in the derivation. Similarly, the first step in Deleuze's argument requires us to be concerned with the logic of derivation.

We would also have to say that the analogy breaks down irrevocably because whereas the attribute is an essence (of substance) the mode is not an essence (of the attribute). Can we say, though, that the mode expresses the modification of the attribute? No, but we could perhaps argue that just as the attribute is a description of substance, the mode is a description of the modification. While this would make sense, it assumes just that which it is supposed to be an argument for. In other words, Deleuze has, yet again, begged the question. Finally, is there any mileage in the description of the analogical definition of essence as power? We could only answer this positively if we could say that the modes are the condition for ascribing to the attributes the modifications and that modifications are, in some sense, equivalent to 'attributes exercising capacity for acting'.

As I indicated above, there are two ways onto the second pathway. The first utilises the point of transitive and immanent causation. The mode can be understood as that which is in an attribute and in transitive causal relations with other modes. The modification, as being in-itself, is caused by God. On the face of it, Deleuze immediately hits a number of insurmountable problems. According to the system, causes must resemble effects, finite things follow from finite things, modifications cannot be substances and substance cannot be identical to, substitutable with, either modes or modifications. Nor can it be the case that what Deleuze means is that whereas the mode of each attribute involves the concept of its attribute, the modification involves only the concept of God because the modification is only expressed, explained, through the mode. But Spinoza himself proclaims that God is the immanent cause of each finite mode whereas finite modes are transitive causes of other finite modes. It depends, he says, on how we consider God: 'The modes of each attribute have God for their cause only insofar as he is considered under the attribute of which they are modes, and not, as he is considered under any other attribute' (2p6). From this Della Rocca deduces that the truth value of certain immanent causal claims is sensitive to the way in which the immanent cause is described. This referential opacity, while necessary for Della Rocca's explanation of numerical identity, cannot apply here. Deleuze is using this referential opacity to argue that there is an extra something that accompanies all numerically identical individual idea–mode units.

The second branch onto this pathway is through the idea of God. Let us remember what Deleuze says about the idea of God. There are infinite attributes, there is an idea corresponding to each attribute, each idea-attribute is distinct, there is no infinity of really distinct infinite minds, there is one idea of God and there is an idea of that idea. The infinite intellect of God therefore consists not of an infinity of infinite ideas of attributes but of one idea (God). Then Deleuze asserts two things about the idea of God. First, 'from the viewpoint of its objective necessity, the idea of God is an absolute principle'. Secondly, from the viewpoint of its formal possibility it is a mode of the attribute of Thought. This second point is easy. Any idea is a mode of the attribute and so has that attribute as its condition. I take the first point to be airing the necessity of a logical 'must': that God understands himself is a necessary premise in the *Ontological Argument* (123). He then claims entailment: 'hence' the idea of God is able to communicate something of substantial unity to modes (127), 'consequently' objects represented will express one and the same modification. I wish to make just two points before moving on. There is an obvious jump between the claim that there are infinite ideas of attributes to the proposition that these form a single idea of God. Secondly, it appears that Deleuze is arguing that we must assume the existence of the single modification expressed by all modes to make sense of the scheme, particularly the parallelism. But, if we require this for the parallelism and the parallelism is required for the *Ontological* and *Cosmological Arguments* and then if we presume the existence of God and work back through our entailments finally arriving at the proposition that there must be a modification, we really have begged the question. Otherwise, all Deleuze means is that it is *possible* that there is one substance – plural attributes and there may be one modification – plural modes (128).

Let me summarise so far. Epistemological parallelism refers to the relationship between the idea and the body. Deleuze claims that the only way to understand this relationship is one of identity: this was the second version of the identity thesis I outlined earlier. Now, the version of ontological parallelism that he concludes with, demands that we accept that there is one mode (or modification) and infinite expressions (modes). This was the first and softer version of identity outlined: the position usually favoured by subjectivists. He has not provided us with any arguments that could possibly convince us that modes differing in attribute form one and the same modification. This would not, of itself, be a problem if we were happy to accept plural individuals. But it has emerged that for Deleuze if substance monism is true and if the numerical identity thesis holds then the parallelism must be true. This argument structure fails, not least because he is unable to come forward with any independent arguments in favour of the numerical identity thesis. And it is this argument, or the assumption of it, which allows for the belief prevalent in postmodernism that there can be plural, multiple interpretations of the same thing: that the thing can, in some sense be identified as or through these multiple readings. It also explains how this can be confused with the harder claims that the thing just is these multiple readings.

Body and mind

Epistemological parallelism presents us with the case for the thesis that the relationship between idea and object is one of numerical identity. Ontological parallelism seems to provide us with arguments supporting the proposition that each of these numerically identical units relates to another thing. I believe that we are now in a position to assess Deleuze's account of the mind–body relationship. The term 'mind' is taken by Deleuze to be co-extensive with the term 'idea'. This means that the relationship between the mind and the body is the same as the relationship between an idea and a body. We would thus expect the mind and the body to be identical, given the numerical identity thesis. Here I wish to explore two things. The first concerns the relationship of idea to its content and the impact that the interpretation of this has on a possible mind–body relationship. The second follows from this and concerns the likely reduction of complex mental activity to brain events.

The numerical identity thesis is an argument to the effect that two modes are the same thing. Deleuze also argues that the content of the idea is the physical modification. We have already noted that there is a significant epistemological problem in assuming this. Aquila puts the problem very clearly: 'a particular brain state might very well be, regarded mentalistically, a particular thought whose object is also some particular brain state, but can we make sense of the claim that it is its own object?' In the previous section we saw how Deleuze attempted to prove by analogy that the same relationship holds between (substance–attribute–essence) and (attribute–mode–modification). But even if there is identity of thinking and extended substance and even if this entails the conclusion that each mode of extension is identical with some mode of intellectual activity, we are not led to this particular conclusion concerning the object of the idea. Indeed, the postulate, as already noted, seems to transgress the rule of conceptual independence. That aside, here I wish to signpost how a simple confusion over this point could lead to a definite position with regards to the philosophy of mind.

Let us assume that the idea (x) x unit is an individual. Let us also assume that the idea only has as its content the physical modification. Further, let us assume that the terms 'idea' and 'mental events' or 'minds' are co-extensive. From these three assumptions it would only be a short step to an extreme form of materialism. Because this is an unexpected consequence of substance monism and attribute pluralism let me explain a little more fully. The position I (x) = x could lead to a variety of different interpretations in the philosophy of mind. But when we define the idea as mind and say that its content is *only* bodily activity then we might as well abandon all talk about the mental realm because it adds nothing to our understanding. The critical step then occurs when Deleuze takes the object of the idea to be the modification of the attribute of Extension, loses the representational content and then identifies that idea as the mind.

This is not actually Deleuze's position, although he is confused about this point. He is not, however, confused about the need to explain how a link can be made between the terms 'idea' and 'mental event'. As we have seen, Deleuze contends that the same relationship holds between the idea and its content as between the idea of that idea and the idea: I(x) and I(I(x)). In other words, the idea can be viewed both in terms of its representational content, its objective being, and in terms of its formal being, that it is a mode in the attribute of Thought. When considered in their formal being, ideas can be considered 'without relation to their object'. The idea of an idea is the idea in its form, independently of the object it represents (131). He identifies 'idea of idea' with 'reflexive consciousness' and states that the idea *qua* attribute of Thought 'has' determinate power of knowing or understanding. The sense we made of this before was that the ideational component separate from the bodily modification appeared to be a simple presence or awareness of bodily modification which itself, can become an object of awareness. I shall further develop this theory of mind during the next chapter. Suffice it to say here that 'idea' and 'mental event' are co-extensive terms.

The allegation that ideational element means 'awareness' is direct from Spinoza. Spinoza himself suggests that where there is a bodily modification and a corresponding idea then there is some awareness, even if there is confusion as to the content. While this all seems fairly straightforward, does it mean that there is awareness wherever there is idea (x) x? Whenever a dog barks or a stone falls down a mountain are there corresponding ideas? Where there is idea (fish) fish, is the fish aware of its movements? Is the content of the idea a modification of attribute of Extension (fish)? Are these ideas to be identified with awareness and if so who, or what, is aware? Is it the fish or the mountain or God? If it is God, because the ideas are 'in' the attribute of Thought, is there a difference between idea (mountain) mountain and idea (cerebral event) cerebral event? Perhaps we could argue that awareness is dependent on complexity, complexity depends on the amount of motion an individual demonstrates and the mountain has minimal, the fish some and the human a great deal. We may dislike this claim because it would lead us to argue that there are degrees of human awareness dependent on the quantity of motion demonstrated by this particular complex modification. Indeed, we may be more convinced by the argument that for each mode there is a corresponding idea, that the human being entertains these ideas, the mountain does not and that there is a qualitative difference between human awareness, *qua* entertaining an idea, and the fish being aware of its physical modifications. However, the problem is that we have now slipped into our discussion an assertion that the 'idea' can be a content of thought which can be entertained. It is this very question of the possibility of complex mental events that Deleuze attempts to answer through the notion of reflexive consciousness. Yet because each and every idea (x) has a corresponding I(I(x)) not one of the problems outlined is addressed.

Deleuze echoes Spinoza when he writes that the soul is the idea of my body (114). A necessary premise of the parallelist thesis is that each and every mode contained in infinite attributes corresponds to an idea.

In terms of the philosophy of mind there are two obvious problems. The first originates from the point that any idea-mode individual is identical to infinitely many other individuals. The second from confusion concerning the status of mind *vis* ideas of the body.

If each mode is to be identified with infinitely many other modes, and with other ideas of those modes, and if my mind is constituted by the ideas of bodily modifications, which are identical to infinitely many other modes, then my mind must also be identical with, or include, all these other ideas. Now, Spinoza argued that the idea and mode relationship is such that the idea is the idea (of) the mode, that it has as its very content that mode of extension. This is not merely a reassertion of the numerical identity thesis but a statement to the effect that the idea has as its very content the bodily modification. To be fair, this allows Spinoza to do two things. First, he can say that the human mind is not to be identified with infinite (distinct) minds which are the ideas of infinite modes of the infinite and distinct attributes. Secondly, it gives him good reason to assume that this idea is my mind because the content of the idea are these physical movements which are this body's alterations.

Deleuze departs from Spinoza by arguing that we can think of these ideas as part of a causally unified whole, if we think of the modification as that which is expressed through all the modes and their unity communicated from the idea of God. This is interesting because, on one hand, Deleuze avoids the problem of reductionism arising from linking the idea to mind and suggesting that the mind is nothing but the physical modification. On the other, he loses the close tie between this idea and this body and thus must extemporise what makes this idea *my* mind. Two points should be made. If we can consider the content of an idea to be, say, penguin waddling forward and accept that this is matched in the attribute of Extension by a series of causally consecutive alterations, then is that idea a mind? We raised this before. Let us leave aside for the time being all problems concerning the representative content of an idea. If it is a mind then what would it mean for *me* to entertain an idea (penguin waddling forward)? If I can entertain this idea, or mind, then can another finite mind entertain the idea of my physical alterations and thus *my* mind? This problem cannot be avoided by suggesting that reflective consciousness can be identified with the idea of the idea and thus that the human mind is peculiarly self-reflexive. This is for the simple reason that, by dint of argument, I(I(x)) relationship necessarily holds for every idea. On first reading, then, it appears as though Deleuze is unable to carve out any private space and privacy is usually considered to be a necessary, although not sufficient, condition for any non-reductive account of the mind. Secondly, the notion of there being one modification expressed through all attributes, while it encourages Deleuze's non-reductive presentation of mind and body, does seem to introduce a thoroughly metaphysical notion of there being an extra 'something', the modification. The definition of this something cannot be given either through mentalistic concepts or through physicalist ones but only through both these and then the infinite other attributes.

When pushed by his own narrative to demarcate a private space, or room for indexicals, Deleuze retreats to a position which merely reiterates that found in the *Ethics*: what we call 'me' is only the idea I have of my own body and my soul in so far as it suffers an affect (146). His answer to the first point raised above leads us back to the second point. According to Spinoza, the mind is not simple but composed of many ideas. If each idea were itself a mind then the mind would be composed of many (other) minds. Deleuze could well argue that my mind is equivalent to the form of all ideas (minds) of all of my bodily modifications and other modifications in all other attributes. I suggest that despite all his metaphysical posturing, Deleuze's attempt to flesh out his non-reductive materialism falls on the twin problems of privacy and ideational content. We shall further explore Deleuze's account of personal identity when we examine his account of epistemology and indexicals.

Conclusion

One Cartesian line of argument, in the general proof of the thesis of dualism, is that the mind can be conceived as distinct from the body and that therefore the mind and the body can exist separately as distinct things. But once Descartes separated and described them as two quite different, material and immaterial, things, he had to explain how they could interact. The Cartesian principle, that mind and body can, in some sense, interact, is rejected by Deleuze. He blocks any form of interactionism with two basic claims: each attribute is conceived *per se* and finite modes can only be in a causal relation with other finite modes of the same attribute. And, by the same token, Deleuze thus endorses the fundamental tenet that the mental and the physical are irreducible. But because he also advocates a substance monism he has to deny that this entails substance dualism. Because he defends a numerical identity thesis and an irreducibility of description we could describe his position in the philosophy of mind as something approaching a property dualism or double aspect theory. This interpretation is bolstered by the underlying thought that one modification is expressed through infinite idea–mode individuals. However, the ontological parallelism cannot rescue the epistemological parallelism from leading to a reductive account of the mind. Given the identity thesis and the confusion over the fact that the idea has as its very content the physical modification I(x) x leads to I(x) = x to x doing all the work, and the idea might as well be redundant. If the idea is identified as mind we can see how a reductionism leads to eliminativism.

A number of questions are left floating. If the mind and body are really distinct, irreducible, then what explains their union? If they are knitted together by conceptual necessity then how can they be diverse? If they express the same thing then how can they be conceived separately? The supposition of a weakened identity thesis fails because it relies upon an invocation of opaque transitive causality and there is, consequently, a blindness to the problem of substitution. I have also suggested that Deleuze's confusion concerning the numerical identity thesis of the mode with ideational content leads him away from a non-reductive account of the mind and moves towards a form of eliminativsm. He is unable to save this account of mind because he can only retain a notion of privacy or intentionality by invoking the identity thesis, which he is confused about and which leads him straight back to a form of eliminativism. This confusion is entrenched, rather than dissolved, when he embarks upon discussions relating to personal identity and knowledge acquisition.

4
The Body and its Passions

In the previous chapter we saw that Deleuze is keen to argue that the mental and physical realms are irreducible[1] and mainly because this would be consistent with his substance monism and attribute pluralism. We also examined his argument that ideas and bodies are numerically identical; that they are the same thing. I suggested that he confuses the proposition of numerical identity with the quite different claim that the actual content of the idea is the body or the physical alteration of the body. I showed how this confusion would be exacerbated if we, as Deleuze proposes, consider the term 'idea' to be coextensive with the term 'mind'. By putting these different postulates together, we saw how Deleuze's account of the mind and body, although explicitly something like a double-aspect theory, is in fact much closer to an extreme form of materialism. I concluded that Deleuze's attempt to flesh out a non-reductive materialism fails due to the twin problems concerning privacy and ideational content. Although I have reserved judgement as to Hegel's explanation for the 'blotting out of the principle of subjectivity' in the *Ethics*, I have advanced the suggestion that we can find the same phenomenon in *Expressionism* appearing in three guises. It appears first in the way that Deleuze is unable to account for the existence, necessary or otherwise, of finite modes. It next appears in the logic of the mind–body argument, such that what is manifestly a double-aspect theory has, as its latent content, a reductive form of materialism.

Deleuze draws his inspiration from Spinoza's *On the Correction of the Understanding*, which he describes as falling into two parts.[2] In the first part Spinoza considers the purpose of philosophy and concludes, according to Deleuze, that through analysing the form of a true idea we come to know our own cognitive abilities. A connection is then established between the acquisition of this knowledge and the acquisition of a higher human nature. The second part of the *Correction of the Understanding* is concerned with the content of a true idea. Once we grasp the content of a true idea, Deleuze believes, we can address ethical problems. The ethics and the epistemology are thus thoroughly entwined. Jaspers claims that this is because both bring awareness of what man is. 'The highest good', he writes about Spinoza, 'is attained through the growth of the philosophical insight in a vision of what is eternal (metaphysical total vision). Such insight is secured by the theory of knowledge. The attainment of such insight is freedom and has as its consequence freedom in practical life'.[3]

It is my contention that when we examine Deleuze's portrayal of human nature we find two things. Contrary to appearances, the individual must be subject to universal and necessary laws. Secondly, the individual is disposed to act in ways we might associate with possessive individualism.[4] To demonstrate the flaws in his argument I shall follow his ethical programme, apparently leading towards ethical maturity, which, I contend, actually leads to the final blotting out of subjectivity. The first step in the programme requires us to become conscious of natures of things. Because it is crucial to take this step, and because Deleuze is more than happy to ruminate on the qualities of the natures in question, it would be a mistake to erase the role and function of 'biology'.[5] The second step is the exertion of our ability to form adequate ideas of these natures. As we climb from the first to second step, we should find ourselves rattling the shackles of *our* overly passionate and determined natures. Incidentally, we will notice the seeds of an alternative to Freudian psychopathology, germinating from Spinoza's account of active and reactive forces.[6]

The individual

At the first step then we must become conscious of the nature of things and Deleuze wishes to connect descriptions of these natures with an account of the ways in which bodies behave. His theory of individual behaviour is the result of hooking the theory of modal essences into an analysis of the laws of motion and rest and then inferring a number of things about consequent behaviour.[7] He believes that there are two ways of approaching the natures of bodies. The first is mechanical and relates specifically to the structure of the body being identified. Deleuze analyses the structure of the body into three components:[8] the essence as degree of power (*puissance*), the characteristic relations in which the mode expresses itself and the extensive parts subsumed in this relation (217). The second way of looking at the body is more concerned with dynamics and involves us considering what the structure enables that body to do. Claims made as to sentience and sensibility are tied in here. Again, this is broken down into three component parts: essence (*puissance*), capacity to be affected (*pouvoir*) and affections that exercise that capacity.[9] Any declarations made, as to the behaviour of a body, require us first to be secure with our principle of individuation and identity: what makes this the same body and the actions the actions of this, rather than that, body.

In his own way, Deleuze pursues Spinoza's thesis that identity can be defined in terms of form. This would mean that if the form were lost, the thing itself would be destroyed.[10] The form of a composite body is defined in terms of its internal relations of motion and rest. For many this approach is a promising beginning to an account of identity. We must assume, though, that the body is in a continual state of being affected by other bodies (210). Once this is accepted we need to develop a clear account of what might be necessary to the body's identity, of which changes are contingent or transient and which amount to the destruction of the body – to the loss, rather than the alteration, of form.[11] Without such criteria there are two possible implications. We could say that all alteration inaugurates a different identity.[12] Or we might say that there can be no alterations.[13]

The solution available to Spinoza was to adopt the scholastic meaning of essence, where a distinction is made between an essence, the properties of a thing and its accidents. In this case, properties are deducible from the essence, and are therefore necessary in some sense, whereas accidents can be lost without change in identity. The modes could be considered to be akin to these deducible properties and unimportant changes in modes similar to accidents. If Spinoza were prepared to ignore the apparent contradiction in assuming that everything in the system is necessary but that there are contingent or accidental events, he might have used the scholastic essence to argue that some changes in a mode are accidental, and therefore do not bear on a thing's identity, while others signal the demise of that thing. However, although this explains how changes might occur, the account presumes that there are things quite necessary to the body without giving us a way to tell what they are.[14]

This solution is not available to Deleuze. Although he does use the term 'essence' to suggest a difference between the nature of something (its essence) and its deducible properties[15] and uses the term interchangeably with the terms 'definition', 'explanation' and 'complete description', he mainly defines 'essence' as 'degree or part of power'. Deleuze accedes to the point that a body can undergo alteration without loss of identity but he explains such continuity through a deeper analysis of the structure of the body. There is, he avers, a natural limit to how much the body can be affected without it being destroyed. The identity of the body is given in terms of the internal relations of movement and rest. The total quantity of the movement and rest of a body remains constant (210).[16] Deleuze links this structural analysis to the dynamic one. When the internal relations are no longer maintained *then* there is no longer any 'capacity to be affected'. As a natural consequence of the organisation of the body, the capacity of the body to be affected also remains constant except in exceptional circumstances (225). This, then, gives us a working definition: the body remains continuous when the internal relations of motion and rest remain constant.[17] Now, Deleuze needs to address the problem of alteration. The suggestion above is that some alteration (affection) can be accommodated. There is an 'elasticity' or a maximum and minimum limit to the degree of possible changes within the system.

Deleuze talks as though the 'capacity to be affected' comprises two powers: the power of suffering and the power of acting.[18] Because the capacity remains constant, these powers must only vary in proportion to one another.[19] These powers, though, are also taken to constitute the capacity to be affected (222). We shall work out the relationship of these powers to the capacity and ultimately to the essence later. Here we are still left wondering why the survival of this individual depends on a, or this, proportion and whether, and how, this individual is to be identified with the limits of its capacity to be affected. Deleuze's arguments are not obvious but can be summarised and presented in four stages.

The rather poor bad quantification of quality argument concluded with the proposition that an essence is a part of power. This conclusion permits Deleuze to state that an essence is never possible but always actual.[20] Now we already know that everything that exists has a power of existing and acting. The second step is the assertion of identity conditions. The necessary condition of physical individuation is that there are extensive parts and the sufficient condition is that the internal dynamics of the extensive parts (temporarily) coheres with a modal essence. In light of this, Deleuze draws an analogy between the mode's essence and its capacity for acting and God's essence and production of infinite things. The argument seems to be that just as infinite things follow from God's nature (essence) so an infinite capacity for being affected follows from the modal essence: as properties from a definition.[21] Finally, Deleuze offers a version of the identity of indiscernibles. No body, argues Deleuze, has the same capacity to be affected. Because the capacity to be affected is a power, no body has the same power. Because power is substitutable with 'power to act', and this power is identical to this mode's essence, no body has the same essence.

The obvious and central problem still lies with the implied coherence relationship. We are supposed to accept that a part of power 'naturally' coheres with a set of extensive parts. Once the coherence occurs then we have a move from the intrinsic to the extrinsic; from being merely in to not merely being in an attribute and from being actual to actualised. From this Deleuze develops his theory of the relationship between the virtual and the actual. If all he means is that we can distinguish between the nature of a body and its actions then this is quite anodyne. However, he wishes to add two things. First, this distinction, albeit a distinction of reason, accredits the finite mode with something 'extra' than its mere material determination.[22] Second, that something 'extra' tells us about the nature of the body, its dispositions and its tendencies.[23] Now, when an essence corresponds to extensive parts the very existence of that mode is constituted. At which point the modal essence is determined as *conatus* (230). So what is *conatus*? Well, it is neither the effort to exist nor is it the tendency either to movement or to self-preservation. The *conatus* just is the existing mode's essence, or degree of power (230).

Initially, Deleuze distinguishes between the *conatus* of a simple body and that of a complex body. Because a simple body is merely determined by other finite modes, any effort to preserve itself would be nothing but an attempt to preserve itself as it has been determined. A composite body, however, as a combination of various bodies, is defined by its structure or by its internal relations. The *conatus* of an existing body has both a mechanical and dynamical function. It is the effort to preserve the body's internal relations of motion and rest and the effort to maintain the body's ability to be affected in a great number of ways. This effort seems to be identified with the mode's power of acting (231). Combining the insights regarding the nature of x with a physics of nature, Deleuze is able to present a positive thesis of the behaviour of bodies: a body is active and actively strives to preserve itself.

A body, as we have seen, strives to preserve its internal relations. Why might this be so? The conclusion that the nature of the thing is not merely active but also self-preservational is derived from the premise that each thing tries to stay in existence and this is derived from the original premise that nothing can destroy itself without outside help. Why might it be said that the nature of a thing involves nothing that is self-destructive? Donagan is prepared to accept the same argument by Spinoza and recasts it in the following terms. A non-external cause is one which follows, according to the laws of nature, from the thing's essence and hence is expressed in its definition. A thing's definition, given this, expresses what causes it to be not what causes it not to be (this step relies on the principle that things are conceived through their causes). If the thing's essence entailed its destruction it would be correctly defined as being such as to cause itself not to be. Therefore, given the second and third propositions, the definition of a self-destructive thing must be a self-contradiction.[24] This is almost identical to the Scotist argument relating to possibility and logical consistency.

However, if no finite thing can have a nature which leads to its destruction, or takes away its existence, and if only contrary natures, natures not included in this nature, could destroy this nature, then we are being asked to swallow a poor argument of implication. If x destroys y, we could say that x and y were distinct and contrary bodies.[25] But by the argument for logical consistency, the term 'contrary' means nothing other than the claim that body y has properties or qualities not included in x (by virtue of the argument that x can contain nothing within itself that would lead to its own destruction). The claim of opposition merely points to an original difference. Spinoza may well assume that 'contradiction' (exclusion of properties) means disagreement but with the benefit of hindsight could Deleuze?[26] This opens a further question. So far, the argument would allow us to say that if this body is destroyed then a contrary and external body must have destroyed it. We are in no stronger position to know what makes body y contrary to body x and we are left casting around for a positive thesis about the non self-destructive nature of x: in what does the 'striving' consist?

Let us insert here the premise that when we consider something as an in-itself we are expecting that thing to contain its own causes. Putting these together, along with the Spinozistic assertion that as an in-itself a thing is active,[27] we have the following: y is neither contained in nor explained through x, y is an external and therefore contrary body, x opposes y, x *actively* opposes y, x pursues its own preservation, x behaves in self-preserving ways.[28] Spinoza put this quite abruptly when he said that the 'definition of a finite thing affirms and does not deny its essence'. Here we find Deleuze making the same point and the same mistake. From a logical point concerning the definition of thing – the properties it may or may not have – Deleuze infers things about its behaviour. The term 'affirmation' introduces this slip. The term is originally used to underline the logical possibility or consistent nature of a definition. Deleuze believes that he can rescue this argument by reasserting that by definition the nature is identical to power and that therefore, to be logically consistent, the nature ought to be active. This does not address the problem that it is active in a particular way, that is, self-preservationally.

Deleuze's positive thesis is given greater depth when he adds that where one body encounters another body, with compatible relations, the first tries to unite with the second. So we now have the complete positive thesis: an individual body acts according to its own essence, nature, if and when it actively pursues its own preservation, that is, actively opposes contrary bodies and actively pursues compatible bodies. Although this repeats the problem of retrospective judgement, there is a much more serious, and general, problem. If we define structure as a system of relations between parts of the body we find a fundamental equivocation. While drawing an analogy with parts of an organism functioning as a whole, Deleuze manages to do two incommensurable things. First he keeps a functionalist description of behaviour in terms of how parts function to wholes. Secondly, though, he slips into the account a quite teleological description of behaviour. The language of 'striving for' and 'effort to' rather masks the difference. With a teleological account of behaviour we presume that there is some practical maxim or end point to which action is directed and for which certain actions are selected. Basically he confuses two types of explanations. The confusion is disguised but can be detected in the way in which behaviour is described: if body y is useful to body x then body x will try to acquire it or to move towards it *because* it is agreeable. The confusion is most obvious with the, supposedly, non-teleological notion of 'appetite' (231).[29]

Let me summarise so far. A logical point, concerning the definition of a thing *vis* the properties it may or may not have, leads to an inference about behaviour. In its favour this account allows us to speak of individuation in a way which appears to rescue the individual's behaviour from the material causal nexus. Against it, however, is the charge that the positive thesis of behaviour is derived from the original argument concerning agreement and disagreement. While Donagan's presentation of the argument would let Deleuze say that the definition of the nature of x could not contain anything that might hurt it or prove destructive to it, he would still have to do two things. He should explain why the definition of x would not also include any other body that looks like not being harmful. He also needs to provide us with a prior notion of the nature of individual x, which does not rely on exclusion, so that we can discern what might or might not hurt it.[30] Surely none of our identity conditions can presume the distinction between internal and external? Finally, we need to be aware that he confuses types of explanation: the functional and the teleological. This radically shifts the suitability of explanations for why bodies may or may not unite. Two people acting together for some common purpose is significantly different from reasons why two organs might act together.

The general theory of knowledge

There are three very Cartesian principles that ground Deleuze's epistemology: the central place given to causality in the acquisition of knowledge, the distinction between *formaliter* and *objectivè* and the belief that ideas can be objects of themselves. Descartes conflated the notion of having an idea and being aware. He was led from the assertion that we are aware of ideas to the interim conclusion that the awareness takes the form of an idea, to the conclusion that all ideas must have the recursive property of being identical with ideas of themselves.[31] We have already covered the distinction between *formaliter* and *objectivè*. Here it might help to remember that *formaliter* refers us to the inherent features of a thing, whilst *objectivè* relates to the meaning and content of an idea – its representational role. An idea can thus have both formal and objective being and it is this distinction which permits Deleuze the 'distinction of reason' between the idea and its form, the idea and our awareness of the idea. It is the causal principle, though, which gives support to the entire edifice of his epistemology.

The causal principle is that knowledge of an effect depends on knowledge of the cause, and involves it.[32] The term *cognitio* has a much broader range than simple 'knowledge' and Deleuze, following in Spinoza's footsteps, takes full advantage of the ambiguity. In the *Ethics* this causal axiom props up the parallelism and we find that Deleuze also insists on using it in this way. Apart from the fact that the epistemologically central notion of the adequate idea is supported by the causal axiom, I can find at least two other ways in which Deleuze seems to be relying on this principle. He requires it for the argument that God understands himself and understanding himself produces all the things that fall within an infinite understanding (101, 116). More explicitly, he seems to believe that this causal axiom establishes the moratorium on causal interaction between the attributes: the independence of the two series (115).

For the sake of clarity it may help to revise our various definitions of causation. Deleuze is never shy about picking ideas and definitions from scholastic philosophy and his discussion concerning causation is no exception. Leaning on Aristotelian definitions Deleuze constantly employs the terms 'formal' and 'efficient' cause. A formal cause typically refers to the way in which the form of a thing is considered to be a factor or the explanation of a thing being as it is. This can lead to the belief that to have scientific knowledge of a thing one must know its formal cause, that is, one must know the definition of an essence of a thing. An efficient cause is not a material cause but can be thought as the primary source of change, that by which change is brought about or the primary agency that produces the change. During our discussion of the *Cosmological Argument* we looked at why the attributes might be described as formal causes. We said that an attribute is a formal cause of substance because if one thing is conceived through another than that thing is said to be the (formal) cause of the former, substance is conceived through the attribute therefore an attribute is a formal cause or explanation of substance. An immanent cause is a cause that produces a change within itself and this is contrasted with transuent cause, something that produces a change in something else.

The general thesis of parallelism runs that for every x there is a corresponding idea in the same order. There is an infinite sequence of ideas, one sequence can be mapped onto the other and for every idea (x) there is an x, where there is an x followed by a y there will be an idea (x) followed by idea (y) and where an x has been caused by a y, (x) will include idea (y). Any mode has its efficient and formal cause in the attribute of which it is a mode and whose concept it involves (115). If we put this together with the causal principle we can see that to know one mode could mean having knowledge of two things: the attribute as an attribute of God and the previous mode, of which this is an effect. Bennett dismisses the same tendency in Spinoza because it is seems to require knowledge of the full causal sequence to have knowledge of this last effect: 'some stratospherically high standard of cognitive perfection... which we cannot have of a thing unless we have just as good knowledge of its cause'.[33] We could though depart from the actual doctrine and suppose, instead, that what is meant is that if x causes y then a *full* understanding of y requires *some* understanding of x.[34]

Deleuze's system carefully combines psychology and physiology. His principal aim is practical. It is to develop an understanding of how we can increase our active appetites.[35] Due to the parallelism, every change in the body will be accompanied by a change in psychology and *vice versa*. From an analysis of how passive appetites can be shifted into active appetites, Deleuze begins to secure his version of ethical naturalism. I shall here trace the move from the passive to the active and demonstrate how this is played out in the separate, but parallel, sequences of modifications. The first stage is referred to as the stage of vague sense experience and the second the stage of common notions and adequate ideas. For there to be therapeutic value to the system not only must Deleuze make the epistemological case convincing but also assure us that alterations can hold across the attributes.

The first stage: first level knowledge

Following Spinoza, Deleuze describes the first stage of knowledge as knowledge from vague sense experience and knowledge from signs. The former is essentially knowledge from perception and memory and an informal induction from what is supposed. The latter is basically knowledge from the verbal reports of others. Not only does this stage afford most of the information according to which people move round the world but it is also the footstep towards the second step of knowledge or insight. In a metaphysical system where every mode has a corresponding, matching even identical idea, and where the mode is itself the content of the idea, in a system where ideas are neither considered nor entertained, it would seem anachronistic to allow for error. Yet proceeding a discussion about what he means by an adequate idea, Deleuze explains how an idea may be inadequate. And it is the notion of 'inadequacy' that carries the whole weight of error. But, more importantly for our discussion, it is the transition from inadequacy to adequacy that marks the progression towards ethical, healthy, maturity. I shall concentrate here on the relationship between inadequacy and error to explore the problem of representational content.

Deleuze's discussion begins by laying out three basic beliefs. The 'object' of an idea is the effect an object has on the body. This means that y causes an affect in the body, x, and there is a corresponding idea: I (x). The (x) is the object of the idea and has to be something like a cerebral event. Deleuze concedes that this means that we do not have a direct idea of the body y that caused the affect x. Secondly, Deleuze brings into play the full force of the causal axiom mentioned above. Thirdly, he shifts into place a vocabulary associated with visual perception and so writes that 'we perceive external bodies only insofar as they affect us, we perceive our own body only insofar as it is affected' (146). The perceptual turn is cemented through a dual description of the image. An image is both a physical affect and an idea of that affect. The image, as idea, is situated in the imagination (150) and memory itself is identified with the sequential presence of ideas.

Parenthetically, it might be tempting to lean on the Stoical influence in *Expressionism* to clarify what is meant by 'image' or inadequate idea. A perception, in Stoic philosophy, is indeed a physical event and it extends to affects on all senses.[36] It occurs when an external object affects the senses and causes an 'imprint'. However, it is also more than a physical event and is experienced by the perceiver as something with content. The content of the image is its representative quality. Even when certain Stoics tried to abandon the 'inner theatre' metaphor, they still considered the content of the perception in terms of its representation of the external object but claimed that this is articulated in linguistic form.[37] It is germane to our discussion that in order to account for thoughts with empirical content, the ideational connection between the external and internal object was insisted upon. This dual function of an image is also present in Bergson's *Matter and Memory* where it occupies a midpoint between a representation and a thing. But again, even if we consider the image as an object in itself we are leaving open the questions of cause and object as cause.[38]

A central criticism of the previous chapter was that Deleuze's confuses the numerical identity thesis with the theory that the content of an idea is the redated physical modification. Now we can add to this the belief that modes are in material causal relationships with one another and we can see why Deleuze might offer the thesis that the direct object of an idea is our physical state and that the external body is the indirect object. And it is at this point that Deleuze, having adopted the vocabulary of (visual) perception, suggests that the image 'indicates' the external body, it is a 'sign' of that body. The proposition that explains the link between the direct and indirect object is that knowledge of one x 'involves' knowledge of the other y. It is noticeable that already Deleuze has done two things. First he has begun to muddy the waters by using a vocabulary which allows him a degree of disingenuous movement between attributes. Secondly, he has brought to the fore the representative features of an idea but tied this to the indirect object. However, it is a moot point whether this gives him a footstep out of the problem of ideational content. An idea of a state of the body, the ideational content (x), is not at all the same thing as an idea of an object causing that physical alteration. This problem is disguised by the language of perception which manages to imply the ideational aspect as well as linking the physical aspect, the image, to the external object. But we must remember, to save any future misunderstandings, that when we do have an idea there is nothing significant about the external object which can enter into the story except in the most minimal sense – that it caused bodily modification x. Deleuze not only exaggerates the role for the indirect object but also trades off its descriptive ambiguity.[39]

Already, in this discussion of the indirect object, we can see him running the risk of obvert inconsistency. Even if, due to the parallelism, I(x) x, if x is the causal product of y, the I(x) x cannot also be I(y) y, which it would have to be if knowledge of one depends on knowledge of the other and this means 'includes'. I think that it is for this reason that Deleuze introduces a variation in the meaning of the term 'involvement'.[40] For the sake of the overall argument, he declares that in this case the term is used to imply that it is only the presence of the cause, the external body, that is linked to the image. If we take this seriously, he means that where I(x) x and y causes x then the idea 'includes' recognition of the causal sequence. While the indirect relationship accommodates a more realistic picture of the relationship between mental states and causes, so, for example, many minds could have an idea of the same object, it leaves too many questions in the air. There are two that I wish to mention here. The first is the same as that discussed by Bennett and is one reason for his description of Spinoza's system as causal rationalism. Suffice it here to say that this relation of 'involvement' would only function within the argument properly if by it we meant something like the following. 'The fact that Fx indicates the fact that Gy if and only if there is some general principle from which, in conjunction with Fx, it follows that Gy'.[41] Without that general principle, and without knowledge of it, then nothing is guaranteed. The second concerns the extent of the space for representational efficacy generated by this argument. I wish to note here that all Deleuze is entitled to say is that if y causes x then x will 'involve something about' y. This might mean that the content I(x) might be, and indeed must be, different from an idea of a cerebral event caused by s but it certainly does not allow for the sort of representation that Deleuze wishes. We can see here the problems accumulating with the account of ideational content and a number of standard difficulties emerging.

For instance, can different things cause the same cerebral event? Can the same thing cause different cerebral events? What status does my 'perception' of a golden mountain or my idea of Santa Claus have?

Obviously if the ideational content somehow maps onto a cerebral event, or indeed *is* the cerebral event, then it makes little sense to talk about the idea *representing* that event. So we can understand why Deleuze might wish to introduce the indirect object, the external object supposedly causing the cerebral event, and use the language of perception – for example, being aware of a cat in one's visual field is very different from being aware of a brain modification. What happens, though, if the cat were to leave the visual field? Well Deleuze is apt to suggest that we could still be in a state where we may or may not affirm the presence of that cat (147). He is forced to this because, like Spinoza, he is not in a position to distinguish between ideas and beliefs and goes so far as to suggest that if I(x) then x so if an idea has as its content 'Santa Claus' then Santa Claus. This is to trade heavily on the indirect relationship because the ideational content is to be mapped onto the cerebral event which may, or may not, have been caused by Santa Claus or I(x) may have been caused by I (y). But that idea needs to be mapped onto y. In the instance of an idea of a golden mountain it is difficult to see just where this mapping relationship could take us.[42] Yet we can see how this might feed into a physicalist theory of mind. If, for instance, I see an 'x' then I am disposed to believe that I see that x and behave accordingly, hence analysing sensory states in terms of beliefs and beliefs in terms of dispositions and behaviour. Once again it must be stressed that Deleuze is not encouraging us to move down this physicalist path but the logic of the argument rather invites us.

For the moment I wish to pursue the problem of Santa Claus. Now, if, by force of the parallelism, for every I(x) there must be x then Deleuze is entitled to claim, as he does, that every idea is 'a true idea'. For sure, every idea that has as its content a brain modification must map onto the cerebral event. If we are to say of that brain state that it is equivalent to an image of Santa Claus and that this correspondence makes it a true idea then that is one thing. But this would severely restrict our domain of truth values: an idea is true (because) it is in an isomorphic relationship with a brain state. How are we to square this principle of parallelism with the problem of error? Deleuze negotiates this through his description of an inadequate idea. An inadequate idea, he says, is both true and false. My idea of 'Santa Claus' is thus both true and false. It is true to the extent that it is an idea of a cerebral event and that the cerebral event is a mode of the attribute of Extension caused by another mode of that attribute and therefore involving something of it. It is false to the extent that I actually lack knowledge concerning the cause of my image (149).

Deleuze does retain two of the most important Spinozistic meanings of the term 'adequacy'. In the *Ethics* the term is used to imply both 'completeness' and that the idea must be caused from within one's own mind.[43] If we were to decide whether or not an idea is adequate, and yet wished to remain faithful to Spinoza's account, we would find ourselves somewhat torn between these two meanings. An adequate idea that is complete refers to the causal sequence that has led up to the ideational content before us. An idea that is adequate with respect to our minds is one where the cause of that idea is also 'in' our minds. We can see here that whereas the first refers us to the object of the idea, the second refers us only to the cause of the idea, which itself must be an idea. Because all perceptions of external things are caused from outside my mind they must all be confused and if confused then inadequate.

Let us take an I(x) x individual and examine how the idea might be confused. The suggestion is that if an external body causes x, then the idea of x will be confused. But this does not actually follow and is a form of category mistake. The physical modification itself cannot be 'confused' all that could be confused is the idea. Indeed we may prefer to say all that can be confused is the person entertaining the idea, but that is another matter. If the idea is the systematic counterpart of the bodily modification then it cannot be confused either. Once again repeating Spinoza, Deleuze simply insists that the inadequate idea is truncated, like a conclusion without its premises (148). All that Deleuze could legitimately say is that the image 'confusedly' indicates the nature of the mode that caused the bodily modification. But this is to use the ambiguity outlined earlier. The image or idea is confused because the bodily modification only involves the nature of the external body and so the causal sequence is opaque. This pans out as the claim that the idea or image is confused because there is a genuine lack of knowledge about the causal sequence. Confusion thus becomes a mental state dependent on lack of knowledge.

However, when he tries to explain how we make mistakes about things, Deleuze rather unwisely parrots Spinoza and works from the notion of confusion to error and claims that error is a lack of knowledge (148). Unwisely because it should be now quite evident that error arises from lack of knowledge. This is not a slight slip as it has crucial reverberations through what might be called his cognitive psychology. By assenting to Spinoza's proposition that falsity has no form, Deleuze clearly wishes to account for a world such there would be no (not-P) in a world where P. To allow himself room to manoeuvre he argues that error is a lack of knowledge and that where the indirect object is concerned there are a multitude of things of which we are ignorant. Unfortunately this leaves him in an impossible position. Because all indirect objects are only in relationships of 'involvement' with my bodily states, there is a manifest opaqueness about causal sequences. There must also be an opaqueness about my own states unless Deleuze wishes to account for the fact that we do not have an idea for, are aware of, every bodily alteration or cerebral event. At the moment this does not matter but we will see the full force of this problem emerging with statements concerning the ethics and later the politics.

Let us add one further thorn to the side of this rather anaemic account of ideas and beliefs. Deleuze wishes to follow Spinoza in the assertion that all images are properly speaking positive. The claim that error consists in lack of knowledge of causes cannot really help with this following problem. If I see a stick in the water and see it as bent then is the perception equivalent to a belief? If not then Deleuze needs to offer a proper account of the difference between belief and perception. If, on the other hand, the two are identical then the perception itself and its idea are not merely positive, as he wishes to say, because I am 'seeing', and affirming the perception of, something inaccurately. Let us add to the problems. If I have an idea or belief about a y because y caused x and therefore x 'involved' y and if we accept that somehow I(x) will also involve (y) what happens if y alters but without affecting my body? I will still have a certain idea or belief about y and it will now be wrong. We can see here that if Deleuze were clear that correspondence holds between the idea and its indirect object he could have ironed out these difficulties but the project is much broader than that. He wishes to lay the grounds for a shift from representational or correspondence theories of truth and this is the first step.

The first stage: passions

We have already outlined Deleuze's positive account of identity: an individual body acts according to its own essence if, and when, it actively pursues its own preservation, that is, actively opposes contrary bodies and actively pursues compatible bodies. The idea that bodies might be contrary disturbs the general theory that bodies are merely modes of one substance. In order to differentiate between bodies Deleuze needs this account of contrariness. He wipes away any metaphysical difficulties with this by explaining that modes, *qua* essences, all agree but modes, *qua* internal relations, may or may not and when bodies encounter one another they may find each other agreeable or disagreeable (238, 244). We have also explored the connection between the mechanical and dynamic analytical perspectives on the physical body. These are the relations of motion and rest internal to a body and the constant capacity to be affected. Every individual body is part of a causal series and can undergo alteration without loss of identity. These alterations can be called affects.[44] If alteration x is explained through the nature of the body X then Deleuze calls this an active affect. If alteration x can only be explained through body Y, that caused affect x, then Deleuze names this a passive affect. Because every individual mode is part of a causal nexus, it will undergo changes which are passive affects.

Each body, as part of the causal chain, is affected by external bodies. The effect, x, is described by Deleuze as a 'corporeal image'. The idea of that affect is an inadequate idea or an imagining (220). In addition to this original effect, modification of the body, there is a secondary affect (*affectus*). Deleuze counts these as feelings. Massumi identifies affect with intensity and distinguishes both these terms form emotion.[45] There are states of the body, x, and corresponding ideas, I(x), there are changes in the body (feelings) and ideas of those changes.[46] At the lowest level then we have passive affections and inadequate ideas, passive feelings (passions) and ideas of those passions.

There are two immediate problems. If we accept each body undergoes changes brought about by an external body and if each alteration either is or is accompanied by an 'affect', and if these affects are all passive, then it is difficult to see just what might be an active affect. The initial step in the solution is based on three rather questionable premises. Firstly, Deleuze associates The 'structure' of the body with a capacity to be affected. Secondly, he identifies this capacity with power – either of acting or of suffering. Lastly, he takes these powers to vary in proportion. Therefore, if we produce active affections our passive affections will be, necessarily, reduced (222). So, all he now needs to do is to show how we can 'produce' active affections. The second, but related, problem is that Deleuze writes that an inadequate idea is an idea of which we are not the cause and that it is the formal and efficient *cause* of a feeling, a passion (221). Similarly, an adequate idea *causes* a different sort of feeling. Because we can be considered to be the cause of this feeling, the feeling can be said to be active and because it is active an action. It would be quite natural to associate 'feeling' with a physical state but this would mean that a mode in one attribute causes a modification of a mode in a different attribute – which is impossible. The two, related, problems then concern the relationship assumed between active and passive passions and the definitional clarity of the terms 'passion', 'affection' and 'feeling'.

With the proviso that only active affections 'exercise' the power of action,[47] let us develop Deleuze's response to the first problem. The capacity to be affected remains constant and is therefore 'all it can be', that is, perfect. Having already identified the essence of an existing mode with its power of action, and power of action with the capacity to be affected, Deleuze feels able to claim that the passive force is a limitation of active force.[48] He names this limit 'imperfection' and strictly identifies it with force of suffering. This would seem to equate the force of suffering with all passive affections. He runs against an apparent contradiction. If the mode's essence is its power of acting, which can be limited, it would seem that the mode is both perfect and open to essential change.[49] For this reason, he distinguishes between two principles: the physical and the ethical. Physically, the capacity, power, to be affected remains constant for a given essence. Ethically, the capacity to be affected remains constant within certain limits.

Let us now try to untangle the parallel sequences of causal modifications. So far we have a body X and a modification x which has been caused by body Y. There is an idea corresponding to x which involves, but cannot fully include, ideas matching the causal sequence of modifications producing x. It is not at all clear whether the change in the body *is* the affect or the affect is associated with the change. The affect on this body has already been called an image, which is both a physical affect and an idea of that affect (220).[50] The image only indirectly represents Y and the idea, which has x as its content, is inadequate. If we assume the latter interpretation then the image, having been caused by an external body, is linked to a 'feeling' which is, necessarily, passive or a passion. Corresponding to this passive feeling is an idea, which has as its content the feeling. For the parallelism to remain secure, the idea of the feeling can only be caused by the idea (x). If we assume the former interpretation then the alteration of the body, resulting in the image, would be described as passive.

Deleuze defines various emotive and cognitive states in terms of three basic affects and, quite in tune with Spinoza's *Ethics*, germinates a complicated, if not altogether clear taxonomy. We already have a general definition of *affectus* that can be used with either attribute: 'the modifications of the body by which the body's power of action is increased or decreased and the ideas of those states'. Deleuze translates Spinoza's term *laetitia* as joy and *tristitia* as sadness.[51] These terms are supposed to be transattributive in the sense of applying both to states of mind and to states of body. An affect is therefore necessarily passive but it can be pleasant or unpleasant due to the simple identification of pleasure with an increase in activity and unpleasure with a corresponding decrease. By direct appeal to the parallelism, Deleuze asserts that where there is an increase in physical activity, there will be an increase in mental activity (256). Hence, if the body is capable of great activity, and exerts that capacity, then there will be proportionally greater mental activity and the feeling of joy.[52]

Because we have already established that it is in the body's nature to act in certain ways, we can now say that when a body, x, 'has' pleasure the body is active and healthy, that is, actively pursuing its own preservation.[53] There are three points to note. The (passive) state of pleasure is supposed to be produced only by an agreeable body. Any state of pleasure means the body is becoming healthier, more vital, and thus nearer to its *perfect* state: acting in accord with its true nature. Lastly, Deleuze presents the case for passive affections themselves causing a response or action. By dint of argument all he is entitled to claim is that passive affections inhibit activity and lower the level of vitality or health in the organism. He circumvents this dilemma in two ways. He proposes that sadness is not just a limit of power it is also part of power. Secondly, he identifies passive affections with desire, allows himself the concept of active passive affects and slips into the account a theory of selective action (231).[54] Although this makes his description of an active mental state more sophisticated, mental agility is not merely a matter of going to the gym more often, the account of desire introduces a number of insurmountable problems.

Desire is the third principal affect and is defined as *conatus* determined by a feeling and accompanied by consciousness. On the surface this means little, so, let us return to the *Ethics* and pick out Spinoza's definition of desire which turns out to be 'appetite together with consciousness of it'.[55] We have already accepted the definition of appetite such that 'having an appetite for x' means 'intrinsic state which causes one to move towards x'. And, according to Deleuze, the 'that to which we are determined' is to be explained through the nature of the body in question (231).[56] Thus, when we put this together with the positive thesis of identity, we arrive at the idea that where there is a desire, there is movement towards something that will, necessarily, increase health and vitality. As we can see this is very similar to our definition of pleasure. The difference is the causal role supplied by appetite, that is, it is, so to speak, the 'push towards' that the organism requires. Pleasure related to the increased vitality or activity of the body and desire seems to relate to the movement towards a thing giving that vital lift.[57] The anti-teleological thrust is retained here. Deleuze makes every effort to explain how passive affections might be able to determine future actions and to explain the direction of those actions through the nature of the body itself: active self-preservation.

If a body Y causes a bodily modification x in body X then there will be a corresponding idea (x), which indirectly represents body Y. Deleuze adds to this a further chain. Where there is I(x), and I(x) is inadequate, then there will be a secondary causal feature: a feeling. If caused by I(x), the feeling can only be an idea. But what is the content of the idea? If it is a sensation then the sensation will have to have been caused by x.[58] The next step is the really contentious one and it is that when body y 'agrees' with my nature the feeling will be joyful. There are three working assumptions of which to be extremely wary. We have seen that Deleuze struggled to ground a principle of individuation and that he relied on differentiating bodies according to contrariness. Earlier this permitted him the positive thesis of active preservation. Here, however, it runs aground. How can there be bodies which are in agreement but still distinct? To answer this, Deleuze is forced to define 'agreeable' as 'that which is useful'. At best this is a tautology. The agreeable body is that which produces modification x in this body and a pleasurable feeling. All this means is that the external body causes a modification which either is, or leads to, a lift in the activity of the affected body. The second problem is the tip of a perilous iceberg.

Deleuze writes that the affection is passive, being produced by an external body and that the idea of the affection is a passive feeling. However, he insists that the feeling is one of joy because it is produced by the *idea* of an object that is good for me or agrees with my nature. Although he needs this as a step in his argument he is not entitled to it. The external body might well cause a physical modification that either is, or is linked to, an increase in vitality, but the feeling of joy cannot be caused by the *idea* of the external body. This is for the very simple reason that I(x) includes only very indirectly an idea of that affecting body. Deleuze cannot have his anti-representational cake and joyfully eat it. We already know that there is nothing significant about the external object which can enter into the story, except in the most minimal sense. But Deleuze attempts to slip the indirect object back into the centre of his account. The most blatant transgression of his own rule occurs when he talks about our relationships with external objects that we love or hate.

Love, he says, is linked with joy, whereas out of sadness is born a desire which is hate (243).[59] When the body experiences joy it is so moved as to preserve the external object causing the feeling. Similarly, where there is hate there is movement to destroy the external body. These two emotions can be linked to the same object. This is either because our own internal dynamics are complicated or because if we were to destroy the external body then we might experience joy. On the surface this seems fairly plausible but let us disentangle the various claims. The external object is the cause of the physical modification x, where there is x there is an idea, whose ideational content is a physical modification. These modes respectively cause a feeling and an idea of a feeling. It is extremely difficult to see where Deleuze could introduce the relevance of the idea of the loved, or hated, object given that the external body is only indirectly represented through I(x). This gives an altogether one-dimensional, and perhaps false, account of our emotional states.

The principal objection must be that an emotive state has a cognitive component involving beliefs *about* the object in question. Our love or hate is surely linked to what we think the person is like? If, in the company of y, I experience sadness then I might well presume that y is the *cause* of that sadness but the explanation for why y causes me sadness might have to do with my beliefs about y. I admit that inserting into any physiological chain of events the relevance of belief states is not without its own problems. But it must be the case that when I experience sadness in the company of y it is because of things I, maybe wrongly, believe about y, things that might have nothing to do with me directly, except that they are my beliefs; that for example y kicks dogs, beats children or is a member of a white supremacist group. So, if in the company of y I experience certain physical changes, it may be because of prior beliefs that I hold *about* y. Deleuze cannot accommodate these representationally relevant characteristics in his theory of emotions. Indeed he explicitly writes them out, stating that judgements concerning what we do not like are retrospective and follow from our feeling of sadness (241). But surely, I may dislike body y or suffer unpleasant affects, not because of physical proximity, which Deleuze requires, but because I have specific and important beliefs about y? In reply to this, Deleuze states quite categorically that only in the presence of a body causing me sad passions will I be moved to destroy it.

The third working assumption of which we are to be wary proceeds directly from the above point and concerns the anti-teleological thrust of the theory. Deleuze has insisted that knowledge of particular things through the senses, signs and hearsay is inadequate and because inadequate misleading and erroneous. He cannot, therefore, base his account, of how to ensure the maximum amount of joyful passions, on an account of behaviour that requires judgement and selectivity. For this reason Deleuze exploits a certain explanatory ambiguity. He claims that when we encounter an agreeable body we will attempt to unite with it, to procure and to preserve it (241). Obversely, when we encounter a disagreeable body we will attempt to destroy it.[60] Trivially, if pleasure were the affect of eating something good for me then, by definition, the object could not be preserved as it had been its consumption that led to my pleasurable state. It is not the case that just because Y is the cause of x and an unpleasant feeling, I would wish to destroy Y. Deleuze recognises that, despite the positive thesis of action, he still needs to explain future-oriented action. We are motivated to act in self-preserving ways but these actions must be directed towards certain objects.

To explain this, Deleuze presents us with a compact version of Spinoza's account of memory. We first desire something to be the case, imagine how to bring it about and, if it accords with our nature, we are moved to so act (240). Consistent with the parallelism, if there are corporeal traces then there will be ideas of those traces. Where the body has been modified in one or more ways there will be an assemblage of traces and ideas.[61] Each trace will be accompanied by, or can be described as, an affect: passive but pleasant or unpleasant. Because the body will do whatever it can to increase its own vitality, the mind endeavours to recall images which were pleasant. In the process, because the content of the idea is the physical modification, and not the external object, corporeal traces are also enlivened. Obviously this whole account could break down under pressure from the parallelism. Not only must the general thesis be true but it also must be the case that, if the modification is not the affect itself, but causes a further affect, then the parallelism must also hold for the feeling as bodily affect and as idea. The account of memory is aided by the theory of ideational content, but this same theory rather thwarts Deleuze's attempt to elaborate a proper theory of action: how can imagining a pleasurable state alter or direct our behaviour?

Absolutely central to the whole Deleuzian project is the thesis that attributes are distinct, are conceived *per se* and that there is no causal interaction between them. This means that it cannot be the case that a thought, an expectation or an idea can *cause* a physical modification. Deleuze could reply that the idea has as its content the cerebral event or physical modification and that, *qua* mode of Extension, this could cause other physical changes. But this would be to confuse the issue. The idea has as its content the (ideational presentation of the) physical modification, not the mode itself. Also, just because we might be able to recall an idea does not explain how this could motivate our behaviour towards an object, for the simple reason that the representational features of the indirect object cannot enter into the physical causal sequence. We must add to this the simple point that the temporal sequence itself cannot be disturbed by an image which then pre-empts physical activity. But this is what Deleuze implies and must mean if he is to present anything approaching an acceptable account of how passive affections might determine future action and it is this account which constitutes the first developmental stage towards emotional maturity (244). Incidentally, if Deleuze's account is plausible it would be a way to answer Spinoza's major objection to teleological accounts of behaviour.

The second stage: second level knowledge

An image, according to Deleuze, is an imprint: it is both a physical impression and an idea of affection. It indicates the existence of an external body, the indirect object, but tells us nothing about the nature of that object. At best the image is a guide to the momentary states of our changing constitution (147). We can think of each image as having two causes: formal and material. Its formal cause is our own mind and its material cause is the antecedent mode in the appropriate attribute. The image, or the inadequate idea, is both true and false. It is false to the extent that it involves a lack of knowledge of these true causal sequences (148). From this first level of rather confused or limited knowledge we can, suggests Deleuze, move to a higher level of knowledge in one of two ways. We can either begin with a true idea or begin by focusing on what is positive in an inadequate idea.

The conversion of an inadequate into an adequate idea is as follows: an inadequate idea is both false and true. It is true, or positive, in a couple of ways. One way leads us to an analysis of idea *qua* idea and thence to the attribute of Thought, while the second takes us to an examination of the content of the idea and so to the attribute of

Extension. The inadequate idea, as any idea, is a modification of the attribute of Thought and so is not only caused by other modes of that attribute but also, by virtue of being an idea, 'participates' in the power of thinking (146). By virtue of the parallelism, for every idea there is an idea of the idea. This is true for inadequate as well as adequate ideas. There is some truth in every idea of an idea: 'just to have a true idea it is enough for it to be reflected; it is enough to know, to know that one knows' (131).

Although we can see a departure from Spinoza with this description of conversion, we have also seen that Deleuze does retain two of the most important Spinozistic meanings of the term 'adequacy' implying both 'completeness' and that the idea must be caused from within one's own mind.[62] To be consistent with the numerical identity thesis, Deleuze would have to argue that just as I(x) = x so I(I(x) = I(x). Because he has not figured the role of representation in the relationship between ideas, their content and external objects, he cannot at this point turn round and claim that there is a significant difference between I(I (x)) and I (x). The distinction between *formaliter* and *objectivè* cannot be deployed here either. As he is so keen to block any referential significance, Deleuze claims that the idea of the idea *is* the form of the idea rather than that it represents the original idea.

If we take this literally, the claim is that the idea of the idea is the intrinsic properties – but of what? There are two candidates. If the idea of the idea is merely the idea then the intrinsic properties must be the ideational content (x). Otherwise Deleuze means that the idea of the idea is the form of the idea (x). Desperate to separate the roles of *formaliter* from *objectivè*, Deleuze does beg us to consider the idea of the idea in terms of the form without reference to representational content (133). This initially sounds quite palatable but becomes less so when we realise that for every I(x) there is an I(I(x)) and an I(I(I(x))) so for every form of an idea there must be a form of a form and a form of a form of a form. Because we cannot differentiate between them, according to what they are about, it does seem that they collapse into one another and we are even left wondering what might be the form of an idea.

The argument, as I take it, is as follows. Any idea can be considered in terms of its objective and formal being. The former refers us to the bodily modification as ideational content while the latter refers us to fact that the idea is 'contained in' the attribute of Thought and, either through the *a posteriori* argument or through the claim that the attribute is a condition of God's existence, we find ourselves back with Deleuze's version of the *Ontological Argument*. Then we can use the conclusions of the *Ontological Argument* to explain the parallelism and with the parallelist thesis come two assertions: that for every idea there is an idea of that idea and that an idea is a 'part' of power and so 'possesses' the power of understanding (130). In short, an adequate idea is the idea of any idea[63] and is the rational understanding of the true causal chain. To conclude; any idea can be inadequate, in the human mind, and adequate, with reference to God. This does seem to be somewhat of a howler as there must be either a change in ideational content or one or more separate ideas that lead through the deductive chain.[64]

The conversion of an inadequate into an adequate idea, through a consideration of content, then looks more promising. Spinoza suggests that whereas truth refers only to the agreement of the idea with its *ideatum*, adequacy refers to the nature of the idea in-itself.[65] The physical modification, of which it is an idea, involves the nature of the indirect object Y (149). Because the external body is only indirectly represented through I(x), we can actually claim very little about that body. Indeed, our perception of the external body tells us more about the perceiving body's physical states. But we do know that an inadequate idea must be caused by a previous inadequate idea and have, as its content, this physical modification. Its ideational content is, or represents, a mode in the attribute of Extension that, itself, was part of material causal chain. Even by postulating this much, we are assuming something that is extremely important. The external body, to have caused x, is not only a modification of an attribute, but is also a modification of the same attribute as the body it so affected. Such an assumption can be unpacked in a number of ways: the causal axiom, the presupposition that the attribute is a form common to all its modes, that there is an immediate mode of motion and rest, that the attribute is a form common to God and to the modes. We form an idea of what is common to the affected and affecting body (150).

This idea is a common notion. In other words, a common notion will be a claim as to the universal organisation of bodies.[66] Deleuze is careful to distinguish between a common notion and an abstract idea. The latter, he asserts, is premised on a perceptual image which is merely an extrinsic sign, that is, it actually tells us very little about the body in question. But, there is a tendency to abstract from these perceptual images a number of traits and to set these up as ways to classify bodies into species, kinds and classes (277). We may also describe words themselves as bodily motions, responses to actions of external bodies. This would mean, of course, that each of us would associate a different image with perhaps the same word and suffer correspondingly different emotional affects. As the individual gathers more experiences, a greater number of images will be connected to the word until the images are compacted together for convenience. This confused character of words cannot be eliminated through the acquisition of knowledge but is the necessary consequence of the action of external bodies on the individual's body.[67] Number is a correlate then of abstract idea, for to be able to count one must know what it is that is being counted and assume the utility of natural types. To know about something means, for Deleuze, to know according to its essential nature which is not, and cannot be, equivalent either to a natural type or reducible to its external relationships or grasped through general words. The essential nature is a composite of the internal dynamics of a body and the ways in which it acts to preserve that internal structure.[68]

In sharp contrast to general words, abstract ideas and number, common notions then take a central place in Deleuze's epistemology. They help him to explain how we might garner knowledge of particular bodies, given that our only contact with the external body is through vague sense experience. When we encounter an agreeable body, and suffer joy, we are 'induced' to form an idea about what is common to the affected and affecting body (282). The verb *induire* means both to tempt and to infer, to reason by induction.[69] What is common to agreeable bodies? There is similarity of composition, there is a certain combination of relations and laws of composition (291). All bodies must be modes of the attribute of Extension.

We can already see two major problems arising. The common notion itself seems to refer to what is common or general to a number of bodies and so seems to be a universal term. This is a symptom of a general problem. Neither Deleuze, nor Spinoza before him, managed to develop a satisfactory account of language. As a result we are left unable to understand how words may convey ideas and how we are to take the function of philosophical language.[70] If Deleuze rejects generic universals then does he mean that only finite particulars exist? Laws are universal structures and the terms naming these laws must themselves be counted as abstract. Are the universal laws ruled out as well as the abstract terms naming them? This leads us straight back to the status of the term 'attribute' with the additional dimension of the common notion; something that names the universal structures of bodies and the laws governing those structures. Charity would require us to accept that Deleuze can adopt a qualified nominalism, where 'natural law' does relate to real and universal aspects of the world. Qualified nominalism works well with his rejection of natural kinds and the substitution of teleological explanations with natural determinism. Yet it may have more honest for Deleuze to accept that both Kant and Hegel had a better solution to the problem of a singular entity (attribute) with a universal function (immediate mode).[71]

Qualified nominalism is a problematic position to hold and it is significant that Deleuze is unable to satisfy any belief condition relating to 'this body in particular' without slipping in an additional premise. From the experience of a pleasant affect we must presume that the bodies in question, or parts of the bodies, will be similar in *relevant* ways. This is an externalist point. But, for the conversion of ideas to work at all, the affected body must also *acknowledge* the logic of the premise. This is an internalist point and as such raises a shadow of doubt as to the comprehensive nature of Deleuze's explanation of cognition as derivative *vis* automatic reproduction of the idea of the idea. Due to the parallelism if x causes y then x must have caused y and the affected body will know 'that y' and know that it knows it. The 'that y', the content of the adequate idea, moves us beyond the empiricist premise, that ideas are caused by external objects, to the recognition that all ideas, *qua* ideas, have material, formal and efficient causes (149). A common notion, *qua* idea, has its formal cause in our power of thinking and finds its efficient cause in God. But we are now left in an invidious position where we have not one but three ideas which have external bodies as their content. We have a representational relation, as outlined by the parallelism, so that to every mode of the attribute of Extension there must be a corresponding idea in the attribute of Thought. There are also the ideas or images, causal affects of these modes, which indirectly represent the external body. Now there are also common notions which claim something about the affected and affecting body through their dependence on God.

Indeed, here we can see the full flush of Deleuze's rationalism. If only finite particulars exist are we now saying that reason is the same in all human beings? For if not then there would be no grounds to assert that it would lead universally to the same result, that is, adequate ideas and reason, for Deleuze, is infallible.[72] It is infallible because error is explained through the existence of inadequate ideas: ignorance counts as error only if inadequate ideas *are* involved and cognition counts as reasoning only if inadequate ideas *are not* involved.[73] The truth of the common notion must, therefore, be self-evident.[74] Indeed, if this were the case, then we would have a science of the physical and a science of the mental, where one causal chain maps onto the other, not through any isomorphic qualities, but through a shared logic. Deleuze has to be very careful here because any suggestion that a physical encounter causes an idea would contravene the no causal interaction thesis. Even to fall back on the notion of 'occasions' would be to invite trouble (287). Yet, at the same time, he cannot surely suggest that we come to a common notion through the perceptual image, which is, by definition, inadequate? Because of this, Deleuze explores the relationship between joy and reason. In the next chapter we will investigate his attempt to resolve the tension between nominalism and rationalism.

The second stage: beyond the passions

Grasping and trying to understand the world, through the particular things that are presented to our senses, is the first stage in the individual's progress towards knowledge.[75] While at this stage, the individual is likely to base his or her opinions on 'signs' and hearsay.[76] Corresponding to this first epistemic stage is the first, immature, emotional stage. This is described by both Deleuze and Spinoza as bondage to the passions and is where the individual remains in the sway of affects, caused by external objects. The reason given for this bondage amounts to an explanation of the causal sequence, but the implication is that an inadequate grasp of this causal sequence results in a confused analysis of the causes of sentiment and therefore a passive physical and mental state. Although all passions are passive, some are joyful and increase our power of acting, while others are sad and decrease or limit it. The developmental challenge, therefore, at this initial stage, is to ensure the maximum amount of joyful passions. This is fleshed out as the individual functioning in ways which are self-preserving. Where knowledge of the first kind is likely to lead to erroneous judgement, knowledge of the second kind, knowledge, through common notions and adequate ideas, is altogether different. This subsequent epistemic stage corresponds to a more mature emotional stage, a liberation from passions and it is here that we will a solution to the problem of transition from passive to active affections.

Deleuze begins by reminding us of the parallelism; where there is an alteration in the attribute of Thought there will be a corresponding alteration in the attribute of Extension and *vice versa* (256). Then he repeats that though all affections are passive there are some which increase the body's vitality and can be described as joyful. The interim premise is that when activity is increased to a certain degree the body will be able to produce affections which are active (262). Reason, here, appears to be given a practical definition. Reason *is* the attempt to link passive joys with active joys (272). It achieves this, initially, by organising chance encounters in such a way so that the above transition conditions can be met (274). The first thing that springs to mind here is that reason has a difficult task in hand, given that it has neither common notions at its disposal nor has it any indexical knowledge. But, reasoning prowess is given a bolster when there are affections which are, or cause, joyful affects. Why is this? The rather bold argument is as follows: there is a power of action (essence), the power of action associated with the mind is understanding, joyful passions increase power of activity, therefore joyful passions increase power of understanding, if reason is the power of understanding then, and so on.

Sadness is an affect caused by an external body modifying body x in a particular way. No amount of thinking this otherwise can alter the fact of causal dependency. Likewise, no amount of considering this causal chain could alter the fact of the chain and therefore the sad passion produced as a consequence of this encounter. Deleuze has two options. He could argue that if I understand the causal encounter then I am entertaining an adequate idea, if I entertain an adequate idea then there will be an increase in activity, where there is an increase in activity there will be an increase in joy. Joy counteracts sadness. Joy is, or leads to an increase in activity. The more encounters, the more likely there is of joy. Or, he could argue that most encounters produce joyful affects, joy increases reasoning ability, reason organises encounters, through knowledge of the laws of physics, in such a way that body x will only encounter bodies which are suited to it. The first option presumes what it sets out to explain: the existence of – or increase in – reason. The second runs foul both of the causal block on attributes and quite explicitly demands a theory of action, presumably ruled out by the functionalist account of behaviour. He argues that when an individual encounters an agreeable body that individual will form a common notion. Because each common notion is, necessarily, an adequate idea it will be accompanied by the feeling of joy. This feeling can now be described as active because it is caused by an idea which is, ultimately, explained through the individual's power of understanding (284).

The outcome of this process, according to Deleuze, is a conversion of inadequate ideas into adequate ideas or common notions. Corresponding to this conversion, is the conversion of active–passive passions into active feelings. When the cause of a passion is analysed and understood, with the help of common notions, the passion, any feeling that is object related such as love and hate, will disappear.

Spinoza likewise saw the potential therapeutic value in detaching passions from ideas of external objects.[77] We may well concur but be somewhat less happy with conceding that emotional maturity is reached when an individual is able to consider encounters, and corresponding passions, as inevitable, according to necessary laws of nature (295).[78] We thus witness Deleuze's Stoic temperament, where freedom is equated with acquiescence to a universal order, that we have come to understand. We can also detect an opposing tendency in *Expressionism*, the belief that knowledge leads to freedom because it helps us to shape, or to act in, our environment.

Deleuze rather falls back on his theory of efficient causes. It is the case that modes are necessarily modified as part of a material causal chain.[79] But there is also a power of acting, which can be understood through, indeed as, the laws of the body's own nature. All affections are passive but some are active and actually increase, or are descriptions of the increase in, the level of activity in the system. Because the body does all it can to preserve itself, and to increase its health, and because action in accordance with the nature of the body is defined as self-activated, then actions will be self-directed towards specific objects. But this obviously confuses types of explanations: reasons and causes. It also opens a whole range of problems concerning the dual theory of efficient causes.

The most relevant is this. The argument referring to internal causal efficacy merely offers a way of describing or explaining events: if a body acts in self-preserving ways then we can explain its actions in terms of its appetites. Deleuze's point must be stronger. It must be more like: because the nature or essence is caused by God then the mode is not completely determined according to the external series of causal events and can act in ways of its own choosing. He needs this for otherwise there could be no explanation for why a body is compelled to move, indeed is able to move, as it will be suffering passive affects and passive affects always limit or inhibit activity (243).[80] It is also interesting to note that Deleuze concedes that the theory of efficient causality is a rather chancy interjection and requires some fast footwork. He has to distinguish between the efficacy of the joyful passions caused by external objects and those explained by the body's own nature. Because of this, he introduces, rather belatedly, the caveat that passive joys increase the body's power and therefore *agree* with reason whereas active joys are *born* of reason (274). It is a rather risky assertion because the claims that joyful passions can be used to form common notions allows him to move from the position where the body entertains only inadequate ideas and, at best, active passions, to one where the body can form an adequate idea, or common notion, and thus be replete with active joy.

Conclusion

My suggestion so far has been that in *Expressionism* there are opposing strands of thought. This is not entirely true because, in fact, one is a step towards the other. Deleuze argues that knowledge, or reason, leads to, and is, the ability the shape one's environment. The individual's environment will be shaped in such a way that suits the individual's nature (determined by universal laws), liberating the individual from passive passions. This liberation will, in the end, induce that individual to contemplate the necessary laws of universal organisation. The equivocation between forms of explanation is quite apparent here and is most glaring with the descriptions of reason 'endeavouring' and 'making an effort'.[81] Deleuze poses functionalist accounts of behaviour against finalist accounts. If he considers the terms 'finalist' and 'teleological' to be co-extensive then this would make sense. Any teleological explanation of behaviour requires some account to be taken of the causal efficacy of the representational features of ideas of external objects. It would also draw upon classifications of objects in terms of natural kinds. This is because only when we have certain beliefs about future states do we have specific reasons for bringing about state x rather than state y and beliefs about the most optimum method for achieving state x. Such an analysis is premised on an ability to make sense of a fairly stable world. Deleuze, instead, collapses reasons and causes when he explains why a body will act in one way rather than another, in terms of efficient causes. The argument that nothing has a final cause, because everything has an efficient cause, is pulled directly from Spinoza and relies on determinism being true.[82] This is obscured through the use of specific terms exploiting ambiguities between causal and purposive explanations but it is only the ambiguity that gives the appearance of coherence to the story.[83]

5
The State of Nature

The conclusion I drew at the end of the previous chapter was that there is a tension in *Expressionism* between two strands of argument. Deleuze argues that freedom can be identified with acquiescence to a universal world order that we have come to understand. But he also suggests that knowledge leads to freedom because it helps us to shape our environment. I proposed that the two tendencies are brought together in the assertion that knowledge or reason leads to, and perhaps is, the individual's ability to shape the environment in a way consistent with that individual's nature. An environment suiting the individual's nature will liberate the individual from passive passions and enable that individual to contemplate the world and its necessary laws of organisation. I will be arguing that this rather archaic attempt to resolve the problem of freedom in a causally determined world does not deliver an acceptable account of agency.

We already know that Deleuze's account of behaviour is informed by a desire to maintain two related philosophical positions. He wishes to provide an epistemology based neither upon the representational features of an object nor on mentalistic accounts of belief-states. In addition to this, he wishes to provide a non-teleological account of behaviour that does not presume a merely passive subject. In order to do this he uses the language of efficient cause. However, while contemporary arguments using the notion of efficient causality have every appearance of novelty they still only work if it is also assumed that determinism is true and they tend to equivocate between types of explanation. This equivocation is the result of collapsing reasons with causes. Due to this collapse we would be on safe ground to describe Deleuze, as Bennett describes Spinoza, not only as an explanatory rationalist but also as a causal rationalist.

A few commentators, for instance Bradotti, have suggested that Deleuze is unconcerned with the 'natural' or essential body. Now, while this might be true of the later Deleuze it is obviously not the case with the Deleuze who writes about the history of philosophy. If there had been a radical break or caesura, as some indicate of Marx, then the story of *Expressionism* would be of merely historical interest. I contend that we can really only appreciate Deleuze's description of the body as a play of forces or a surface of intensities within the metaphysical system of this earlier work. The underlying logic of that system, I have been arguing, leads not to a fleshed out, or embodied, account of subjectivity but to the utter blotting out of the principle. And this explains the curious tension discerned by tenacious readers such as Bradotti in the later works of Deleuze.[1]

I have already identified three places where this elimination occurs. The first is where Deleuze attempts to derive the finite mode from the infinite but is actually unable to account for the existence, necessary or otherwise, of finite modes. The second is with his description of the finite mode which is manifestly a double-aspect theory but which has as its latent content a reductive form of materialism. The third occurrence is with the exploration of the connections between epistemology and ethics. Here Deleuze implies, contrary to appearance, not only that the individual is subject to universal and necessary laws but also that the individual must assent to their subjection. In this chapter I shall develop the thesis that there is a distinction to be made between the manifest and latent content of Deleuze's account of ethical maturity. The purpose of these arguments will be to illuminate the consequences of this description for Deleuze's political philosophy.

Ethical maturity

During his discussion of Spinoza's contribution to the history of philosophy, Hegel considers the moral system developed in the *Ethics* and states that it is dependent upon a number of conceptual dichotomies.[2] He contests that because of this original philosophical framework, Spinoza produces a description of liberty that is the 'empty abstraction of independence'. Perfectly in harmony with Spinoza's project, Deleuze's statements on ethics fall into three broad categories. The first can be called a negative metaphysical thesis; arguments against metaphysical moral realism. The second category involves an explanation as to the causes of metaphysical moral realism. The final category is the substantive thesis.[3] We shall return at the end of this chapter to review the distinctions as discussed by Hegel with reference to Spinoza and ask whether Deleuze too operates within these basic and fundamental dichotomies and whether his account of freedom is as empty. The first port of call will be an analysis of Deleuze's negative thesis.

The negative thesis

The negative metaphysical thesis falls into two sections: arguments against monotheism and arguments against theistic dualism. The former also sub-divides. There are a few initial remarks suggested by Deleuze concerning Plotinus and these are followed by a number of arguments indicated as a response to the monotheism associated with the Judaic-Christian tradition. Deleuze is keen to prise apart Plotinian ideas that add something to his overall project from those which compromise it. We have already seen that while he is taken with the materialism of the Stoics, he also appreciates the spiritualistic monotheism often associated with Plotinus. We have also noted that the promise of Plotinian Platonism coalesces around the doctrine that intelligibles are not outside the intellect, and that the main problem for Deleuze with Plotinus lies with emanation (174). Because Plotinus believed that the first principle (of) being must be absolutely simple, he argued that there must be some simple thing 'beyond being'. The One is simple in the sense that it transcends or supersedes any composition and thus stands apart from the complex real and representations thereof.[4] It could be argued that Plotinus initiated a discussion concerning simplicity and uniqueness that defined later Hellenic monotheism and which was then absorbed into the Abrahamic tradition.[5] Throughout the first chapter we explored Deleuze's positive thesis that the One is also the Many. These arguments are supposed to block the move from the conception of the One, as unique, simple and distinct, to the conception of the One, as transcendent, to the monotheistic conception of a transcendent deity.[6] I have suggested that Deleuze encounters and does not answer the problem of first principle. Without the *Principle of Sufficient Reason* the Deleuzian system would be unable to begin.

During our discussion of Deleuze's monism, I suggested that we could detect echoes of the Stoic concept of fate. The Stoics maintained that the universe is ordered and ordered according to a rational plan identified with the divine *logos* and they also believed in a connection between rationality and the uninterrupted series of cause and effect. But there was some consternation as to the moral implication of this general thesis, because in a determinist world there seemed to be little room for moral accountability. If an action is determined and the agent determined to act, then where the action is evil the agent must be thought as determined to do evil. As part response to this, some Stoics argued that our final end is to live in accordance with nature and suggested that we do this by first interrogating cosmic nature and then conforming ourselves to its requirements therein discerned. Surprisingly this suggests both that the individual has a final end and that the individual should live in accordance with natural law. We must understand the Stoical ethical thesis as a dialogue with, and response to, eudaimonist ethical theory and here we can see that various answers to the problem of moral agency were defined within a language of ends more suitable to eudaimonist ethics. Although his arguments against theism provide the background against which Deleuze explains ordinary value judgements, he is also faced with the task of addressing this Stoic dilemma. Without using the language of final ends, he must answer the following questions: how can evil exist in the universe? Is the world determined in such a way that there must be evil? If an event or act can be described as evil, and all events are caused, is an individual determined to act in an evil way?

With an eye then to the problem of theistic dualism, Deleuze unravels the appearance of evil. In accordance with fairly traditional monistic theories, Deleuze has identified the whole as a singular individual (235). In the general taxonomy we have infinite attributes and infinite modes which follow from these attributes. These modes are the laws of nature. The infinite mode of motion and rest follows from the attribute of Extension and performs two functions: contains eternal essences and constitutes the extrinsic bodies of individual finite modes. The infinite mediate mode is the series of finite modes. Deleuze then takes an existing individual finite mode and claims that each has three aspects: its essence, its relations and its extensive parts. To each aspect corresponds an order of nature: an order of essence, an order of relations and an order of encounters (237). The first order, that of essences, is one of total conformity. The second order is identified with laws which determine the *eternal* conditions for a mode to come into existence. The final order *effectively* determines the conditions for a mode to come into existence and is referred to as 'the Common Order of Nature'. It too has three aspects: an order of extrinsic determinations, an order of chance encounters and an order of passions (238). It is at this level where the moment of the mode's existence, the duration of that mode's existence and its destruction are determined.

Deleuze wishes to argue not only that Nature is not determined in such a way that there must be good and evil encounters but also that individual natures are free from such determination. He advances arguments both at the level of essences and at the level of relations. Through what I consider the rather poor quantification of quality argument Deleuze established, to his own satisfaction at least, that there is an infinity of essences and that each essence is a part of divine power. It follows that because essences are, by definition, outside time and that destruction is a temporal term, no essence can be destroyed.[7] If we identify the concept 'bad' with the concept of 'cessation' it also follows that at the level of essences there is no thing, or event, that can be described as bad (249). Deleuze appears to claim that at the second level there is *only* composition On the face of it this just seems false. Most, if not all, cases of compositions will *depend on* the decomposition of other relations. For this reason Deleuze states that there is a positive viewpoint in nature – the viewpoint of composition (248). This is somewhat disingenuous. If nature is identified, in any way, with the series of finite modes and if the judgement 'bad' is a relational term, indicating the type of encounter of one body with another body, and if these encounters do occur, then we would have to say that good and bad encounters are part of the natural world; these are the facts of the matter, it is not a question of viewpoint. The real problem though lies somewhat deeper and is the problem of agency. Deleuze's only option at this point is to suggest that at a general level all changes can be explained through the Nature of the One and that therefore all changes can be defined as good.

Let us recall that an individual acts according to its own essence, nature, if and when it actively pursues its own preservation, that is, actively opposes contrary bodies and actively pursues compatible bodies. This principle of individuation relies on there being a mechanism of coherence existing between the essence and parts. This was neither specified nor explained by Deleuze but is suggested here merely as a relationship of composition. By using the idea of efficient causality, whence it is assumed that the individual's behaviour can only be explained through its nature and that (therefore) the individual will do whatever is useful to it, Deleuze addresses the above two points. First, *contra* dualistic theology, that there is no evil in Nature. Secondly, he argues that because all encounters can be explained through the individual's nature, at the level of relations, no individual is determined to do evil (249). Deleuze indicates the deeper problem of agency when he advocates the use of the concept 'viewpoint' as a way to meld the notion of efficient causality with behaviour to avoid using language more consistent with ends or intentionality.

Deleuze clarifies why an action might appear to be, but cannot be, intentionally wicked at the level of encounters. The clarification forks into an argument against there actually being wickedness at this level and an explanation as to why we might believe that there is. First he argues that it is not an evil when a body's internal coherence is adversely affected by an action – even from the viewpoint of the body in question. His explanation for this is that the body is always as perfect as it can be and that no relevant deprivation can occur. The notion of relevancy is crucial. Spinoza had defined evil as the passage from greater to lesser perfection and this turns out to be a comment on a comparative bodily state of a mode. Likewise, for Deleuze, a movement does occur, diminution of the mode's power of action. But essence, or *conatus*, is eventually worked out in terms of power of action. If power of action could be impeded then the essential nature could be destroyed or harmed and this would contradict his previous assertion. Some fancy footwork is required here and Deleuze does not disappoint.

No variable state can be identified with the nature of the body (251) and a body's power of action can be adversely affected but, given this, the body is always as perfect as it can be. This is because the mode's capacity to be affected is exercised rather than constituted, by affections and the limits of that capacity are a consequence of the body's relations of composition. This is all highly questionable. If by nature we mean either the internal structure, or the active principle by which the body seeks to preserve itself, then it is quite clear that by removing that body of one or more qualities it may be deprived of its ability to fulfil its nature. Secondly, he narrates the origin of our errant belief in intentionality in the context of ethical judgement.

The common person's judgement

His general ethical thesis is presented against both eudaimonist virtue ethics and the moral systems associated with monotheism. The starting point is that the terms 'good' and 'bad' do not represent actual properties inhering in things. Consistent with the theory of sensation we can say that an individual is part of a causal nexus, such that body Y will cause a modification x in body X. Due to the parallelism, where this happens there will be a corresponding idea (x) which indirectly represents body Y. When body Y 'agrees' with body X then there will be increased activity and a feeling of joy.[8] Agreement, let us remember, is defined in terms of usefulness. When body Y disagrees with body X then there will be diminishing of activity and a feeling of sadness. Disagreement is the obverse of usefulness. Deleuze defines this reduction, and the decomposing of a body, as 'an evil' (247).[9] Likewise, an increase in activity is 'a good'. Thus to claim that 'x is good' is to claim that 'x has relation R to y' and it is this relation which is being described. Deleuze is happy with this relational account of ethics; indeed, he cites Spinoza approvingly and says that 'we judge evil from our viewpoint'. Good and bad, he says, are so only in relation to human ends.

Let us sum up so far. Deleuze has established to his satisfaction that there is no evil in Nature and there are no actions that can be properly classified as evil. He has also established that ethical judgement concerns a relation such that where x has relation R to y, and R means x is useful to y, then the relation can be categorised as a good one. This is a truth claim about the nature of substance and the relationships holding between modes of that substance. But if there is no error how can we account for the fact that most people presume that 'good' and 'bad' are monadic properties rather than relational terms? Why do people refer to 'evil' rather than to 'bad' actions? Why do people believe in the fact of moral accountability? Deleuze attempts to answer these questions by tracing the causal origins of these confused beliefs.

Confused ideas are divided into two main groups: those of vague sense experience and those of signs (2p18s). It is the latter which are relevant here. A 'sign', for Spinoza, is equivalent to 'hearsay' or to 'word'. We have already noted that 'word' may refer to a bodily motion, a response to an external body, or to an image of the bodily motion. Bodily motions that have occurred together may well recur in attendant circumstances and led by apparent resemblance, we tend to link different images with single words. Due to the logic of involvement,[10] our experience has as its content our constitution rather than an external world.[11] Yet despite this, we compress various images and form a universal idea of the external object. These universal ideas, or words, are then upheld as models to which particulars ought to conform. Fitting in with this account, Deleuze distinguishes three types of signs: indicative, imperative, revelatory (181). Each sign has its origin in experience.

When an idea, that cannot represent an external body, is used to infer something about that body, or the causal sequence, then the sign is described as indicative. For our analysis of the ethical story, the indicative sign is relevant in two ways. First, it explains how words, that are supposed to have universal significance, merely reflect contiguity and imply our interest. Secondly, it helps to explain the transition from relational to property based morality. If body x is decomposed in relation R to y, the relation is bad from the perspective of x and accompanied by an affect of sadness.[12] Thereafter, the image of y will be associated with the relational affect. Here it seems we have started to talk of the affect itself as good or bad and this projected outwards to the object that caused it. An imperative sign presents natural law as a moral law. One account for this, drawing on Humean empiricism, might be that where there is a sequence of events, the events will be seen to be in a (causal) relationship.[13] If an idea or impression forms of this sequence it might suggest a necessity. This feeling, or idea, of continual necessity is then linked with a singular image or word which tends to be a deity, a singular necessary being. There is also the rather Nietzchean suggestion that we confuse the image of cause and effect with the idea of act – punishment (254).[14] Finally, we have revelatory signs. These are signs, or words, which are thought to be about something which has faculties analogous to humans and which is also thought to be superior to the human. The explanation appears to be that we have a confused idea of the attributes as common to all things and this is transferred to an idea of a God in all things and we then predicate of a singular being absolute power (182).[15]

Deleuze then asserts that when we impute moral intention we are describing a particular association of an image with an action.[16] Where the image is of an agreeable body, whose internal structure would be destroyed by the action, we tend to judge the action, or person acting, as evil. Argumentatively, then, the association of an image of a disagreeable body, with an action which would destroy its relations, would not be described as intentional wickedness. For this to be substitutable with our notion of moral action, Deleuze must stress the connection of the image of an agreeable body, with an action, or an image of an action, which will decompose that body. According to what criteria though might we choose these images? During our discussion concerning the problem of future-oriented action, we saw Deleuze implying that images somehow have a causally relevant role. Now, to give some content to the notions of 'endeavouring' and 'trying' to bring about certain states, he stresses the causal role of these images. Either the image has no causally relevant role or it has. If it had not, and we must be convinced that it cannot, then he is merely repeating an aspect of the deterministic story. If it has, then this is inconsistent with his parallelism. Yet the presentation of action in terms of formal and efficient cause and association of images must explain both the origin of our confused idea of moral responsibility and provide the basis for this substantive account of ethical action.

If we pull together these aspects we can get a more rounded version of the origin of apparently false moral beliefs. Let us return to the points raised above. In answer to the question 'why do we judge things, rather than relations, as good or bad?' Deleuze responds with his account of signs. Universal terms are supposed to refer to various particulars and each particular is supposed more or less to satisfy the universal term (IdS). Particulars are then judged in terms of how well they exemplify their universal, the presumption being that a particular *ought to* coincide with its universal. The 'ought' implies a moral aspect to the judgement. This categorical judgement is a transposition of a judgement of practical necessity – in order to bring x about I ought to do y (ImS) – and is supported through monotheistic foundationalism (RS).[17] Once we have formed our universal concepts and judged individuals in terms of how well they satisfy their concept, we then judge between the universals and place them in a hierarchy of moral worth. The choice between models, however, is made according to our interests (IdS).[18] Thus the ensuing ethical system is identified with morals rather than functions and properties rather than relations.

The second question is answered through his account of revelatory signs. Finally, if someone were to ask 'am I morally responsible?', Deleuze would answer that moral values are words which have a metaphysical crust but which contain a germ of rational truth. One can only be blamed for bringing about y or not bringing about x if one either ought to have done or not done so. The past participle indicates a prior commitment to a present condition such that here are things that one ought to 'endeavour to' or 'try to' bring about. This commitment itself requires an assent to an original belief that x would be a good thing to happen.[19] We can see that the truth of a value judgement lies in its apprehension of a state of affairs that is of interest to the organism and the inference that it would be in the interests of the organism to bring the state about. That said, to believe in one's own responsibility for an action, is to mistake the relationship of cause and effect. To believe in the moral worth of an action is to be party to the general confusion outlined above. The implication is that as all events are necessary, in a strict sense, the belief in free, willed and intentional acts is an error that can be explained through a causal, empirical, analysis of belief formation. It is not, though, at all clear whether we can have an idea of moral responsibility without some sense of free-will.

Before moving on to Deleuze's substantive account of ethics, I would like to make a few preliminary comments. I do not believe that this account of empirical psychology provides a thorough explanation for the move to property attribution. Bennett explains Spinoza's account in the following way. Spinoza begins by asserting that initially we believe we are at the centre of the universe and we also believe that God has made everything 'for us'.[20] This leads us to believe that what really matters about a thing is how it suits us. This, in turn, encourages us to attribute to the good 'in-itself' various powers and qualities. The truncation of 'this is good for me' to 'this is good' is endorsed by subject–predicate grammatical structure. Even this explanation is unsatisfactory. The account runs adrift in the somewhat choppy waters of mental content.[21]

Deleuze defines the term 'sign' as something like an imprint or an image. Here the term seems to signify the imprint, an idea of that imprint, articulated in language, and then our belief about that idea. So, for example, during his exposition of Spinoza's three types of signs, Deleuze suggests that we form beliefs from confused imprints and this explains why we mistake natural for moral law. We can see here that in order to explain error, Deleuze finds himself borrowing from the language of cognitive apprehension. But the sign can never indicate anything *about* the indirect, external, object and we can see now that there is no groundwork for the conceptual apparatus Deleuze needs in order to explain the origin of our moral beliefs. Following from this, because he denies talk of belief-states, he makes it impossible to open the process of belief formation to critical scrutiny. It is with the description of the origin of the revelatory sign that this problem reaches its apex. Let us recall that the revelatory sign is explained as a result of confusing an idea of the attributes, as common to all beings, with the idea of a God. Not only does Deleuze not clarify why the confusion of 'bad' with 'evil', takes place but he also does not answer why we reify the idea and 'lend God determinations analogous to our own (Understanding, Will)'.[22] We can see that Deleuze's naturalised epistemology blends seamlessly into an a-historic account of belief formation and all that is entailed.[23] He unfavourably contrasts the language of the imagination, constituted by inadequate ideas and signs, to the natural language of philosophy (of the intellect)[24] and in doing so betrays his advocacy of materialism with a latent, but overriding, rationalism.

The substantive thesis: model behaviour

Deleuze's ethics are naturalistic but it does not follow that they are either relative or open to the vagaries of individual judgement. Reason, in accord with nature, demands only that 'everyone should love themselves, seek what is useful to themselves, and strive to preserve their being by increasing their power of action' (264). Thus the philosophical and political anthropology cannot be considered apart from the ontology. Aside from the fact that it would be a testament to his ingenuity if he could devise a universal ethic system, which remained true to the principle of qualified nominalism, the political consequences of an ethics based on the concept of 'self-affirmation' are severe. For the sake of simplicity I shall present Deleuze's substantive thesis in three parts. I shall first discuss his idea of model behaviour the 'what is being affirmed' then proceed with an investigation of the harm principle and the principle of unity. The rational and collaborative ethics that is supposed to follow from the nature is then examined.

Deleuze, following Spinoza, reintroduces us to the term *entia rationis*. These 'entities of reason' have no independent status and function as a guide to correct thinking. Thus they cannot be judged as true or false, adequate or inadequate. According to Savan, these entities of reason may help assist our thinking in three ways. When one image is compared with another, they help us to discern what is true in the imagination. They help us to construct general models or examplars. By doing this, we can see how a collection of things share certain fundamentals. Finally, they help us to see that terms such as 'negation' and 'non-being' merely help us to understand and do not actually subsist.[25] The relevant point is that these entities form a bridge between our intellect and our experience; they explain the conversion of inadequate into adequate ideas. There is a distinction to be made between an inadequate abstract idea and an idea, which makes certain universalistic claims but which is, nonetheless, properly understood to be a thing of reason. These ideas are also known as models and for Deleuze the choice of the appropriate model is the crux of the whole issue of ethical behaviour.

Central to Deleuze's project is his belief that a transvaluation of moral to ethical values requires a revision of our idea of human nature. Spinoza mentions such a model in the *Ethics* [26] and Bennett describes his rather cursory comments as a 'palimpsest'.[27] The idea of models is more central to *The Correction of the Understanding* and this explains why Deleuze has a tendency to highlight echoes from this work in the *Ethics*. He believes that by considering an individual physical structure we will glean a proper understanding of that individual. This, he stresses, does not imply a reductive materialism because given the parallelism, there is a parallel sequence of modifications, so that where I (x) there will be an x and *vice versa*. There is no causal interaction between them but a strict isomorphism does pertain. This means that if we apprehend the mechanism of individuation of the finite mode in the attribute of Extension we will also be well placed to understand the mind of that mode. Once this is apprehended we will be able to discern what is objectively in the interests of that mode and advise of suitable, ethical, behaviour.

Although the model is based on descriptions and analyses appertaining to the individual, it should not be confused with a common notion or an adequate idea. In two ways we can say that 'the body' forms the basis for Deleuze's model. Through an investigation into the laws of nature we arrive at knowledge of the body and discover our first principles of science (mechanism) and ethics (dynamics) and the former gives us a strict account of identity conditions and from the latter we derive the working principle of self-love.[28] Secondly, from an assessment of the points of influence between the mechanistic and dynamic aspects of the body, Deleuze believes he can draft a picture of power that is neither based on a notion of actualising the possible nor on the idea of development towards an ideal.

So, there are two modal triads: the mechanical and the dynamic. Centrally, both insist on the existence of a unique part of (divine) power (*puissance*). Mechanically the relations that compose the body give rise to the dynamical constant capacity (*pouvoir*) to be affected.[29] By virtue of the fact that any affect caused by an external body results in a passive affect, this capacity translates as a force (*puissance*) of suffering. The capacity to be affected by active affections is translated as a force (*puissance*) of acting. Because the capacity to be affected remains constant these two powers (*puissance*) are related proportionately. Then Deleuze argues that the power of suffering is passive and is therefore derivative, a limitation of the other active force. He concludes by stating that the essence (*puissance*) of a mode is to be identified with the active force, that is, 'active force' is coextensive with 'the capacity of this body'. Thus, he writes that because we do not know how to produce active affections we do not know our power of action.

Because he has established that every mode is all it can be at each moment, and that the essence or *conatus* of a mode is identical to its force of action, Deleuze feels satisfied that he has shown that the rule of proportionality need not be identified with a teleological notion of perfection. Yet this seems to leave his modes in a rather neglected state and his ethics without any anchor. So he argues that if the power of acting is inhibited it is so to a greater or lesser degree and, if the *conatus* is identical to 'force of action', then the *conatus* itself is open to variation (224). Mechanically we have defined *conatus* as the 'endeavouring to preserve the relations of composition' and defined it dynamically as the 'endeavouring to maintain the body's ability to be affected in a great number of ways'. The strong claim is that the dynamic account replaces the mechanistic one as the foundation for the ethical naturalism. The ethics is thus to be governed by the question 'what is the extent of my power?' and the practical ethical imperative is 'act in such a way as to increase the extent of that power' (269). The question can now be posed as 'what could I do if I were not interfered with?'.[30] However, due to the necessitarianism, this becomes 'what *would* I do if I were not interfered with?' and the matter of ethics must be acknowledged to be an interrogation into causal interactions.

We have seen Deleuze describe the developmental stages through which the individual begins to behave in such a way as to ensure the maximum amount of joyful passions and then to transform active passions into active affections. It became clear that for this process to begin, and then to be embedded, the individual would need to organise chance encounters in a way that would suit its nature. An individual acts according to its own nature, essence, when it actively pursues its own preservation, that is, actively opposes contrary bodies and actively pursues compatible or agreeable bodies. The terms 'agreeable' and 'useful' are co-extensive in this context. Deleuze struggles to explain future-oriented action because the representational features of an indirect object cannot enter into the physical causal sequence. This means that an image or idea (x) is only a causally irrelevant and indirect image of the body Y which might cause x in the future. The empiricist suggestion, that when we remember something we recall the causal chain whereby we were originally modified and that this then also recalls the physical state and that this newly recalled state effects future action, also fails. We must then be suspicious of any assertion appearing to relate to purposive behaviour. When Deleuze claims that good and bad are relative to human ends, he means that when I say 'x is good' I mean that 'x is good for me' and that this is explained through my nature, which is determined to pursue that which is useful.

The identification of the terms 'usefulness', 'good', 'increase in activity', 'pleasure' and 'power' is, then, supposed to guide our thinking or behaviour. Deleuze's arguments are from a tradition that includes the moral philosophies of Hume, Nietzsche, Mill and Bentham and are intended to demystify moral statements and to uncover and then bridge, through shifting the terms, the logical gap between is and ought, facts and non-natural moral properties. Yet the questions 'is everything that gives me pleasure, good?' and 'is every action designed to bring about a pleasurable state, good?', still seem to be meaningful, in a non-trivial way.[31] Because his story of ethical transposition is inadequate, these questions remain pertinent. Indeed, Deleuze's definition seems to raise a number of questions. Just because x is useful to me, is identified with a pleasurable state, *ought* I to endeavour to attain it? *Should* I treat, or think, of every x from my viewpoint? Is every increase in power *justifiable*? Is it the case that every sad passion is the result of tyranny? Similarly, is the sad person necessarily in bondage to his or her passions and is that *bad*? In other words, Deleuze has attempted, and failed, to close the gap between the question 'what sort of actions are right?' and 'is performing such actions the right way for me to live?' The proposed naturalistic solution, a form of consequentionalism, though is only supposed to be an intermediate state between old style moral values and the completed transvaluation of values, which is a particular type of psychology and character. The continual upgrading of ethical judgement is supposed to reflect Deleuze's commitment to Nietzsche's non-teleological or evolutionary sense of becoming-Übermensch.[32] Without this, it is difficult to see any normative impulse, anything that might delineate his 'ethology' from a description and classification of behaviours.[33] Indeed, we might hope to find something additional in the form of a harm principle such that not all actions which bring about an increase in activity in the systems of an organism are justifiable.

The substantive thesis: the harm principle

It would be right, to describe Deleuze's ethical position, just as one would describe Spinoza's, as rational individual egoism. This is not the full story however. There are specific things that the individual ought to do to bring about a situation which would deliver that individual from its passionate nature and thereby release it from bondage. Deleuze wishes to explain that the rational individual ought to enter into compact with other rational individuals as this will help it mature from the first to the second level of knowledge. For the sake of argument, let us call this his interpersonal ethics – practical maxims guiding our behaviour towards others. The principle of ethical responsibility works with the principle of efficient cause: if we can explain an action in accordance with the nature of the individual in question then we have some purchase on the notion of practical necessity, what the individual ought to do in a given situation. The principle of co-operation is the conclusion of various arguments, which begin with the assertion that when an individual encounters an agreeable body, it will attempt to unite with it in ways so as, 'to procure and to preserve it' (241). Here I shall concentrate on the latter part of the claim.

I have already suggested that there is no good reason to suppose that just because object x causes a feeling of joy that it would be right, or indeed possible, to preserve it. More importantly though, in fact, we can see that there is no injunction against any type of other-related behaviour. If a body always acts in ways so as to procure that which is useful to it, unless it would gain some pleasure from acting against the agreeable body, it just would not do so. Indeed, if there is pleasure in the decomposition of body x, because we have jettisoned language of purposes, we would retrospectively claim that body x was in fact disagreeable. Deleuze might wish to prevent this occurrence and could offer an argument relating to natures; that it is against my nature to harm a body that is useful to me. Because acting against my nature causes a disagreeable affect, acting against my nature is not in my interest, we could conclude that it is not in my interest to harm an agreeable body. But this does not answer the point at all. If I encounter an object and act in such a way that I experience pleasure then the action is good for me, whether or not, and sometimes because, I destroy or harm the body in question. Hence, we know that any action against a (disagreeable) body is acceptable. This account is all the more harrowing given that if x and y have different natures then those natures are, by definition, contrary: x and y are different individuals because one 'has' properties, or a structure, not included in the other. If y is different from x then x will find y to be a disagreeable body and will seek to destroy it. So, as a last point, we should note that by virtue of Deleuze's logic of identity every other body must be defined as contrary and therefore disagreeable and that, therefore, any action permissible.

Empiricists, such as Hume, have presented accounts of moral psychology based on various statements as to universal features of human psychology, such as a tendency towards sympathy for others' feelings. Spinoza avoids Deleuze's conclusion by slipping into his argument the claim that relevantly similar individuals tend to imitate the emotions of others. This, if nothing else, could provide a good reason not to harm an agreeable body, maybe even a disagreeable one.[34] There is some intimation of a similar doctrine, of interpersonal psychology, at work in *Expressionism* but nothing substantial.[35] Reflecting Nietzsche's comments on pity, Deleuze defines pity as a sad passion and therefore something to be freed from (271). Although there is nothing necessary in the slip from a self-regarding ethical theory to a solipsistic or selfish 'ethics', without an accompanying interpersonal psychology the move to universality is, at best, problematic. It is because there is no properly worked out theory of 'otherness', or intersubjectivity, that Deleuze struggles to explain the move into compact. We can now add that because Deleuze has jettisoned but not replaced representational theories of belief, there is no room to include the causal efficacy or relevance of the 'aboutness' of the other; we simply move and experience intensities.

The principle of unity

According to Deleuze, the germ of rational truth, contained in ordinary value judgements, is that there are some states just in the interest of the organism to bring about. Compact is one of these states. Deleuze commences this explanation of compact with the premise that individuals will attempt to unite with bodies that are agreeable (257). 'Agreement' is co-extensive with 'useful' and the relation of agreement between two bodies depends on a similarity thesis. The second premise in the overall thesis is thus that 'man' will attempt to unite with 'man' (261).[36] This is an immediate problem. Let us assume that where x and y have similar natures, they will act in similar ways to preserve their composition. In a situation of scarcity it is this very fact that might lead x and y into conflict over attaining some scarce, but mutually appealing, good. Likewise, if x and y have relevantly similar natures, and if there is a situation such that some s is a threat to beings with natures such as theirs and only one body could escape, then conflict is not only likely but necessary *qua* the self-preservational doctrine. Indeed, this is the idea of rational egoism clearly articulated by Hobbes in his *Leviathan*. If two, rational, individuals desire the same thing, which they cannot both enjoy, they become enemies and endeavour to destroy one another. It is because one knows that the other is relevantly similar, that they both pursue the same ends, that one learns to distrust and fear the other. This, for Hobbes, is the rational response to natural law. Deleuze attempts, and as we can see fails, to provide an ethics which avoids talk of belief-states by appealing to the natures of individuals.

Deleuze argues that x and y must recognise that compact is in their rational long-term *mutual* self-interest (264). Thus the ethical judgement 'this is good for me' is substituted for the ethical judgement 'this is good for me therefore this is good for you' and a temporal qualification added 'this is good for me and therefore you, in the long run'. Why is it that compact is in mutual self-interest? Well, Deleuze advances three reasons. First, all men (sic) have relevantly similar natures, these natures are agreeable thus each will be affected with joy in the encounter. Secondly, this means that the quantity of active passions will be increased in each individual and the individual's power of action will be increased. This is in the interest of each individual. Finally, the individual bodies unite and through this third relation compose a single body. Although each body is preserved in the new combination, the new body is 'twice as strong'. Because it is a single body it will seek to preserve itself and because it is a single body it will contain nothing within it that could lead to its dissolution.[37] The ethical judgement is ultimately transformed into 'this is good for us in the long run'. Following Spinoza, then, Deleuze could claim that under the guidance of reason, there would be nothing that the human individual would desire for him or herself that she or he did not also desire for the rest. But, to reach this point, Deleuze must presuppose that all human individuals are relevantly similar and reasonable and there is nothing in the argument supporting this.

Because Deleuze, it seems, does not adopt Spinoza's imitation thesis, he has to rely on his description of the composition of the third body, to explain why it would be in the interests of one body to unite with a second. Yet there is no secondary argument to demonstrate that the third body will be twice as strong. This may make sense if, and only if, every encounter with every relevantly similar individual is a happy one. We have already demonstrated that this does not hold. Similarly, because he is keen, due to the political implications of doing otherwise, to insist that each body retains its integrity, he cannot really argue that it is a single body. If he cannot use this then he cannot argue that there is nothing in the united body that might cause its destruction. The one option is this. The individuals function together and thereby pursue ends common to the single body. The functionalist description of individuals acting together could eliminate the need to talk about the apprehension of a common end or interest. Except that Deleuze can only persuade us of the merits of the argument by illegitimately helping himself to a teleological and cognitive description of action through a thesis which prioritises similarity of natures: individuals act in certain ways *because* it is in their common and natural interest to do so.

The civil state

What then is the political consequence of these propositions? Armstrong identifies a curious relationship between Spinoza, Deleuze and Hobbes. Although the contract theories of Hobbes and Spinoza share certain premises, Deleuze, she claims spots and endorses a divergence between the juridical and anti-juridical versions of contract between authoritarian and anti-authoritarian state of nature arguments.[38] Picking points out from Deleuze's preface to Negri's *Savage Anomaly* she identifies four characteristics of juridicism. The first is that the forces have a private or individual origin. The second is that these forces must be socialised to engender relations that adequately correspond to them. In order to achieve this, there must be a mediation of power (*Potestas*). Finally, the horizon is inseparable from a crisis, war or antagonism for which the power is presented as a solution. I shall be arguing that while this appears to be the case, the conclusion of Deleuze's rendition of contract theory shares the juridical elements of the Hobbesian account.

Deleuze's argument begins with the attribution to the individual of a natural and utter egoism. From this is supposed to follow a rational and collaborative ethics. His state of nature argument is intended to do two things. First, it has to explain how the individual can move from a position of ethical immaturity to maturity given that no one is born reasonable (259). The paradox Deleuze has to address is this: if you were to live according to your nature, you would organise encounters which would maximise your joyful passions and understanding. But, the ability to organise encounters in this way depends on joyful passions having already been maximised. Thus, Deleuze concedes that a City-State, and its organisational powers, may be a solution to this riddle. Secondly, he needs to demonstrate the natural origins of collaboration. It appears that, unless one immediately states that the power of the individual is that of being, we do have a thoroughly private or individual origin and Armstrong's first condition is fulfilled. The role attributed to the City-State satisfies her second condition. I shall demonstrate that because Deleuze does not present a substantial account of interpersonal morality, he has to concede to Hobbes the logic of the argument: thus satisfying the third and fourth conditions.

As any exposition of a hypothetical social contract, Deleuze's versions of the state of nature and move to compact is also intended to answer a number of philosophical and political problems. To secure the overall cohesiveness of his ethical naturalism, Deleuze must justify the identification of the terms 'power' and 'right'. Otherwise put, he must convince us that Rousseau had misunderstood the relationship when he wrote, 'force is physical power, and I fail to see what moral effect it can have. To yield to force is an act of necessity, not of will – at the most, an act of prudence'.[39] I shall suggest that Deleuze can only supply the normative content by making a virtue out of force. The concept of 'legitimate' power is evacuated[40] and, because the individual is compelled to act in accordance with natural law, terms such as 'duty' and 'obligation' and even 'consent' become redundant.

Commentators on Spinoza's political theory often maintain that there is a significant rupture between the *Theological-Political Treatise* and the *Political Treatise,* due to the centrality of social contract theory in the former and absence, in the latter, of such references. Against this, Curley postulates a seamless development in Spinoza's ideas on the question of political legitimacy. Deleuze's mixing of references from these two works indicates that he would agree with Curley's interpretation. In accord with contractarianism, Spinoza bases his social compact on a promise. Interestingly, in the earlier work Spinoza notes that this promise is in-itself insufficient, as here:

> Though men may promise with definite signs of an ingenuous intention, and contract to maintain trust, still, no one can be certain of another's reliability unless something else is added to the promise. For by natural right each person can act deceptively, and is bound to stand by the contract only by the hope of a greater good or fear or a lesser evil.[41]

Curley, I believe quite rightly, surmises that the supplement is the existence of a sovereign with the power to enforce contracts. He argues that the situation only arises because while it may be in the individual's rational interest to keep contract or promise made, not all individuals are rational all of the time. While I agree with Curley's conclusion, I would replace this last contention with something more like Bennett's argument that the move to supplement the social contract is not only itself rational but born out of peoples' quite reasonable distrust of other rational individuals. In *Expressionism* Deleuze cites Spinoza's four foundational political principles approvingly.

These begin with a restatement of the self-preservational doctrine and the association of this theory with a doctrine of natural law. When a body x encounters body y, it either suffers good or bad passive affects. If it were to suffer from good affects then it would attempt to unite with body y. If, however, it were to suffer from bad passive affects then it would avoid y. Now, because there is no account of purposive behaviour, we would have to describe a body's movement towards body y as caused by, or explained through, its nature. Because the mode is causally determined and logically derived, its behaviour is a result of causal processes, which are both natural and logical. We can then explain the body's movement in terms of its own nature: 'appetite as efficient cause'. This bears striking similarities to Hobbes' contention that, so long as an individual is not interfered with, it will do whatever is in its power to gain what is useful to it, which is, in the end, more power. 'The object of man's desire', Hobbes writes, 'is not to enjoy once and for one instant of time but to assure for ever the way of future desire'.[42] The only significant difference is that he concedes that the objects themselves exert an attraction and he is thus able to explain movement towards an object with that in mind. The law of nature is for Hobbes a general precept or rule discerned by reason, whereby the individual is forbidden to do that which is destructive to life or to take away the means to preserve that life. The law of nature is, for Deleuze, a statement of the self-preservational doctrine within its causal nexus.

Just as life in the Hobbesian state of nature is nasty, brutish and short, so life for the Deleuzian individual is brutal, insecure and wretched.[43] The state of nature for Deleuze and Hobbes, is pre-civil, pre-social and pre-exists moral codes.[44] The finite individual is at the mercy of chance encounters, and lives with the continual, reasonable, thought that other individuals are a threat to security. Indeed, all other individuals pose some sort of threat. Those who are different will, in all likelihood, attempt to destroy or to assimilate the individual's body and those who are relevantly similar might have good reason to do the same. The merit of this type of account is that the conventional and contingent nature of law is broadcast. The downside is that by identifying social bonds as conventional or law-like these can be 'de-naturalised'. While it may be critically acute to notice the historical nature of social relationships, the rhetorical device of the social contract defines the individual as that which pre-exists and enters the social bond. Attributions of personality types or 'natural' characteristics can then be used to explain why laws and contracts were formed in the way they were. Because all this is hypothetical, we achieve a retrospective justification, or indeed criticism, of current social conditions through descriptions of natural types.[45]

Because there is a natural law it follows that we can deduce from this certain things about the bodies. Hobbes offered us 19 such maxims, all which suggest ways in which the individual ought to behave given his or her nature. Obligation and duty are thus practical, if categorical, matters.[46] Deleuze identifies natural law (*loi*) with natural rights (*droit*) and argues that the individual is not only within his (sic) rights to do whatever is required to preserve his body, but also that the individual is categorically obliged to pursue what is in his interest. Here Deleuze seems to be repeating Spinoza's general thesis that the right of each thing extends as far as its power. Curley underlines the disturbing nature of this thesis and also that, while there are similarities with Hobbes' assertion that in the state of nature every man (sic) has a right to everything, it even goes beyond Hobbes in two ways. Spinoza applies it to all individuals not only to human beings and he does not qualify it by saying that it applies only to individuals in the state of nature.[47]

In the *Theological-Political Treatise*, the co-extensiveness of 'right' and 'power' depends on the assertion that God, as supreme authority, has a right to do all things. Because the 'power of nature' is substitutable with 'power of God' we could argue that nature has a right to do whatever it can do. Because nature is nothing but the power of all individuals, we could thus argue that everything in nature has a right to do what it can do. This argument cannot ground Deleuze's ethical theory. God, as infinite being, is not identical to the infinity of finite modes. Deleuze dismisses reasoning from analogy, otherwise it would have been open to him to argue that, just as infinite things follow (logically and causally) from God's essence, so an infinite capacity to be affected follows from a mode's essence: as properties from a definition. The secondary claim, that any mode has a *right* to exercise its capacity to be affected, to exercise its power, can only be justified either through analogy or through the strict identification of right with natural law and natural law with the causal and rational sequence of production.[48] Which is exactly what Deleuze does do: 'the law of nature is never a rule of duty, but the norm of power, the unity of right, power and its exercise'.[49] This means that if the encounter with body y causes an affect which is an increase in activity in the system, a feeling of joy, then body x is within its rights to (endeavour to) unite with, or to assimilate and certainly to use, body y.

From this, Deleuze deduces that 'nobody has authority to decide my rights'. At first glance this is just empty and as a working political principle of autonomy worthless. He has argued that it is within the rights of body x to do whatever it must to, or with, body y. Because his harm principle is so severely flawed Deleuze undermines his own position. Through an encounter, body y may well find that it suffers sad passive affects and that its power of action is diminished. If we define rights in terms of power, and the exercise of power, then clearly body x has affected the rights of body y, and, most importantly, was within its rights to do so. The concept of decision-making is drafted into the account and, due to his previous position on cognition and belief-states, should not be accredited with any seriousness. This argument is supposed to link authority with consent and is a necessary foothold in Deleuze's climb from the state of nature to Civil Society.

The Hobbesian and Deleuzian individual is, quite *reasonably*, in a state of fear and distrust (260). He knows that when he acts in a way consistent with his nature, he is likely to come into conflict with any relevantly similar body. In this state, he suffers passive passions and these are likely to be mainly sad. It is in his interest, therefore, to enter into contract with other individuals. Hobbes saw that the central task here was to secure a path which would lead people to act in accordance with the qualities which would dispose them to act rationally, and thereby to seek peace. The obligation to seek peace, whilst living without security, must hold *in foro interno* only. How might rational egoists, with a completely reasonable distrust of one another, enter into a compact and form a government? In a similar fashion, Deleuze argues that individuals in the state of nature must 'seek to organise encounters', to form an association of men in relations that can be combined. I shall not rehearse here the points raised above which demonstrate that his account of universality is too flawed to be of use. But let us add that he has no right to help himself to any purposive account of behaviour and that the notion of expectation can not fulfil the function Deleuze wishes. Deleuze must concede this and the next point to Hobbes.

It is in the interest of the individual then to move out of a state of fear and distrust. Through an initial compact, the individual renounces his or her natural rights (266). Hobbes built in to his political programme a device to eliminate the instability that bedevils co-operative systems. There would be a single enforcement agency, with a guaranteed monopoly on coercive power, which would terrorise those who might otherwise contemplate breaking the co-operative pact. At any point, if the individual were to be tempted to invoke a strategy of active aggression, to ensure maximal and *rational* pay-off, he would find the process irreversible. More than being a simple political and social constraint on passions, the Sovereign ensures a constant and optimal return on interest. In this way, Hobbes deduces, from clear descriptions of human nature, steps that need to be taken to deliver that which is really in each individual's long-term interest.

It is at this point that Deleuze is supposed to diverge from a Hobbesian or juridical model. Rather than assuming a consent doctrine premised on an alienation of powers or rights, one could interpret the 'body-politic' image as a form of direct, all-embracing, democracy. Now, Deleuze argues that there has to be a power to organise social relations in such a way that the citizens 'are forced to agree and be compatible'. He claims that this can be delivered through the body politic itself rather than a separate third individual, which is why Gatens also describes this as an anti-juridical political model.[50] There are two immediate objections. First, Deleuze does insist that the individual gives up his or her right to judgement (267) and, secondly, he has already had to concede to Hobbes the logic of the move to compact through a sovereign power.

Thus we arrive at a definition of legitimate power and begin to see the influence through Spinoza of Machievelli's republicanism. The individual abandons the right to ethical judgement and, at the same time, transfers his or her power to a third body: a common body and soul.[51] These powers are, of course, executed. Where it is understood that right is coextensive with power, we could say that rulers of the City govern with right only to the extent that the subjects consent to their rule by obeying their commands. One could argue that the naturalistic description of the individual imposes specific limits to any power a sovereign may have: the right of nature does not cease in civil order. This impediment is supposed to work in two ways. First, it operates as a limit to the actions of the executors. Secondly, we can say that 'the City' is itself a body and as a body it must act in accordance with its own nature. The self-preservational doctrine then admonishes the executors to 'aim as far as possible for reason's ideal' (267). Some citizens suffer more sad passive affections than others and the bonds of servilitude are broken when the individual comes to use his or her own understanding. The slaves, the weak and the foolish must be guided by the wise who are able to grasp the laws of nature. I use the term 'guide' rather euphemistically. What Deleuze actually says is in harmony with Rousseau's exaltation that we are to be forced to be free. 'The sovereign City', he writes, 'then has power enough to institute indirect conventional relations through which citizens are forced to agree and be compatible' (266).

The meaning of 'good' in the term 'good city' is supposed to run parallel with the ethical naturalism, where good refers to an object that is beneficial to the individual. Either, then, a city is good when it is in the interests of the individual, useful to the individual, increases the individual's power of action (267) or, as a body, when its powers are properly exercised and its power of action increased as far as possible.

Deleuze has stated that we alienate our right to judgement. Without a properly worked out epistemology the meaning of this is rather obscure. Yet he needs this caveat, because otherwise, in a situation of scarcity, there would be absolutely no guarantee that the body politic could or would maintain cohesion. There may well be competition amongst group members for the instruments of power enabling individuals to realise their capacities or achieve their own ends. If we allow the suspension of judgement and the principle of unity move, there is still a question to be posed. What is to stop this one group committing all sorts of acts against another group? Indeed, if we concede the third body metaphor, this body politic could well behave in the same way as any individual confronting a similar, but hostile, other. The solution to this is that there is one good which is never scarce and that is reason or cognition of God.[52]

Before moving on to a discussion of the state of blessedness, I would like to summarise so far. The ethical system is a carefully elaborated and systematic rendering of the types of judgements we do make. The exegesis is premised on the belief that from an analysis of the structure of bodies we can derive a typology of motivations and passions. These then provide the foundation of the ethical naturalism. The terms 'good' and 'bad' have objective content because they refer to relationships between bodies and objects. Because the relationship concerns individual bodies which endeavour to unite with other agreeable bodies, the ethics is supposed to take account of perspective, be context specific and partial; 'this is good for me, now'.[53] If we tease out the actual position it is like this: we know that all emotional states are passive: modifications produced by external bodies. Some of these diminish our power of acting. Spinoza spells this out when he writes that 'human lack of power in moderating and checking the emotions I call servitude. For a man who is submissive to his emotions does not have power over himself'.[54] If it is the case that all (passive) emotional states are caused by external bodies, that only affects can mutate affects, and if it is the case that no individual can escape physical encounters then we can do no better than encounter objects which cause pleasurable affects. Agreeable encounters cause rational insight. What does rational insight deliver? Freedom. When we properly understand and analyse the causes of our passions, any feeling that is object-related will disappear and our power of action will correspondingly increase. The process is the same, and as mysterious, as the transformation of inadequate into adequate ideas and joyful passive passions into active affections (262).[55] The powerful individual, it seems, is one who controls his or her emotions and this is achieved through detaching affect from object.

Conclusion

We have already detailed how various philosophical problems make the account quite untenable. However, I would like to conclude with a few remarks concerning Deleuze's political legacy. There are three axes on which the political programme turns, and these should cause us some consternation: the role of power in the Republic, the interpersonal ethics and the necessitarianism. Deleuze's arguments concerning the transition of inadequate into adequate ideas requires an interjection of an organising force. The hypothetical compact explains this, but requires the original principle of unity. But his entire personal morality, required for the universal thesis, is based on an interpersonal psychology, in which the first thought is not 'the individual is human' but that 'this individual is like me'. The second thought that must follow from this logical judgement of identity is that 'this individual is like me, and therefore I ought to fear him or her'. If we had taken the republicanism seriously, and assented to the idea that the Republic forms a third body where 'power' can be defined in terms of the ability to act (in concert), this rational egoism must make us pause. The underlying logic of the argument is such that individuals will only act in concert, indeed consent to an original contract, if there is a coercive body enforcing specific rules of organisation. Rather than this power being limited by the natures of the individuals in the Republic, in fact the description of the individual natures gives it legitimacy. The laws of organisation, supposedly receiving their content from nature, only have as regulative ideas the poorly thought out harm principle and a principle of maximisation. The former is nothing but the 'assertion that nobody has this authority to decide my rights, which is a poor version of the liberal principle of non-interference because, as we already knew, it is within the rights of body y to do whatever it must to or with body x. To accept the latter we have to presume that all joyful encounters are to be encouraged and all sad encounters discouraged. Indeed, we also have to presume a distinction between interests and wants and a scientific primacy attributable to the former.[56] Because this throws us in to some confusion with reference to his qualified nominalism, Deleuze advises us that the foolish must alienate their judgement to the wise, who can grasp common notions.

The Stoics argued that an impression must, in some way, faithfully represent the external object and that the apprehension of the perception coincided with assent to it. The Sceptics suggested that as there are perceptual errors, Stoic faith in the causal sequence was misplaced. In response, various Stoics argued that the kind of impression we have depends not only on propositional content but also on the way in which the content is thought.[57] This propositional attitude involves an emotive response to the proposition in question. Now, although Deleuze does not have a similar notion of propositional content, he does have an idea as to the emotional affects caused by object encounters, and in various ways also uses this to explain error. In terms of the political programme, however, we must stress that according to Deleuze it is in the individual's long-term interest to separate himself from emotions caused by all objects. It is extremely worrying to note that some of these objects are also other subjects. It is part of the ethical project, perhaps as an interim step, to validate the use of these other subjects. Any one or thing should be used to increase this individual's joyful passions. The principle of identity of indiscernibles does not protect the individual because the ethics turns on a rational egoism, such that every interaction with every other individual is defined as necessarily limiting. We can now see why the lack of an interpersonal psychology, or rigorous harm principle, creates such a vacuum in his moral and political philosophy.

Finally, the logic of the system is such that each individual mode is determined to behave in the ways in which it does. Each finite mode is part of a causal chain and its passions, whether joyful or sad, are thus determined. To waylay the full force of this mechanism, Deleuze, following Spinoza, attempts to argue that we can intercede in the causal series with images and affects that follow from these images but we have already seen that this fails. This is critical to the political philosophy as Deleuze presents us with finite modes *endeavouring* to create joyful encounters. Let us then define what it would be for an individual to have an increase in its power of action. Well, at first sight it seems that it should mean that this individual is causally determined to behave in such a way as to encounter many more individuals and is able to select between possible encounters. Once again we find the familiar equivocation with levels of explanation and the problem of intentionality raises its head. All Deleuze is entitled to is a functionalist account such that 'if x happened and x was good then y endeavoured to attain it'. This principle itself has to be reformulated as 'if x happened and x increased levels of activity in the system then x was good and this increase can be explained through the nature of y′. At a certain, rather mysterious, point, the individual comes into full possession of his or her reason, inadequate ideas are transmuted into adequate ones, and the individual is able to contemplate the causal processes.

The hypothetical contract pictures the individual with given interests, needs and purposes. The State, or civil society is pictured as a set of possible social arrangements which more or less meet individual interests, defined by their natures. The individual in the Deleuzian project is as functionally abstract as the 'mushroom man' of *Leviathan*, indeed as in many modernist political philosophies.

> For the moderns, under the influence of Christian and Stoic individualism, natural law, as opposed to positive law, does not involve social beings, but individuals, i.e., men each of whom is self-sufficient, as made in the image of God and as the repository of reason. This is to say that, in the idea of jurists in the first place, first principles regarding the constitution of the State (and of society) have to be extracted, or deduced, from the inherent properties or qualities of man taken as an autonomous being independently of any social or political attachment. ... To deduce from this logical or hypothetical state of nature the principles of social political life ... is the task which the theorists of modern Natural Law have undertaken, and it is in doing so that they have laid the basis for the modern democratic State.[58]

It is thus instructive that, after he demarcates a careful distinction between private and public uses of reason, Deleuze basically outlines the principal objective of the political philosophy. Political philosophy, the politics of positive difference, is the elaboration of the ways an individual can learn to use his or her own understanding, to be proceeded by the breaking of bonds of servitude. The concertina effect of various, fairly standard, Enlightenment beliefs with an underlying Utilitarian, or consequentionalist, ethics, disguises the fact that this political philosophy speaks straight to the Natural Law tradition which gained a certain hegemonic force from the middle of the seventeenth to nineteenth century. Deleuze, however, argues that it is the primacy of the concept of power that marks his project as absolutely different. He insists that his proofs employ premises about practical rationality and the genetic structure of human affects, derived from a systematic reflection on human life. While his conclusions may be or may not be true, it is the case that his epistemological naturalism, based as it is on the parallelism, is a step aside from the thought of mediation and any critical purchase that the idea of social context might have. One example of this is his explanation for the reification of various ideas ending with the concept 'God' and another is his definition of servitude. For example, servitude is defined in terms of being tied to passions, overly affected and limited by separate others, where the individual is determined to do that which will increase his or her own power and where what is 'good' is defined by the use to which others can be put.

Before moving on to the final state as envisaged by Deleuze, I shall return to Hegel's criticisms of Spinoza. If we recall, Hegel argued that Spinoza operated with a number of conceptual dichotomies and these resulted in a system unable to sustain a meaningful concept of freedom. Spinoza distinguishes between God and nature, human consciousness and the corporeal. According to Hegel, Spinoza considers 'that true Being lies in what is opposed to the corporeal'. We can see that for Deleuze, again contrary to the apparent materialism, bodies always limit other bodies and the free man is the one who begins to think himself apart from the sensuous world. The abstract individual of the hypothetical contract is pre-social and, although with a nature, surely without a personality. The fall into a personality is the fall into intersubjectivity, finally redeemed in the free State of Reason. The contract, as presented in *Expressionism*, shows not only the truth of this but also suggests ways in which individuals can think themselves as part of the One. Deleuze's definition of freedom as rational insight into the rational whole ought to strike some as a cause for alarm. Even if we conceded the principle of free will we might prefer to assume that a subject is free to the extent that she or he faces a field of possibilities.

In the Deleuzian system there is no thing or event that is possible and is not necessary. Deleuze's later work is indebted to this system and due to his influence on some strains of postmodernism it is worth pausing here. Where the material world is identified with unfreedom there is always a tendency to reify the world, or experiences, or that which exists outside time and therefore causal laws, and find freedom there. Because the world is not actually so split, we find that laws are, in effect, the 'material' laws of the social world. Where laws and motions of the market govern that social world then we could say that these laws have been projected onto the blank sheet of the mythical state of nature. This then reflects back the lack of freedom within the social order as a natural necessity. But the meaning of the term 'freedom', just as the concept 'legitimacy', has been emptied of all content, and becomes, in effect, merely an acquiescence to a causal order and the claim that freedom is a matter of the individual using his reason correctly.

6
The Blessed State of Reason

As previously indicated, Deleuze advocates Spinoza's idea that ethical maturity is achieved when the individual commits to a political programme that is designed to improve the intellect – the objective of which is to distinguish, appreciate and achieve the one true and eternal practical good.[1] Describing a passionate nature as one in bondage, Deleuze presents us with his vision of a free individual. He offers us a negative definition of freedom – we are free when we are freed from our passions. This occurs, according to Deleuze, when the individual gains an understanding of the causal origins of the various affects he or she is suffering [2] and manages to grasp the fact of the causal series by applying common notions to the evidence of his or her senses.[3] Deleuze also assumes that when the individual entertains a common notion she or he will experience a certain affect, which is persistent and permanent.[4] This is the second stage of knowledge outlined in the earlier chapter. There is, though, a third kind of knowledge: intuitive knowledge. Spinoza writes that:

> After experience had taught me the hollowness and futility of [the] everyday thing that is ordinarily encountered in daily life, and I realised that all the things which were the source and object of my anxiety held nothing of good or evil in themselves save in so far as the mind was influenced by them, I resolved at length to enquire whether there existed a true good, one which was capable of communicating itself and could alone affect the mind to the exclusion of all else, whether, in fact, there was something whose discovery and acquisition would afford me a continuous and supreme joy to all eternity.[5]

Third level of knowledge

The classification of types of knowledge and general epistemology differs between *The Correction of the Understanding* and the *Ethics*. The latter is concerned mainly with knowledge of the second type but professes interest in 'fixed and eternal things' rather than 'singular changeable things'. This obviously raises the problem, already mentioned, of indexicality and gives little guidance regarding knowledge of these things in our environment. The gap between sense and reason means that although one might be able to deduce, from the general laws of nature, what sort of finite things might exist and anticipate their general features, one would never be able to deduce a fact about this particular thing, here and now. There are various reasons for this. To know anything about a thing in my environment I must be able to perceive it, identify it and perhaps even classify it in relation to other things already so identified. This sort of knowledge is knowledge through vague sense experience and fully vilified by both Spinoza and Deleuze. A more extreme example of this problem is the problem of self-knowledge. How can I come to know my mental states and behaviours when I am unable to think simple things about body Y causing my internal state x? Indeed, while it is nigh on impossible to talk with impunity about the facts of my environment, talk about my personal history is ruled out altogether because this would rely upon memory. There are, in addition, more general problems of introspection and a peculiarly Spinozistic difficulty in thinking or talking about the self under one or both attributes. Deleuze argues that the idea of the 'common notion' had begun to make its presence felt in the *Correction of the Understanding* precisely to bridge the gap between sense experience and reason. He believes it imperative to prove that the bridge was secure because the ideal ethical life is such that one has clear and distinct ideas of one's own situation and emotional states.[6]

In fact Deleuze suggests that knowledge of the third kind owes nothing to that of the first kind but is somehow indebted to knowledge of the second kind. However, unless intuitive knowledge includes a sensory, rather than intellectual way, of identifying its particular objects then it seems unlikely that it could illuminate our actual environment. Because knowledge from sense is fallible one option for Deleuze would be to take Spinoza as a necessitarian and argue that the actual course of history and futurity, taken as a whole, is the only possible one and is as necessary as are the laws and structure of Nature. In this case, a sufficiently powerful intellect could know the full facts about each particular thing as specified descriptively. The solution to this puzzle lies in the dual function of the term 'intuition'.

The term 'intuition' has a rather chequered, but certainly protracted, history. Locke, for example, distinguished between the terms 'demonstration' and 'intuition'. A demonstration takes one from premises to a conclusion. At each step a further premise is affirmed. The separate acts of the mind, which affirm each step, are intuitions. The whole, though, is a demonstration.[7] This is certainly implied when Deleuze insists on the fact that we see God 'at a glance'. Yet, he also says that we reach the idea of God as quickly as possible. In a manner reminiscent of the *Meditations*, Deleuze prescribes the steps that should be taken to reach the idea of God. These form a rather informal argument. First, there is something positive in an idea. The inadequate idea can be transformed into an adequate idea. By definition, the adequate idea refers to its cause and, avoiding infinite regress, to the cause of the cause. God is the sufficient reason of each and every cause. Each common notion, or adequate idea, refers the enquirer to God. This obviously involves a series of steps, and although there may be intuition involved, this third kind of cognition is still inferential. Bennett draws out a further strand to the meaning of the term 'intuition'. He reminds us the term refers not only to the method of cognition but it also indicates something about the intuited object itself. Here intuition might mean the way in which the mind is directly related to a *particular* or individual object.

Deleuze refers to a rather well-known example from the *Ethics* considered by Spinoza, at least, to clarify the distinction. Let us take a basic arithmetic problem. Say we are given three numbers and asked to find a fourth, related, number, then we will in all likelihood discover certain things about the different ways in which the answer can be found. 'Tradesmen', says Spinoza, 'have no hesitation in multiplying the second by the third and dividing the product by the first'. This is the method of the classroom. If we choose simple numbers for our procedure we find that is an alternative way to reach the conclusion. 'In the case of numbers 1, 2, 3 everybody can see that the fourth proposition is 6, and all the more clearly because we infer in one single intuition the fourth number from the ratio we see the first number bears to the second'.[8] Wilson points out that although in each case we come to know that a certain number is the solution to the problem, there are different ways in which we reach the answer: fortuitous external inculcation, the application of rigorous proof or by direct intuition.[9]

If we reach the answer according to the first way, a way associated with the first stage of knowledge, then we are merely, and probably blindly, following a rule. That said, the intellectual operation does seem to carry a certain necessity. It is as though we *must* multiply the second number by the third and divide the product by the first. Deleuze explains this appearance of necessity by the imperative quality of the sign. Such signs, he says, appear to tell us what we *must* do to obtain a given result, achieve a given end: this is knowledge by hearsay (289). When we reach the answer in the second way, the application of rigorous proof, we begin to understand the real epistemic distinctions. Deleuze contends that if we were to understand the rule of proportionality through a common notion then we would 'grasp the way that the constitutive relations of the three numbers are combined' (291). The second type of knowledge, or epistemic method, differs from the third in requiring steps of reason, as distinct from direct mental vision and it fails to arrive at the inmost essence of things. The implication is that the second type of knowledge is concerned with properties of things rather than with their essences. There is, thus, a flattening of issues of epistemic method and content. The third level of knowledge is characterised both by its method, direct mental vision, and content, essences not properties.

The crucial phrases are 'ideas of the third kind are defined by their singular nature' and 'they ... give us knowledge of particular essences as these are contained in God himself' (300). Here we see the function of Deleuze's qualified nominalism. Common notions can also be intuitions, intuited, because they are singular and of particular essences, that is, attributes.[10] To grasp something intuitively, one must proceed from an adequate idea of the attributes of God to ideas of the essence of things. Common notions are, according to Deleuze, the conditions for intuitive knowledge; they determine us to form the third kind of knowledge, to enter into 'direct vision' (301). Because essence is identified with a thing's nature, and adequacy is characterised in terms of completeness, then we are looking for an immediate cognition of a thing's complete nature. What things are we talking about? According to Deleuze, there are three ideas of the third type: things, myself and God.

Deleuze links the first two (myself and things) to the third. Spinoza suggests that the more we understand particular things the more we understand God[11] and that insofar as our mind knows itself and the body under the aspect of eternity it necessarily has cognition of God. So Deleuze writes that everything we understand within the third kind of knowledge, including the essences of other things and that of God, we understand on the basis of conceiving our own essence (that of our body) *sub specie aeternitatis*. I can detect three arguments that may help us to understand what Deleuze means, although they rely on the *Principle of Sufficient Reason*. This is the first. We know a thing through its (efficient) cause and the cause is the sufficient reason of that thing. If the definition of a thing includes the idea of this cause then the definition is complete. If the definition is complete then the idea is adequate. No finite individual is a substance. No finite individual is self-caused. God causes all finite individuals. The definition or full description of an individual thing must include this causal dependency. If it does then the idea of this thing is adequate. This is the second. We know a thing through its cause and the cause is the sufficient reason of that thing. Finite individuals are in causal relations with other finite individuals. The causal sequence must have a first cause. Only God can be this first cause. To know a finite thing then would be to know it through its (first) cause. The third argument depends on the *Principle of Sufficient Reason* and the principle that where b is understood through a then a can be said to be the cause of b. The finite mode is understood through one attribute or another. The attribute is a cause of the finite mode. An attribute is not a substance. Only God is a substance.

As previously noted, the finite mode is not supposed to be subject to a dual causality: a vertical relation between God as cause and a horizontal material causality. But the finite mode is subject to determination in two ways – its existence is determined from the standpoint of relations as eternal truths and through material causality. This is one reason why Deleuze stresses the need to conceive the thing under consideration *sub specie aeternitatis*. Greene emphasises the connection between knowledge under the aspect of eternity and the thought that all things are necessary rather than contingent.[12] In perceiving things as necessary, reason perceives them in relation to the necessity of God's nature. Because the principles of reason are common to all things, they must be conceived without any relation to time, but under the aspect of eternity. The point here is that each finite, or singular, thing can be considered as a thing following from the eternal necessity of God's nature: its force of persevering.

The object of the intuition is therefore the nature, or eternal essence, of finite things. The intuition itself is the immediate apprehension of this. Matheron writes that it is as though Spinoza 'simply wants to say to his readers: "Follow me all the way to the end and you will come to know your nature, starting from the nature of God, in the same way and just as well as you understand the equality 1 / 2 = 3 / 6"'. Deleuze highlights the immediacy time and again. He has already led us to a position where there is no 'free' volition, and no error and he has also been quite clear that there are no faculties of will or intellect only individual acts of the mind.[13] Yovel phrases the position in the following way. 'By an intuitive flash all the causal information is now reprocessed in a new synthesis that lays bare the particular essence of a thing and the inherent way in which it flows by logical necessity from one of nature's attributes'.[14] But, let us remember that there is a problem with indexicals – we cannot actually make any claims as to this essence, here, now, in front of me. Even if, by virtue of the identity of indiscernibles, essences are distinct, and by virtue of the argument from power, each is a *res physica* (303), we can only comprehend the nature of an essence is the most general way. Thus, we can surmise, not only can one not know anything about this particular object here, now, but also one should not be interested. The individual is to concern him or herself only with what is true about each and every thing considered from the viewpoint of eternity and known immediately.[15]

The term 'adequacy' implies not merely completeness, as in complete description, but also suggests an internal rather than external cause. How might one have a complete idea of a thing without being affected by that thing, that is, without there being some external cause of the idea? We could recall that an adequate idea has an element of causal self-sufficiency.[16] Now, while this is problematic for the general epistemological thesis, it should not surprise us. Deleuze is at his happiest when considering the form of an idea. We have already noted that Deleuze makes full use of the scholastic notion of 'distinctions of reason'. These are nothing but philosophical entities of reason such as the distinction of God's essence for existence, power and properties, opposition, order, relation. The cause of ideas can also be classified as 'internal' because they are explained by the individual's power of thinking and begin with the individual's idea of his or her own essence. Deleuze advocates both but the latter position acts as first premise in the argument towards blessedness.

Third level: blessedness

Deleuze returns to his distinction between the intensive and extensive features of the attributes to clarify the partition of second level knowledge and affects from third level knowledge and truth. The argument from powers, and the argument concerning the quantification of the qualities, provides Deleuze with the material to explore, and finally to justify, what he means by intuition and blessedness. Blessedness is the description of the end-state of emotional maturity.

Contrary to his explicit statements on this matter, Deleuze does split the mind into something like faculties (311).[17] There is the imagination and there is reason. Both operate according to laws and the former is directly related to sense experience. There are four laws of the imagination which concern us here. The first and second are the laws of contingency and of transitoriness. When an external objects affects someone, he or she will form an idea of that object.[18] Deleuze intimates that at the level of sense experience, the individual perceives the external object as transitory and therefore as contingent but would like to perceive something permanent in that object.[19] The third is the law of intensities. When an object is perceived as necessary, the affect is less intense than if the object is perceived as contingent. The fourth is the law of multiple affects. A feeling is much stronger the more causes act together to provoke it (295). There are, correspondingly, four laws of reason. The first two are the laws of necessity and permanence. Reason perceives all things as necessary. A thing is necessary due to its causal relations, material and logical. It is causally dependent on the attributes constituting the essence of God. We can think of these attributes as 'properties' of the finite mode. To put it otherwise, although we can talk about the attribute of Extension we can also say that the mode is extended. Thus, reason can perceive something permanent in the object, its properties or (its causal dependence upon) the attributes. The third law follows from the first. Because objects are perceived as necessary, the passion caused by that object is less intense. However, only affect can effect an affect, so Deleuze has to add that there is an affect associated with reason itself and this is 'more' active than that caused by the external object. Lastly, reason uses common notions, a common notion applies to more than one thing, it is frequent and lively.

Let us hold aside a certain scepticism that is raised by this anthropomorphisation of the faculties because there are a number of issues to consider before moving on. We previously mentioned the problematic use of the term 'perception' and here we can see that Deleuze employs the ambiguities fully. In some cases he is asserting a physical modification and in others the comprehension of that modification. It is the intellectual comprehension, though, that commands the authority in the transition of affects and it is precisely such mental agility which Deleuze is not only unable to explain but also, quite explicitly, rules out. There is no good argument offered, by either Deleuze or

Spinoza, to evidence the law of intensities: that the more causes involved in producing an affect, the more powerful it is. Indeed, physics appears to offer some counterexamples. Finally, Deleuze accepts the assumption that pleasure is, *ceateris parabus*, more powerful than unpleasure. This is, of course, unproven.

Common notions are supposed to straddle the two 'faculties' and help us transform passions into actions (294). Given the various laws of the imagination there are a couple of different techniques. First, where body Y causes modification x in body X and this modification is unpleasurable Deleuze extols the therapeutic strategy of separating the idea of body Y from x. The parallelism makes this nonsensical. It was not the *thought* of Y that caused either x or the related affect. We discussed this more fully in a previous chapter. The second technique is to reflect on the necessity of causal sequence. There is no proper argument offered as to why any passion would be transformed into joy through the consideration of determinism. Indeed, we could cite a case of fear as a good counterexample. The fact that I am aware that events are so determined – that I will be attacked as I sleep tonight – does nothing to quell the unpleasurable affect. The last technique is such that we are advised to form clear and distinct ideas of the affect or passion – we can form actions from passions. Where the modification is accompanied by a pleasurable affect then body X will be induced to modify I(x) into a common notion. By the law of intensity, the common notion will occur with further pleasurable affects. These affects will counteract affects caused by the external body. Given the *Principle of Sufficient Reason*, every common notion is accompanied by an idea of God. The idea of God appears with another affect, which we may classify as love.

There are two points to be made here. If body Y, an external body, caused x, then the indirect object is an external object and the idea of Y an idea of an indirect and external body. Such an idea is inadequate. It would be rather stretching things to argue that the ability to form a common notion can be explained through the nature of X and that therefore the idea is adequate. Secondly, we can see that Deleuze interjects the common notion between sense experience and the understanding to provide the individual some purchase on their particular states. But, if we take the 'essence of x' to be coextensive with 'a complete description of x', the latter need not actually be about x. Bennett puts this nicely. 'Suppose that F is the complete nature of an individual person living on the far side of our galaxy and that by sheer coincidence I have a thought involving the concept of F: "It would be nice..if there were an F person". Is it not clear that thought is not about the actual F person? My thought fits him but is not about him'.[20] This is just one reason why we will have to accept that there is no bridge between knowledge from sense experience and knowledge from reason. This holds, even if we replace 'complete description' with *res physica*. If we cannot actually think about object Y causing affect x then we cannot even begin to move from passive to active affects.

Although the attributes, common between many things and between the finite mode and the infinite whole, constitute the essence of God, the actual idea of God is something different (294). When we grasp the fact that a common notion has, as its content, the various attributes we come to realise that each attribute, common between the finite and infinite, is singular and each is an essence of God. This determines us to form the third kind of knowledge, 'to enter into a direct vision' (301). Each common notion leads us to the principle of God as sufficient reason and is, supposedly, accompanied by a specific affect: joy. Deleuze also suggests that the affect of joy can be described in terms of desire and love: desire to know more about the world and love of God. This is because the notion, as an idea, is caused by the individual's internal state. But this description does as well for joys associated with reason and the second stage of knowledge. The difference is that when we make the transition from an inadequate to an adequate idea, we carry with us the passive passion associated with the former. Now, an adequate idea of an essence is 'contained' in the attribute of thought. It would certainly be strange to presume that intuition of an essence must be accompanied by a passion.[21] So, Deleuze concludes that when we intuit an essence, specifically our own essence, there is a corresponding feeling of joy or beatitude. The assertion is that when we intuit our own essence we come into immediate contact with our 'being' as it is in the attribute (315).

Spinoza could maintain that wherever there is an idea of God there is an affect, described as love, because he insisted that whenever an idea is clear and distinct there is a pleasant affect. This is derived from his assertion that an adequate idea, or a common notion, is 'lively'. When an idea or image of cause accompanies pleasure then the affect is love. Intuitive knowledge would thus have to be an immediate apprehension of various particulars, essences, and a concomitant intuition of the *Principle of Sufficient Reason*, all accompanied by an affect properly described as love. Such an account might well make sense but rests on an illegitimate step where Spinoza, and here Deleuze, requires a belief to be a cause. If we were to ask 'why do I love God' and answer 'because the idea of God causes a pleasant state', this would seem at best vacuous. Since intellectual love is a species of pleasure, and God is not affected with pleasure, it would make sense to argue that God does not experience love. Yet Deleuze claims that God does, both towards himself and towards human beings. If we recall, pleasure is really activity, shifts towards and away from death and perfection, and the link with intuitive knowledge seems to be made in one of two ways. First, it is to do with the eternity of the mind and secondly with the nature of essence.

There is in God an idea of the essence of the human body, as opposed to an idea of the actual existing body. The existing body is part of a causal nexus of modifications and passive affects. Knowledge of the first and second kind concerns this axis. By definition, essence is something outside time. An essence is a *res physica*, a part of divine power. Each must be conceived through its cause and each is necessary. Because the mind is nothing but a collection of ideas of the modifications of the human body, and there is an idea which pertains to the essence of the body then there is (a part of the) mind which contains ideas of an eternal thing. The idea that expresses the body's essence is necessarily eternal (313). Because everything has a cause, this idea can be explained through the individual's power of thinking and ultimately through God. The individual, therefore, has the power to conceive all other bodies *sub specie aeternitatis*. The power of thinking parallels the power of action. The individual has power of acting *sub specie aeternitatis*. To each power corresponds a capacity. Incidentally, it is this, the set of necessary truths about essence, power and capacity, which remains when we die – when the eternal, intensive part is removed from its extensive parts (315). Frankly, this is all I can make of Deleuze's postulations concerning the identity of being and joy. The overall picture is a mélange of assertion and purported derivations. In death the body is no longer causally determined and because it is not causally determined there are no passive affects. Where there are no passive affects there is no power of suffering to limit the power of action. Therefore in death the soul fulfils its potential. Deleuze insists that when 'we' form an idea of the idea of essence x, the soul experiences joy. This is explained through the principle of adequacy (316).

Stepping closely to Spinoza, Deleuze equates having a part of the mind that is eternal to being in a state of blessedness. The basic assertion is that the more ideas we have like this the more ideas we will have of things that are eternal and therefore the more eternal will be the mind. If x is an eternal truth about my body then I(x), the thought or idea of that eternal truth, must itself be eternal. Because Deleuze does not distinguish between the idea and the entertaining of that idea, he slips between this and the inference that the mind itself is eternal. Apart from this glaring error, there are two further problems. Up until now Deleuze has struggled to give positive content to ideas. Mental content has either been of the physical modification or of the form of the idea and here we can see that Deleuze must mean propositional content. There is also a problem to do with the conception of 'effort'. He implies that the existing individual must make every *effort* to think these eternal thoughts, to increase his or her power of action while alive as this leaves the essence in good standing when the individual's body has unravelled (317–19). The argument is poor but we can see that Deleuze wishes there to be a significant difference between living well or ethically and living badly. The equivocation concerns the role of 'must'. Deleuze suggests that it is a practical maxim: if you wish to enter the state of blessedness then these are the things you need to do. This is a mistake. The *res physica*, and the idea which has it as its content, always had and always will obtain and would have obtained, however I behaved. How we come to these ideas is thoroughly obscure but what is clear is that any path we take is always already determined.

We can distil from the above some very general points concerning our psychologies. It is not that far off the mark to note that individuals can choose an 'objective' or 'reactive' attitude to an event that occurs to them. An objective attitude could be defined as one looking to explain the event, interested in the causal mechanisms. A reactive attitude could be defined in terms of 'gratitude' or 'ressentiment'. Strawson indicates the close family resemblance between these responses and religious sentiment: moral approval and disapproval. Even if all events are causally determined we are not compelled to erase these latter responses. Rather than trying to rid ourselves of these uncalculated, emotional, passionate responses perhaps they should, and do, form the centrepiece of a rich and interesting intersubjective morality.[22] Indeed, we could go one step further and argue that a number of emotional responses just cannot be classified as reactive. Not only could pity be a response born of an objective attitude but also without it, or anything like it, it is difficult to frame an ethical response to a particular other. But, then, neither Deleuze nor Spinoza is that concerned with particulars.

The method of Expressionism

I would now like to bring together the ethical thesis with the philosophical method. We are presented with a triadic expressive relationship. Substance is said to express itself, the attributes are the expressions of substance and essence is what is expressed. Philosophically, the thesis of expression is supposed to provide a solution to the problem of the relationship between the one infinite thing and many finite things such that the ensuing system is pantheistic without an identity holding between the two terms. The rôle of the attributes is key in understanding this pantheistic or univocal system. They provide the philosophical bridge in ontology, metaphysics and epistemology. Being is said to be univocal because the attributes are forms or expression of being common to both infinite and finite things. Metaphysically, they ground univocal production; God is an immanent cause, because the attributes are causes or explanations of God and finite things. Finally, there is univocity in epistemology because every idea tends to an idea of an attribute. It is through grasping the function of attributes that we can come to know the structure of the whole. Throughout the preceding chapters we have explored how Deleuze attempts to solve various philosophical conundrums by collapsing reasons with causes. Thus, when he extols the virtue of being unwinding or unfolding we find that he means that the causal sequence is, at the same time, a logical sequence.

It is my contention that *Expressionism* unveils and revises a thoroughly disingenuous form of argument. Rather than alluding to an aesthetic of irony, this lack of sincerity conceals an epistemological framework which appears to be pragmatic or one that may facilitate perspectivism, or multiple readings, but which is, in fact, thoroughly dogmatic. Without doubt Deleuze heralds the philosophical innovativeness of the system of expressionism and seems to consider it as an answer to the intellectual problems encountered not only within Spinoza's *Ethics* but also within various other naturalist theological projects. Apart from this ambition to rigour, the term also enables Deleuze to exploit its Husserlian or phenomenological and aesthetic timbre.

I find it intriguing that Deleuze's writing is thought antagonistic to the three Hs (Hegel, Husserl and Heidegger) but here we find that he has formulated a system mirroring a number of Husserlian themes. The parallelism tilts his theory of language or meaning towards the use of Voice in interior monologue whereby ideas are immediately present, reproduced and form the basis for a proper insight or grasp of the causal properties of being. Just as Husserl sees 'true' language in terms of 'expression', where expression is expression of meaning as willed and intended by an utterer. In *Expressionism* all ideas are present in the intellect of God who intends insofar as we understand God to be the sufficient reason of the series and sequence. Without pursuing this in detail, it seems as though Deleuze retains the Husserlian notion that verbal meaning is subjected to mental states, by identifying meaning with finite modifications of the attribute of Thought, which have as their content modifications of the attribute of Extension. This content is secured through the general arguments for the parallelism. At the same time, the (physical) affect, or intensity, of an encounter is separate from the idea caused by the encountered object and is perhaps more interesting as it may lead to emotional maturity and activity in the individual's system. Yet this affect is not only strictly determined but is also secondary and perhaps really rather irrelevant, if quite pleasant.

When we consider the generation of meaning, we see that the parallelism does remove any central role assigned to the individual consciousness and also the functional place of the (external) object. Deleuze encourages us to believe that the primary referential relationship holds between the idea of the idea and the idea rather than between idea and its corresponding mode in the attribute of Extension or even the indirect object which causes the modification of the mode's state. Although I(I(x)) has I(x) as its referential content it also signifies the structure of being and it is this structure to which all adequate ideas attest. Philosophically ambiguous, finite modifications of Thought seem to be minds, things tied to corresponding physical modifications and things that can be entertained by other minds. Thus, in places maybe sounding more like Derrida than Husserl, Deleuze hints that individuals are in the same position as recipient and sender. Similarities abound when we meditate on Derrida's attempts to unite causal force and meaning which is both mystical and mechanical, 'discarding the ordinary mental push of individual minds and allowing ideas an objective impersonal deterministic movement of their own'.[23] This peculiar mixture of mysticism and mechanism, metaphysical materialism, is abundant in *Expressionism*. Deleuze goes further than Derrida, who incidentally has little time for neo-Platonic theories of univocity, and anchors this mystical mechanism with its proclivity to infinite regress, to the theological *Principle of Sufficient Reason*.

Comparing Deleuze's method to that of the aesthetic movement of the turn of the century known as expressionism, Macherey suggests that his method is at odds with the demonstrative rationality adopted by Spinoza. Expressionism is associated with eighteenth and nineteenth century Romantics who considered art to be the expression of the artist's emotion evincing an emotional response in the audience.[24] The comparison between this aesthetic movement and Deleuze's philosophical work is not unproblematic. For example, if the purpose of art is to express feelings of the artist then should we take Deleuze or God to be artist? Is there content to the feeling? Deleuze's arguments tend to rule out such 'aboutness'. If we take the artist to be God then does God actually feel, have emotion, about anything? Deleuze is clear to distinguish emotions of the first and second level from beatitude of the third level. This distinction must be firm because God cannot experience actual emotions because emotions are the effects of external bodies. Where God is concerned there is no external body. Thus we must conclude that for Deleuze expression cannot refer to a relationship between behaviour or feelings and language, as this would be to locate the thesis at the first and second stages of apprehension.[25] Alternatively, we could consider expressionism to be the externalisation of an intuition of a unique object, and the reproduction of said intuition in the recipient, an account familiar in Croce's work. This would bring us much closer to Deleuze and Spinoza's actual method with a place for both demonstrative rationality and intuition. But we would then be forced to pursue certain questions relating to the rôle and function of the concept of intuition.

In an informal sense, our intuitions often conflict. One person can claim to know one thing by intuition and another person could contradict this. How might we decide between conflicting intuitions? Any appeal to a further intuition, or a 'superintuition', would be unstable. It does seem as though we would have to go outside the realm of intuitions to prove which intuition was right. Even if intuitions never conflicted that is no guarantee that the object of the intuition is accurate or true: everyone might agree that a certain proposition 'p' was true, and claim to know it by intuition, and this would still not prove 'that p' was actually true.[26] Indeed, it could be argued that the term 'intuition' is often used to disguise a degree of ignorance as to how a thing was known, if it were known at all. Deleuze explains what he means by truth and adequacy through an account of definition. Overall he describes his method as synthetic but articulates three stages: reflective, genetic and deductive. He opposes this method to Cartesian scepticism and to Kant's transcendental argument.

Cartesian inferences

Deleuze applauds Spinoza's assertion that 'truth is its own standard'. Their mutual antagonism to the hyperbolic doubt is rooted in their shared anti-Cartesian metaphysics. The hyperbolic doubt presumes an original distinction between God and individual, such that a God might deceive the enquirer. Deleuze's argument against the Cartesian method revolves around the central claim that because Descartes inferred cause from effect he had to insert various other principles, which meant that, in the end, his reasoning turned out to be circular. If God is the cause of adequate ideas then the proof of God's existence, and the description of God, cannot itself rely on the intellectual comprehension of the idea of God. Neither, though, can the axioms used to prove God's existence be merely stipulative, if they are to lead to a conclusion with truth value. As a way out of this, Deleuze looks to Spinoza's correspondence with de Vries where Spinoza draws a distinction between two types of definition.[27] The distinction is between a definition that explains a thing as it exists outside our understanding and a definition of a thing as it is conceived, or can be conceived, by us. Only definitions conforming to the former criteria are properly speaking propositional or axiomatic and 'ought to be true'. In response to a remark made by Tschirnhaus, Spinoza extends this and points out that a true idea will express efficient cause and from it can be deduced all other properties.[28]

Deleuze's theory of ideas can also be seen as an attempt to offer an alternative to representational theories of meaning, which, he believes, still suffer from the same problems as those present in Descartes' *Meditations*. Broadly, an outline of the Cartesian position might be that: all that the mind knows it knows by means of that of which it is directly aware. The only things of which it is directly aware are things immediately present to it. The only things which are immediately present to the mind are mental things or things which are in some way in the mind. Thus all that the mind knows it knows by means of that which is in the mind. But the mind is said to know non-mental things. Its knowledge of non-mental things must take place by means of its direct awareness of things in the mind. Thus the mind knows non-mental things by means of its ideas which are representations of non-mental things.[29] But if this is the case then there is a problem. How can the mind distinguish between ideas representing their objects as they really are, and ideas which do not? Descartes appeals to the principle of clarity and distinctness. If an idea has internal characteristics of clarity and distinctness, then it can be said to be true. But this then means that we have to come up with satisfiable criteria for clarity and distinctness even before we can answer a simple question such as 'is this proposition true'? The criteria need to satisfy without reference to truth.[30] Descartes bridges this gap by means of a divine guarantor.

Deleuze wishes us to adjust our understanding of representation, away from the fairly standard inner object theory of perception and the parallelism offers such an opportunity.[31] The relation between the idea and its object is given in terms of a distinction between objective and formal reality whereas the relation between the idea and what it represents is given in terms of the resemblance of the thing represented to the object of the idea. The object of the idea, and the idea, are related as formal reality to objective reality. A thing has formal reality in so far as it exists in itself. It has objective reality in so far as it is thought of. We know that ideas have as their objects modifications of the body and that they only indirectly represent external bodies. We have already seen the problem that this position causes for the overall account. Here it is simply relevant to note that the ideas of bodily affections do not represent external bodies by mental pictures or images.

Ideas are supposed to represent external bodies to us by containing objectively something which the external body, as cause of the affection, contains formally. For an example let us take the idea of the sun. This idea is not a mental picture of the sun but an objective reality of the affection of body. The affection is produced by the action of the sun. Since the sun is the cause, and since there must be something in common between cause and effect, there is something in common between the sun and my bodily affection. My idea represents the sun because its object is an affection that has something in common with the sun. The relevant resemblance is not between the idea and the sun but between a bodily affection and the sun. It would seem that if the idea represents anything, it represents a causal relationship between specific structures of bodies. If it indicates anything, it indicates the natural laws of motion and rest derived from the modes of an attribute.

Kantian deductions

Transcendental arguments, it could be argued, begin with an hypothetical judgement and the necessary and sufficient conditions, which would make the proposition true, are then deduced. Kant's method famously relies upon the relationship of implication such that if p then q where p is a type of experience and q is the set of conditions, both necessary and sufficient, for p being the case. There are two main problems with such a transcendental argument. It seems that we must take 'p' as given and beyond question. An argument moving from fact to conditions can be described as 'regressive'.[32] Because of this it is rarely considered to be conclusive but only probable. Otherwise, we must assume that these and only these conditions could, and do, bring about p. These problems really come down to one: is the argument actually deductively valid, that is, do the conclusions follow analytically, by the laws of deductive inference, from their premises? One could argue that the argument form is only valid if by experience we mean 'conscious experience of specific objects', if it is analytically true that all experiences must be 'owned' and if by object we mean something that is extended, obeys causal laws and has certain properties.[33] However, this seems to contradict Kant's own assertion that we are actually adding to knowledge, bringing together different concepts rather than clarifying a definition.[34] If we are to concede synthetic necessity, then we could say that there are *synthetic a priori* relations between propositions or concepts and that Kant's method is, in fact, the 'expression' of his fundamental philosophical beliefs.[35] While this sounds very neat, the argument, if it were to work, would rely on three basic assumptions.[36] Due to this it is perhaps the case that the best that can be said for Kant's argument is that it gives us an idea of what we as human beings tend to, given our psychologies, believe to be the case.

Deleuze believes that the method deployed in the *Ethics* helps to free us from these problems. The method also uses two features apparent in Kant's transcendental argument. Its first premise is hypothetical, a general hypothesis, and from this premise certain consequences are deduced. These consequences are then 'checked' and confirmed against data. Where there is nothing to contradict the conclusions a weaker set of confirmations run back upwards. Picking up the point that an argument moving from fact to conditions is regressive, Deleuze argues that despite all appearances to the contrary, it would be a mistake to interpret the method he has been discussing as regressive. What does this mean? He contrasts the hypothetical premise of Kant and the determination of the necessary and sufficient conditions required for p to be the case, with the hypothetical premise of Spinoza, where we come to know the effect through knowledge of the cause. An example offered by Deleuze requires us to consider an *a priori* proposition or a geometrical image, an idea of reason, such as a sphere.[37] Deleuze recalls the fairly archaic general theory of entities of reason and this underlies his method in *Expressionism*. A thing of reason is a thing of the intellect, it has no existence outside mind but is a mental aid, an abstract fiction which still manages to help us to come to a proper understanding. Let us recall that we can move from the first to second stage of knowledge by grasping what is positive in an inadequate idea and thereby converting that idea. Or, one can begin with a true idea. Because there is no object in nature to which a true idea, such as an abstract geometrical image, corresponds we are *forced* to consider the image through our knowledge of its cause.[38] Two possible causes spring to mind. The first is that *qua* idea its cause is our power of thinking. The formal definition of truth is the idea insofar as it is explained by our power of knowing. The method here is reflexive.

Or we can posit a 'material' cause. In the case of a circle we might form an idea of its cause, say a straight line revolving around one of its points (134). With this example we can see that the efficient cause lies 'outside' the concept of the circle (22) but once this cause is asserted then the properties of the figure can be deduced. This would then satisfy the principle that a 'real definition' must concern something outside the understanding and can conceive this to the extent that it grasps the essence of an object, which is the object's own internal principle and its efficient cause (18). Here is the interesting move. Deleuze recollects the *Principle of Sufficient Reason* (135). This principle can be described as the principle that nothing can be so without there being a reason why it is so. This reason has to ground contingency in necessity, that is, why this actuality rather than another possibility. This principle can be taken in a formal or logical sense where the premises of an argument are the sufficient reason for the conclusion. He then suggests that the cause of a thing, now understood as its sufficient reason, is that which, once given, results in all the thing's properties and if it were to be withdrawn then all the properties would be withdrawn with it. This is the same definition as that given for essence. As previously noted, the finite mode is not supposed to be subject to a dual causality: a vertical relation where God is seen as cause and a horizontal material causality. But the finite mode is subject to determination in two ways – its existence is determined from the standpoint of relations as eternal truths and through material causality. Deleuze resolves this apparent contradiction through the claim that God is the immanent cause of all things. However he also emphasises the point that each mode has, as its essence, its own degree of power, admittedly from God. The material definition of truth is the idea insofar as it expresses its own cause and expresses God's essence as determining cause (139). Deleuze defines the method here as genetic.[39] A genetic definition is the description of the construction of a thing. Because of this 'constructive' aspect it is also considered to be 'dynamic'.[40]

Once we accept that God is the immanent cause of all things then we will also have to accept that one thing follows from another in a necessary way. In understanding that God is the cause of all things then we understand more about this finite mode. By this argument Deleuze is offering us a solution to the Kantian problem of implications in the transcendental deduction. Fs and Gs are *causally* linked. This link is not a brute fact; the sequence occurs as it does through absolutely necessary causal laws. In this way, material causality and logical causality are collapsed. If x causes y then there is a causal link between them and the cause relates to the effect as a premise does to its conclusion. Where cause and effect are not obviously linked then the premise appears to be detached from its conclusion. I take it this is what Deleuze means when he says that we start with the idea of God and then deduce ideas one from another. These ideas are linked through their content but the content is determined by the sequence. The sequence of ideas reproduces reality. But we can see that any representative content depends on the parallelism and any judgment of veracity comes after we have first affirmed the logical and causal necessity of that parallelism (160). At which point we can say that there is an identity of form and content (138). Deleuze defines the method here as deductive. We can see that before we are convinced by Deleuze's solution to the problem of deduction we must first accept the soundness of the principles of causal rationalism and explanatory rationalism. Incidentally, any assertion that the Deleuzian system is fundamentally different from a logic of being, I think is to miss the point that without such logic of the One, there could be no sense to claims relating to the nature of forces or power.[41] Just as without the idea that an attribute is conceived *per se* there would be no sense to the proposition that being is affirmation.

Explication and affirmation

We have examined Deleuze's description of his method and begun to analyse how it is supposed to give epistemic foundations a security unavailable to Cartesians and Kantians. If the argument works it enables Deleuze to write with impunity about the third stage of knowledge, intuitive knowledge, and to bridge arguments in the disparate 'fields' of ethics, politics and psychology. Baugh claims that the term 'intuition' means a form of interpretative insight, capable of relating an empirical actuality to its causal history or genealogy, it is the goal rather than starting point of knowledge. We would have no real disagreement so far. Unfortunately, he continues, this occurs 'not according to some antecedently given schema or method but creatively in such a way that differences and singularities can be grasped by their uniqueness and positivity'.[42] But the concepts of singularity, positivity or intuition only have a critical purchase through the rationalist metaphysical system we have been outlining. Deleuze summarises the method of causal rationalism as 'explication'. Here I would like to extract the explicit comments relating to the method of presentation, truth and assertion and consider the connection between these comments and Deleuze's notion of affirmation. I will conclude this section with a number of comments concerning the content of the idea of 'affirmation'.

Before we reconsidered his version of the *Ontological Argument*, we briefly examined what Deleuze might mean by the term 'explication'. Explication, as a form of argument, seemed to support the proposition that if a being is fully defined then it is self-explanatory and if self-explanatory then self-caused. The argument I attributed to Deleuze is that if one thing is conceived through another than the latter is said to be the cause or explanation of the former and that the attributes are the formal causes of substance. If the set of definitions is complete then that which is defined has no appearance outside the expressions it describes. So, with reference to God, Deleuze could say that the attributes are the formal causes of substance and the concept 'substance' is fully defined or self-explanatory and that therefore God is self-caused.

Deleuze rightly points out that this method has a long history. Leibniz's monadology depends on the logic of inclusion[43] and Spinoza chose it as a strategy to refute scepticism and, more specifically, sceptical problems raised by philosophers such as Sextus Empiricus of antiquity and revived by philosophers such as Montaigne.[44] The principal sceptical problem goes by the name of the 'diallelus', or 'The Wheel' and the issue concerns proof of first premises and the criteria to distinguish true ideas from false ideas. The solution proposed by Spinoza, and I contend adopted by Deleuze, could be described as an 'intuitionist theory of truth'. Within the theory there are ways to ascertain the truth of a proposition: by inference and by intuition. I can do no better than quote Delahunty:

> He has discovered the true philosophy because he has applied the correct method – that of making truth-preserving deductive inferences from premises which are known to be true. The choice of an admittedly cumbersome geometrical form goes hand in hand with an intuitionist theory of truth; for with no other presentation will the flow of truth from premises to conclusions be so manifest and so incontestable. The reader will ideally resemble a 'spiritual automa-

> ton': since his 'perceptions' in thinking will be rightly 'ordered', and will put first the essence of the universal cause, his mind's activity in working through the consequences will mirror the true order of causes in Nature.[45]

Indeed, once again, we can see the influence of the ancients on Deleuze's work. Merlan suggests that our understanding of the relationship of implication and explication ought to be consistent with the use made by Nichlaus of Cusa. He argued that a causal explanation, an explanation of an event that includes how one thing acts on in space and time, does not even approximate an explanation for that event. The neo-positivist move to replace this with a description does not suffice either. The metaphysical conviction which solves the pyrrhonist dilemma is thus that Nature and logic can be brought together, which means that to explicate something is to discover things that follow in sequence, be they things of nature or properties from a definition.

This leads us to final comment concerning the concept 'affirmation' in *Expressionism*. When an enquirer comes to consider his or her mental contents, she or he does so within a parallelist system, where there is no interaction between the attributes of Thought or Extension and where no idea is caused by the action of a body but where a fundamental isomorphism pertains. The concept 'affirmation' ties an expression or proposition with assent and truth. Herein lies the truth and error in Macherey's description of the method, at once rational and affective, evincing through the process receptivity in the reader – who will come to affirm the truth of the argument. We have already discussed Deleuze's consideration of error and noted that for Deleuze, philosophical insight, the intuition of basic truths, is beyond the ken of ordinary folk. If one is not moved, one must resign oneself to the 'lumpen'. The New Ageist illusion that one is being offered 'a perspective' is belied by the drama of causal rationalism defining not merely the position but also the content of the perspective.

Due to the fact that there is no actual mark indicating assertion in ordinary language, some have argued that the utterance of a sentence in the indicative mode is naturally assertoric: one might say that 'p' automatically says 'that p' unless you obstruct it from doing so. Deleuze identifies the assertoric nature of expression with an act of assent. Assent, as we have noted, does not require an act of will but is the same has 'having the idea in mind' and failing to see any reason to doubt it. Once again the Stoic influence is clear. Epicetetus argued that we must assent to certain propositions, Galen suggested that we are naturally disposed to assent but could always choose otherwise and others suggested that certain truths almost drag us to assent. Deleuze is rather taken with such references to natural and causal connection, the supposition of a link between facts and our beliefs. He likes the ideas that certain states of affairs are such that once they come to our attention we are thereby caused to believe that they obtain, mainly because this would allow him to maintain that causal connectedness secures the foundation of our knowledge. He could also, then, argue that our basic beliefs are 'natural beliefs', beliefs towards which nature leads us, that is, 'those beliefs which we are naturally caused to have by the very facts which the beliefs express'.[46]

Instead of considering the will to have a role in assenting and denying ideas, Deleuze propounds the Spinozistic doctrine that, although free will is not required for the act of assent, it remains true that assent could be called free. How might this be? According to Spinoza, when I am drawn to affirm 'that p' by an adequate perception of the truth of 'p', I am maximally free because true freedom is nothing other than to be determined to a certain response by the perception of compelling rational justification. But not all ideas are of formally real existents or essences. There are, for example, ideas which we create and which represent non-existents and perhaps non-essences. We might like to say that these ideas are materially false, even when asserted. Deleuze responds to this problem of error by claiming that any inadequate idea is premised on an ignorance of the true causal sequence. I am ignorant of the true causal sequence at the point when I am struggling with inadequate ideas. We could say that I am unfree, likely to err, to the extent that I am embodied.

Thus we can, finally, demystify the frequent statements referring us to the philosophical role of affirmation and can make sense of the claim that being is 'the object of a pure affirmation' (333). The idea of affirmation is dependent upon the thesis of parallelism and a philosophy of perception, which answers the problem of error by arguing that the proper object of (rational) perception can never be falsely intuited. By virtue of the theory of affects, where there is asserted an adequate, true idea there is a corresponding affect of pleasure: a movement of the body. In this way, Deleuze ties philosophical insight to psychology, the emotive affect, and then to ethics through his ethical naturalism. Here we can see the result of Deleuze's various question-begging moves. Deleuze would, of course, not admit to begging the question, using later arguments to justify primary ones, but at the points when he is most concerned to demonstrate that this is not the case, he appeals to further extraneous metaphysical principles, such as the *Principle of Sufficient Reason*. In the end, the confirmation of the position is supposed to be 'experiential'. If such confirmation is not given, Deleuze can always describe the doubters as 'foolish' and 'weak', where the blessed, on the other hand, can penetrate the truths of nature, as here:

> (the concept of immanence) claims to penetrate into the deepest things, the 'arcana'. ... It at once gives back to Nature its own specific depth and renders man capable of penetrating into this depth. It makes man commensurate with God and puts him in possession of a new logic: makes him a spiritual automaton. (322)

The politics of Expressionism

As Deleuze embarks on his conclusion to *Expressionism*, he introduces a few speculative comments concerning the role and value of philosophy. With reference to the former, he highlights the relevance of philosophical context to the labour of philosophical argument. 'It sometimes happens', he writes, 'that those concepts are called forth at a certain time, charged with a collective meaning corresponding to the requirements of a given period and discovered, created or recreated by several authors at once. Such is the case with Spinoza and Leibniz and the concept of expression. This concept takes on the force of an Anti-Cartesian reaction led by these two authors' (322). Without wishing to deny that philosophy enjoys a relative autonomy, as do all cultural activities, it seems that Deleuze manifests a relationship between social, rather than philosophical, context and argument.

Before closing the general argument, I would like to connect the ethical thesis with the political treatise and indicate the relationship between the philosophical system and certain unavoidable political consequences. I shall begin by recording the state of nature argument, suggest an analysis of the function of such hypothetical arguments and assess the conceptual structure. Early state of nature arguments, presented by such as Hobbes and Locke, acted as a looking glass in which early bourgeois thinkers reflected their own social situation. Because their situation itself included elements of distortion, they reflected a distorted picture, magnifying some elements and distorting others. To this original distortion, we can also say that in the state of nature myth 'the bourgeois male recognises his flaws, his fears and anxieties as well as his dreams'. And to this, Benhabib adds that,

> the varying content of this metaphor is less significant than its simple and profound message: in the beginning man was alone. ...

> The female, the mother of whom every individual is born, is now replaced by the earth. The denial of being born of woman frees the male ego from the most natural and basic bond of dependence.[47]

In *Expressionism* there is a significant relationship of dependence, a straightforward patrilinear line from God to son: such that each particular is in some sense son of God. If the first step, in the state of nature myth, consists in individuals confronting each other in fear and hostility, the second step is taken at the point each individual agrees to form a 'fraternal' bond with the others, to call for a rational cessation to hostility.[48] It is not that each individual is textually gendered, it is that the space carved within the philosophy, for the progressive rational deliberation which frees the self from the passions, excludes those who are tied or encumbered in any way. We find that Deleuze's text silently incorporates the values of fraternity and thereby positions actually embodied subjects while explicitly deriding the affect of 'contingent' factors, such as gender.

From the second to third stage of emotional and political maturity we find that public deliberation is dependent upon, but separated from, any 'private' sphere of 'family' or quotidian and emotional life. Deleuze's naturalised epistemology dissociates reasons from passions and looks to find explanations for belief elsewhere than in the location of the knower.[49] Not only is the political context definitionally irrelevant to the process of ethical maturation but so too are relationships of any type, except to the extent that these enable or impede the knower gain mastery of his passionate nature. Here, again, we can see how the celebration of the passage from nature to culture, from conflict to consensus, condemns those who remain emotionally connected to others to immaturity and bondage, which can now be described as prisons of their own making. Many feminist philosophers would maintain that these are the founding moves of very traditional philosophical argument.

Commenting on Deleuze's remark that 'eating bored him', Shukin investigates *A Thousand Plateaus* and discovers that Deleuze and Guattari dichotomise nomadology (the raw; the intense) and the regulatory (domestic). This is a surprisingly old fashioned duality between nature (power: movement of the infinite: the involuntary) and convention, where convention is judged according to the ethical criteria discerned in nature. Shukin develops this point: 'Deleuze expresses boredom with eating because he can take it for granted; the labour of women who (historically) prepare it is precisely not involuntary, and therefore devoid of interest ... . Women's actual, embroiled lives are sacrificed in the text'.[50]

Such dichotomies are integral to many portraits men have painted for themselves, where the autonomous self strives to unite the rational and the passionate sides of his nature while characterising his emotions as unruly, chaotic and burdensome. The idea of nature as the archaic realm, as 'irrational' force, is the underbelly of Enlightenment thought. Here we can see that Deleuze appears to accept a number of dualisms and to value nature, typically associated with the feminine, over convention, typically associated with the masculine. However, this appearance is soon dispelled when we learn that the principles of nature are those of the *logos*, the *archē* of being. Convention is constituted as the place of mediation and sensibility, blocking the individual's immediate and joyful intuition of the One. Bodies are only relevant instrumentally to the overall narrative, stepping-stones from convention to grace. The description of the body as 'a site of intensities' is the consequence of these various philosophical propositions.

The resulting ethical theory embeds these dichotomies even deeper and, like contemporary universalistic moral theory, repeats the binary distinctions of autonomy and nurturance, independence and bonding, the sphere of justice and freedom and the sphere of personal, private relationships. These underlying metaphysical conditions, which carry a repetition of the laws, determined the form and consequence of Deleuze's ethical naturalism. This suggests that the attempt to 'think differently' or to 'think difference' within Deleuze's system would only have the appearance of novelty or content.[51] When Bradotti speaks of reading Deleuze with sceptical perplexity, because he seems unable to account for sexual difference, we can now respond by saying that he is unable to account for any difference or specificity, sexual or otherwise.[52] More profoundly, he repeats the rationalist dream of neutral judgement and disembodied coincidence with the Godhead, rehearsing the archaic chant that each dispassionate self can discover God, the father, moving within him, moving him to feel in the proper sense. As feminist theorists tend to challenge the century-old identification of the thinking subject with a universal subject and offer various critiques of philosophies of disembodied judgement, connecting these to an underlying positionality, perhaps we need to look elsewhere for our inspiration.[53] Deleuze's philosophical method in *Expressionism* is itself ripe for such a critique and certainly cannot deliver a radical and alternative account of corporeality.[54] It is for this reason that, throughout my commentary, I have retained the gender-specific pronoun.

Conclusion

The dichotomies, already pointed out by Hegel, tend to organise philosophical argument and become charged when philosophy and politics coincide at various points of rapid social change. We have identified a number of salient moments in the argument, leading us to presume that Deleuze's Spinozism is not inured from context. These moments have related principally to the characterisation and eventual elimination of the subject. To these three moments, we can now add that the principle of the quanitification of quality, a principle that leads Deleuze to endorse a thoroughly Cartesian *mathesis universalis*,[55] and the principle of instrumental rationality incline us to argue that Spinozism actually shares a number of notable features with Cartesianism. Deleuze thinks otherwise, and believes that his Spinozistic project breaks from the Cartesian tradition in a number of ways. There is the insistence on a 'physicalism' from which we are supposed to derive an ethical theory and an epistemology that, putatively, relies neither upon representational features of an object nor on mentalistic accounts of belief states. Our questions are these: do these features really break from the central characteristics of previous philosophical systems? And, if not, are there any consequences?

Deleuze presents a version of pantheism, highlights the primacy of the concept of power and infers from this an ethical theory according to which the individual is determined to do whatever will increase his power. Actions are judged in terms of their consequences and other subjects are cast in terms of utility. The return to Spinoza, and the revision of ethical naturalism, is surely a symptom of the failure of the Enlightenment project and a hope that psychology can provide a view of human nature that might assign new status to moral rules.[56] Utilitarianism, though, itself faces a number of moral dilemmas. Critics hold that a consistent utilitarian must allow 'injustice' or harm where the promotion of utility requires it, where the answer to the question 'what is the right thing to do?' might require us to override the constraints of ordinary morality. The constraints, in *Expressionism*, which might have blocked the shift into aggregation of uses, such as the harm principle, were found to be implausible. The moral theory is unable to take into account actual particulars and entails two conclusions. First that one ought to abandon any moral philosophy concerned with concrete individuals and relevant moral categories (responsibility, bonding, sharing) and moral feelings, (love, care, sympathy and solidarity). Second, that one should endorse a moral theory which is, at best, a form of rational egoism. Thus we can see that the erroneous dichotomies, outlined earlier, transcribe themselves into our ethical theory and make us choose between two specious alternatives with an illegitimate either/or.

The question with which we are faced concerns the relationship of this type of ethical theory, constructed as it is through a number of false oppositions, and the social context. I contend that we find a utilitarianism, consistent with the morality of the market, and a rational egoism, consistent with the politics of enlightened privacy. Cutting through both these is a 'techno-Benthamite' instrumental rationality. This means that others enter our ethical landscape only as means to ends which, supposedly, we ourselves decide. Our final end state is one without determination, except in the most minimal sense, where individuality is guaranteed, but unknowable, by the rational principle of the identity of indiscernibles. The fall of the particular into this 'abyss of annihilation' is a consequence of the relationship that is taken to hold between the infinite and the finite.[57] Deleuze's causal rationalism concedes freedom to rationality and actually removes it from empiricism, which might, in different worlds, realise that freedom. The description of the world of material affects as one that holds us in tutelage, is both true and false. It is true to the extent that individuals do confront material determination and their actions are compelled. It is false to the extent that this is neither necessary nor rational. This, I maintain, is evidence of the inverted, and somewhat distorted, reflection of social context in the 'state of nature' myth. Its reified effects are felt most strongly when Deleuze transposes the position of those who are compelled to do certain things, for example women's relation to domestic labour, with those less compelled, yet at the same time managing to glamorise the latter at the expense of the former. Principles of organisation are displaced from the realm of cognition, convention, to the realm of physics, nature. But these organisational principles *are* interested and they reflect *social* principles of organisation. Which is why it is so suitable that the philosophical system ensures that we lose the tools with which to criticise and explain the rôle and function of mediation. We can thus see that the principles of organisation are retained but the emancipatory or liberational hope within Enlightenment thought is lost.

If it is the case that arguments or problems tend to gain a profile at specific junctures then our first question is 'what changes are we undergoing at the moment?' Amongst other responses would be globalisation and the political confrontations of various identities. The profile of Deleuzian philosophy might be explained by the fact that it is ideally suited to the former. As to the latter, following Faludi's warning of a backlash,[58] I can only quote Shukin:

> Philosophy even lightly brushed with an ethnographic zeal is liable to find women of interest only in their capacity to quicken the blood: carriers of strange winds and estrangement that provide Western man with the conduit he needs to abdicate himself ... . When its material actualities can be bracketed, the feminine provides a perfectly exotic minority medium.[59]

I hope that I have shown why these material actualities are so problematic within the general *schema* and now we can begin to see the consequences of a philosophical system that denies to thought any critical or referential, rather than reverential, purchase. Critiques of 'the subject' tend to be critiques of the 'concept of subjectivity'.[60] Although the 'quarrel of the subject is ... a scholastic quarrel' it raises questions concerning the role and function of theory. More precisely, the ways in which representations, or images, are moulded may effect the positions which embodied subjects can adopt. Indeed specific formations might well be congruent with definite interests.

Conclusion

Problems relating to identity, representation and truth have gained an academic profile over the last two decades. Deleuze draws together this constellation of concepts, writing, in *Difference and Repetition*, that 'modern thought is born of the failure of representation, of the loss of stable identity and of the discovery of all forces that act under the representation of the identical'.[1] The critique of representation is a theme common to all postmodern philosophers concerned with questions relating to identity. As the feminist philosopher Ollkowski has it, Deleuze is central to the postmodern move which links the analysis of existing conditions to the critique of structure of representation in order to produce the ruin of representation.[2] Deleuze assures us not only of the immanent demise of representational theories of truth and meaning but, by premising representation on identity, also advocates a general rejection of the philosophical principle of identity.

Psychological theses concerning self-reference aside for the moment, critiques of principles of identity are, in various postmodern texts, either premised upon, or offer arguments for, the belief that metaphysical realism is a failed ontology and that representational realism is a failed epistemology. To rather simplify the matter, representational realism is the theory that there is a transparent correspondence between word/concept and object and that truth-conditions are satisfied by accurate correspondence. The principal feature of metaphysical realism is the belief in a mind-independent world. The relationship between these two philosophical theses is complicated. For instance, one can be a representational realist and maintain that there is no mind-independent object. One might be an idealist and an empiricist, such as Bishop Berkeley. Or, realism might lead to a position where it is consistent to maintain that it is possible, although not necessary, that the world differs radically from the way in which it appears. A rigorous empiricist, such as Hume, might hold that we cannot justify our belief in permanent identities, either of objects or of the self.

Common sense tends to lead us to assume that the objects about we which we raise epistemological questions have identifiable features or properties and that these properties, such as 'redness' are instantiated in, perhaps expressed or exemplified by other individuals. Although the ontological question 'what types of things are there?' is distinct from the epistemological 'how might we know?' there is a close connection. Both answers suppose it possible to identify what is being talked about at an abstract level. This point is not merely simplified but obscured by the relationship of entailment between representation and identity in the above quotation.[3] In fact one could be an anti-realist or an internal realist and still have a notion of identity. Just as one may be a metaphysical realist without an ontology of stable objects. It is true, though, that without an ontology that includes stable objects and identity conditions, it would be difficult to be a representational realist. That said, without some sort of working principle of identity, it is very difficult to see how any claims relating to the world of experience, indeed talk of the experience itself, or of its causes, would be comprehensible, let alone claims as to the nature of the world.

The appraisal of this particular constellation of issues – identity, representation and truth – begins to take shape as a reassessment of the term 'materialism'. There are three types of materialism relevant to this study. The first sort of materialism (M_1) concerns a mind-independent world. This type of materialist need neither dismiss the existence of consciousness nor believe that there is direct access to the world and we should not confuse materialism with empiricism. The term 'empiricism' usually denotes the belief that a proposition can be confirmed or denied by immediate sense experience. Empiricism attempts to tie knowledge to experience in such a way that anything that cannot be immediately before the senses, or inferred from a class of things observed to be true, is not considered to be a legitimate road of enquiry. The second form of materialism (M_2) of interest is often linked with physicalism and is prevalent in the philosophy of mind and cognitive sciences. It is the theory that everything that exists is material. This version of materialism suggests three approaches to the problem of 'mind': eliminativism, reductionism and a sort of property dualism or double aspect theory.

Throughout this work I have indicated places where I believe that Deleuze exhibits tendencies from (M_2) and (M_1) as well as touches of empiricism. There is a third version of materialism from which Deleuze is keen to distance himself: dialectical or historical materialism (M_3). This materialism was first fashioned as a response to Hegel's idealism. Hegelian or Objective idealism is basically the doctrine that the world is essentially a mental construct or image, contrasted with the common sense realist view that there is something 'out there', mind-independent and distinct from the perceiver. Marx concedes that the human world is fashioned from human activity but makes a sharp distinction between this sort of activity and the 'production' of concepts or thinking. The second aspect of Marx's materialism relates to his methodology and can be referred to as a 'context-principle'. Taking from Hegel the idea that each thing needs to be understood in its relationships with other things, Marx 'turned Hegel on his head' and argued that the relations between things are not conceptual but are historical and social. To grasp what a thing is we must first place it in context, which is at once social, political and historical. Any attempt to analyse a thing extracted from its context will lead to erroneous and often ideological judgement. Historical materialism is thus a theory of relations such that individual identity is considered to be a consequence of antecedent processes. Lastly, the term conveys a commitment to a scientific method of enquiry. This brings the two previous points together. It is the belief that there is a mind-independent world, that events in the world can only be understood in context and that the situation of the knower might well effect knowledge claims. Economic, social and psychological processes are open to scientific assessment by a method able to accommodate change, non-conformity and difference. The only scientific method with sufficient explanatory potential is dialectical and the underlying epistemic position fallibilist; we can make truth claims with the understanding that what counts as true might alter over time.

Reminiscent of Frege, Deleuze saturates his work with commentaries on sense, bracketing the problem of reference.[4] But even when invoking the singular mental event, or affect, or series or parallelism, the puzzle of identity re-emerges. This was true in his discussion of ethics when he postulated an individual that remains significantly the same throughout change and alteration (identity), as it was in his state of nature argument when he made judgements about things (properties, etc) that these individuals share (abstract universals). The fault-line ran through the initial, founding, arguments relating to the nature of substance: singular being and multiple attributes. The only real shift is a general scepticism with regards both to the descriptions associated with the universal terms, the epistemological status that the terms ought to occupy,[5] and with the assumption that a natural correspondence is a necessary and sufficient condition for political action.[6] But if we take the thesis to be a rejection of realism in epistemology, we would mistake his theory of causality, the logic of sense, and we would be unable to subject the thesis to proper analysis. If we take his claims at face value, not only would we mistake the epistemic tools he requires for his project but we would be left without a critical armour and be unable to investigate reasons for his philosophical position. It would be extremely difficult to argue, with any conviction, about the causal origin, effect or even nature of the material practices in question (M_3).

The same points can be made if the focus is shifted from the individual to 'practices' and is especially salient to talk of the 'science' of singular events or forces – the alternative to permanent identity.[7] The materialism linked to Deleuze, or to a Deleuzian approach to philosophical questions, is not realism about *objects* in a mind-independent world nor is it dialectical materialism. It does, however, pull on a theory of 'stuff' which precedes our cognition or representation; subterranean forces. That claims, as to the principles and constitution of experience, underwrite the critique of representation and are the 'new scientific basis' for ethical judgement or action is a fact lost in a general quagmire of epistemological relativism. Deleuze slides out of this problem in two ways. Firstly, he can say that the truth of the demonstration can be immediately intuited. Secondly, he offers through an image of the body, a philosophy of action, which can be used if it suits, and that will be known through trial and error. These would be quite disingenuous retorts. The former assumes a truth that is the content of the intuition, the latter hides the factual claims relating to bodies under a pragmatist veneer. Indeed, there is nothing more totalising than a philosophical system which refuses to reflect on either its own truth assertions or its context.

The issue of context brings us to the topic of mediation. Now, we have seen that in *Expressionism* Deleuze introduces a notion of philosophical practice characterised by a relationship between ideas, so that the idea or mental event becomes the referential object of enquiry. We have also seen that Bennett's criticism of Spinoza also holds for Deleuze, not only are we unable to give content to the mental event but also, with no language of mental activity, such as 'entertaining a belief', the ideas form an infinite regress of 'formal plates' (1(1(x))), (1(1(1(x)))). The loss or redundancy of the substantial object mirrors the speculative role attributed to philosophy that is unable to account for its own context. This, in turn, reflects an epistemology that leaves us without proper tools to analyse social mechanisms. I contend that in spite of its critical appearance, and in spite of the genuine criticism that is contained within *Expressionism*, one can see concealed a germ, as a secret potentiality, of uncritical positivism and equally uncritical idealism.[8] Throughout this exegesis, I hope that I have begun to show how reductive materialism and idealism are sides of the same coin.

In his rather touching essay comparing the ideas of Deleuze and Adorno, Toole suggests that the aforementioned philosophers help 'to restore the sense of something grim and impending within the polluted sunshine of the shopping mall – some older classical European-style sense of doom and crisis'.[9] But the works differ not merely in approach but also in content and the systems of Deleuze and Adorno, contrary to the shared appearance of radicalism, have quite separate political and ethical commitments. If the motivation for embracing Deleuze's poststructuralism is political or ethical, then a germane question might be: 'is the problem really the principle of identity?' Perhaps it is only possible to examine the implication of thought, and the social conditions of the thought, through the (insufficient nature of the) judgment of identity.[10] But the social conditions still need to be thought and thereby identified. To separate these philosophers of 'difference' and 'non-identity', one must see how the poles of subject and object operate within their philosophical system.

Dialectics not a standpoint

In *Nietzsche and Philosophy*, Deleuze writes that

> the dialectic proceeds by opposition, development of the opposition or contradiction and solution of contradiction. It is unaware of the real element from which forces, their qualities and their relations derive; it only knows the inverted image of this element which is reflected in abstractly considered symptoms... . Dialectic thrives on oppositions because it is unaware of far more subtle and subterranean differential mechanisms.[11]

This statement clearly delineates Deleuze as a philosopher who is concerned to develop a philosophical approach distinct from those embroiled in Hegelianism. Cornel West once remarked in an interview that 'Deleuze was the first to think through the notion of difference independent of Hegelian ideas of opposition and that was the start of the radical anti-Hegelianism which has characterised French intellectual life in the last decade'.[12] If Deleuze does have this profile, it is interesting to note that *Expressionism*, although an early work, provides the metaphysical frame of reference for many of Deleuze's later philosophical interjections. It is then even more interesting to note that Hegel shares with Spinoza not only common ground but a deep philosophical affinity. Differentiating between Hegel and Deleuze's Spinoza would be much simpler if Deleuze was merely a fellow traveller with Nietzsche. However, by stressing the immanence of God and his identity with the whole of reality, Deleuze distances himself from Nietzschean atheism. As Deleuze shares this with Hegel, the difference between Deleuze and Hegel seems more perplexing.

For Hegel, Spinoza occupies a privileged position in the history of philosophy. He believes that Spinoza's absolute monism, combined with his revival of early Greek thought, provides the necessary substrate and beginning of all philosophy.[13] As Yovel puts it 'in Hegel's *Science of Logic*, it is Spinoza's system, duly modified, which brings to a climax the whole march of traditional philosophy, crystallised into 'Objective Logic''. Indeed, Hegel in characteristic flight writes that:

> It is therefore worthy of note that thought must begin by placing itself at the standpoint of Spinozism; to be a follower of Spinoza is the essential commencement of all Philosophy. For as we saw above when man begins to philosophise, the soul must commence by bathing itself in this ether of the One Substance, in which all that man held as true has disappeared.[14]

Hegel, though, condemns Spinoza's formal-deductive method for not tracing the 'inner movement of its subject matter'; in other words for its non-dialectical presentation of philosophical proof. Deleuze adopts and adapts Spinoza's method, precisely because he believes that it does follow the inner movement of the subject matter, which is not dialectical. Ostensibly, then, the point of difference lies in the characterisation of being in dialectical terms and the methodological rôle accredited to 'negation' and 'affirmation'.

Affirmation and negation

In a pragmatic identification of content with consequence various philosophers have exalted the philosophy of Deleuze as a theory of affirmation. Colebrook goes so far as to couple this philosophy of affirmation to feminist theory, as though the concept 'affirmation' actually has content and the content uncontested. Feminism, she says, has always been a question of what concepts do, how they work and their consequences.[15] Although speaking from a different position, Malabou also suggests that the primary philosophical question to pose is whether or not one begins from an originary 'no' or a limitless 'yes'. Because Hegelian dialectical method evades this question, it is, in turn, limited to a simple procedure. Thus, she says, one must examine the interests and motives underlying any such system.[16] Throughout this work, I have indicated how in *Expressionism* the logical theory of judgement is tied to the psychological thesis and, ultimately, to a scientific hypothesis concerning nature: power, desire or energy. Now, I would like to explore how a philosophy of affirmation can be described as 'uncritical positivism', a term which can in turn be unpacked as a format, and that this means 'reductive materialism'. My contention is that philosophies of affirmation rather than performing a critical function are secretly aligned to the interests of the *status quo*.

Deleuze considers Spinoza to have demonstrated two things. First that negation is nothing and second that 'non-being' or 'nothingness' is never included in the nature of something.[17] Let me take the latter point first. Following Grossman, I think it helpful to distinguish between three notions: nothing, negation and non-being. He maintains that 'nothing' is a something; it is a linguistic entity or a logical quantifier, to be distinguished from the 'not' of negation, but he argues that the term 'non-being' does not add anything to our ontological vocabulary. Briefly, whereas Hegel suggested that, on reflection, we must concede a unity to the state of being differentiated and of being undifferentiated, a unity to being and non-being, Grossman sees no such implication. He summarises Hegel's argument in the following way. Being *qua* being has no properties and stands in no relations. It is not differentiated from other 'things' by having this or that property, or by being related to other 'things' by this or that relation. Pure being is absolute negation, since it is not this, that or the other. And absolute negation is nothing, that is, it is non-being.[18] Grossman disagrees over the points that being without determination is still being and that there is no such entity as non-being; no property or feature. For Hegel, when we think 'Being' without determination we find we are thinking 'no-thing', and when we think 'no-thing' we find ourselves speculating on the nature of being. That said, the real point of contention is whether or not there is being without determination and whether determination is associated with negation. This takes us first to an analysis of the term 'negation'.

Deleuze describes the idea of 'negation' as an abstract entity of reason; others include non-being, limit and falsehood. All these terms, he claims, in a thoroughly Kantian manners, are tools of comparison and do not suggest any characteristics of being itself. In other words, he suggests that if I were to affirm that (it is not-dark) I would be merely denying the corresponding positive state of affairs, and would be saying (not (it is dark)). Negation here disappears from the states of affairs and reappears as a cognitive act of denial. In fact though, when we analyse how 'negation' functions we can see it is category indifferent and combines diverse things into existent wholes. Grossman puts the alternative case and summing up his thoughts as to the operations of negation, he suggests that: 'negation in combination with a number of entities, yields an existing fact ... it makes something out of nothing ... it creates fully-fledged existents out of disjointed bits and pieces'.[19] As Frege might have it, negation belongs to the content of what we say.

If we maintain that negation belongs to the content of what we say, it seems that there is an argument building which would allow us to describe determinate being by using the concept of negation. To clarify this I shall briefly examine the relationship between the terms 'affirmation' and 'negation' and being by analysing the value placed on the copula by Kant and Hegel.

The 'is' in the proposition 'this table is brown' signifies different things to the Kantian and the Hegelian. Kant would have it that the 'is' signifies a judgement, the bringing together of two concepts. Due to the complicated taxonomy of pure concepts and concepts, the 'is' also indicates an affirmative judgement, which is also a judgement concerning what is real. The judgement presumes that each individual is subject to the principle of determinability, according to which, of every two predicates, in the same category, only one can belong to the subject. When the concept is brought to intuition, when it is schematised in time, it is subject to the law of non-contradiction. If we were to consider a colour, say blue, in its relationship to other colours, the colours of the rainbow, then we would be subjecting it to the principle of complete determinability. This would be to commit an error and would indicate a confusion of content with logical form.[20] From this confusion, we might be fooled into believing that to know a thing we would have to know every possible predicate and must determine it thereby, either affirmatively or negatively. Because the idea of complete determination requires all possible predicates and because this can never be delivered in concrete, there can never be the experience which is necessary for such a judgement to take place. The notion is thus based on an Idea which has its seat solely in the faculty of reason. We can only think negation, maintains Kant, by basing it on an original affirmation.

The Hegelian response, which transforms this dialectic of illusion into a dialectical of knowledge, is premised on the belief that the original judgement is, in fact, the conclusion of a deductive syllogism. We may not be able to know the content of the field but we can come to grasp the logic of judgement. The disjunctive syllogism demonstrates how we arrive at a particular through a process of determination, qualification and limitation from within a field of possibilities. Hegel writes that 'quality as determinateness which is, as contrasted with the negation which is involved in it but distinguished from it, reality'.[21] A thing, he continues, is what it is only in and by reason of its limit. Therefore the limit makes the thing what it is. But, the negation is not an abstract nothing. Blue might well be determined through the field of colours and limited as such by being not-orange and not-brown, but these negations are also somethings. Otherness thus negates or determines the quality at the limit or boundary and is, at the same time, something in-itself. There is for Hegel an endless alternation between the two terms, each of which calls the other up. Here we can see one example of dialectical contradiction. The limit constitutes the thing as it is but is also its negation, it is also what it is not. Because the thing is constituted at its boundary, it carries otherness into what it is. It would not be what it is, were it not for determination by the other. It is otherness which makes the difference and so difference is carried within any judgement of identity.

Neither Kant nor Hegel would really disagree that the 'is' is only fulfilled in the relationship between subject and predicate. This begins to make sense of Hegel's claim that being is always determinate, as well as Kant's criticisms of Descartes' *Ontological Argument*. In other words they presume that a proposition can only be true if the particular is instantiated. The dispute between Kant and Hegel concerns the function of the copula. For Kant, the 'is' suggests that a bringing together of two concepts has occurred in a judgement and that if the concept is instantiated we might say that the object exists.[22] But, due to the general scheme of the deduction, when an object of perception is asserted in a proposition, this assertion involves the logical idea of affirmation and the deduced concept of reality. Any further negation is derived from this initial assertion. Hegel, on the other hand, contends that any assertion of a thing involves both the thing's negation and its affirmation. This means that 'the real' is thought to include both negation and affirmation and any intuited particular already combines its concept and substance.

Hegel, in summary, suggests three ways in which 'negation' can function and to this I would like to add a fourth. First, Hegel's idealism insists that objects are determined by concepts which are determined by all other concepts. It is possible to distinguish between the idealism and the claim that concepts and objects are in determining relations. Second, if we do separate out this from the idealism we can see that the concept of negation may indicate an interdependence of meaning, uncovered by a synchronic linguistic analysis of conceptual relations.[23] Third, the claim that being is only determinate through negation, once separated from its phenomenological roots, can suggest that any particular gains its form in context. If we were to say that the context is social or 'material' in a loose sense then we see how the relational account of identity can afford a concept of subject embeddedness. Finally, if we say that the negative function of thought is to negate something, and if that something is already a negation then we are negating a negation. This idea is fleshed out in the claim that if we are presented with an assertion which conceals an original negation, or one which asserts a false identity, then to negate that claim would be to clarify what the state of affairs may be like.

Now, Deleuze is keen to extract from Spinoza an argument very similar to Kant's – that negation is derivative and always depends on an initial assertion of a thing. Assertion is, as we have already discussed, identified with the logical category of affirmation: to assert something is to assign it positive truth value.[24] In the *Ethics* Spinoza argues that to be finite is to be limited and this involves a denial in part.[25] Deleuze attempts to marry Kant's description of judgement and Spinoza's analysis of finitude, given his opposition to Hegel's insights into the nature of determinate being. There are two principal issues I would like to discuss here. The first concerns the nature of the object of perception, as well as the act of judgement, and the second refers more directly to the 'is' of predication. I shall suggest that Deleuze is so keen to stress that the real contains no negativity that he throws the baby out with the bathwater.

Deleuze uses and develops parts of the *Ethics* to present a case against the rôle of negation in determining objects. To grasp his alternative we must first identify the object in question and its relation to concepts or ideas. There are two sorts of relevant objects. The second stage of knowledge acquisition as presented in *Expressionism* has as its object modes and their properties. These modes either are or can be known through adequate ideas. The third stage of knowledge acquisition has as its object essences and these are grasped through a direct mental act of vision. Let us take this latter case first. In the second chapter we examined Deleuze's quantification of quality and found that an essence is an intensive degree of power which is 'explicated' in a relationship. An essence is, by definition, 'positive', a part of power.[26] When we intuit an essence we *assert* it as the object of intuition and because assertion and affirmation appear to be co-extensive, we *affirm* it. Where essences are concerned, therefore, there would be no sense to the idea of a 'determined' subject, no sense to the subject of a judgement being informed by its idea. Determination and negation are also extraneous concepts with regard to the process of judgement.

Let us now examine the first sort of objects we mentioned above, modes and their properties, to see whether or not determination plays a rôle in their formation. We investigated the relationship of explication in the fourth chapter and discovered two things. Modes are explicated in characteristic relations, these do involve a limit, and modes are in determining relationships with other modes, when extensive parts are subsumed in the mode's characteristic relation. Determination is limitation and hence negation – *omnia determinatio est negatio*. Deleuze is initially interested in the limit of the correspondence between essence and extensive relations. Modes only determine one another in material relations of cause and effect. But this determination implies negation only in the loosest sense. We might wish to say that x negates y, or an aspect of y, where x interferes with what y would have done otherwise. Although at this level, modes do affect one another, the significance of the affect is a moot point. For sure, the modes are causally determined to act in certain ways but the relationship between cause and limit is not at all clear. Indeed, Deleuze is happy with the notion that extensive determination is real distinction in a weakened sense. Ideas are isomorphic, although it is not clear whether they are isomorphic to the mode or to an event. It is clear, however, that to have an adequate idea one must grasp the logical and causal dependence of the finite mode on the infinite.

So modes are only determined by other modes in a weak sense and not at all by their concept or idea. Determination actually comes into its own for Deleuze in the relationship between the finite mode and the infinite and the critical issue is the role played in this determination by the attributes.[27] Although both substance and some modes are extended, the relationship to extension is best summarised as F(a) where modes are concerned and a = F where substance is concerned.

The 'is' is an 'is' of identity in the latter case and of predication in the former case. Yet even in the former case, we saw that Deleuze struggled to convince us that F(a) is meaningful and that he resorted to the claim that things are modally, not substantially, individuated – that intensive quantity can only be understood as extensive through a process of abstraction. We can now see that his rationalism concedes the principle of determination to the 'eternal' attribute through the quantification argument and to the infinite modes of the attribute, for instance of motion and rest, in the arguments concerning mode identity. Only by grafting into the account various transattributive features can Deleuze make any sense at all of the principle of determination or difference.

Hegel's logic led him to posit a relational account of identity and we saw how this could be transformed into a context principle. In his desire to proceed without the concession that the real, and our way of thinking about that real, contains something we may wish to name 'negation', Deleuze offers us an account of an individual striving to preserve its identity *despite* its relationships of embodiment. Deleuze insists on the individual's embodied state, that is, its natural dispositions to behave in x way. The description of individuality concludes with a disembodied account of that nature. His eulogy to disembodiment begins with the assertion that all relations must be described from the point of view of affect, a necessary and causal effect. We saw that little or no content was given to the mode's characteristics or properties; let alone to those of the affecting modes. Indeed, despite a sort of *identity of indiscernibles* argument, at an abstract level each mode is overwhelmingly similar and it is only the similarity which is interesting. This same abstraction is present in the epistemology which exalts the individual to form clear ideas of logical and causal dependence on the infinite, by disengaging from passions, passions which are caused by and through relationships with other modes.

Self and other

The description of the individual subject nicely illustrates the different philosophical approaches for us. Hegel would not dispute the claim that thought must begin with an individual x, nor, indeed, that there is a relationship between x and its essence. However, according to Hegel's depiction of maturity, at an early stage, a conscious individual attempts to posit itself as essential or independent, and this drives it into conflict with others. Hegel suggests that each one attempts to subjugate the other, to negate the other, to make the other being-for-self. The driving force of this, Hegel contends, is that I need another subject's recognition to be an object to myself; to be self-consciousness. At this first stage of negation, this other subject is slave to my desires, is without recognition or personhood. The other, in the Hegelian account, transforms or negates the negative relation, her being-for-me, through activity and this takes her back to a being-for-self. The negation is thus also a something; there is content. Although the other marks my boundary, she is also a positive something. From an original position, where there was a bare personality, I negated the other. Settled at my boundary, the other is for me, but this other is not just as being-for-me, I am not the other-as-being-for-me. This tension is finally resolved when I realise that I am myself and I am myself through the other but that these others are also determinate individuals. This is the disjunctive syllogism applied to people. The principle of personality, Hegel maintains, is the principle of universality. The conclusion of this process of active differentiation, is self-consciousness, the development of personality and the recognition of the logic of the whole. The materialist transformation of this by the Young Hegelians and Marx needs little comment. Except to note that the idea of a self, constituted through his or her relationships, has this dialectical origin.

In his comparative study of Sartre and Deleuze, Boundas argues that for Deleuze neither the self nor the other are primordial. Other and self, he says, fall together and the transcendental field reveals itself in all its purity.[28] But this is true only to the extent that we allow not merely the existence of power but also confer a constituting role to power and its principles of organisation. Deleuze's non-relational account of identity is subsumed and disguised in the doctrine of self-preservation. Deleuze argues that when an individual follows his or her nature she or he will conflict with others. A good encounter increases activity of the system and a bad encounter depletes it. The more bad affects the less likely we are to recognise the causal sequence producing the affect. But he holds that it is sufficient to have an idea, to have an idea of the idea and he defines mind as a collection of ideas, an idea of that aggregate would, perhaps, be self-consciousness. These ideas are all produced automatically. An inadequate idea can be transformed into an adequate idea, and this is facilitated through 'good' encounters. The other is not actually negated: unless one counts destruction as negation. The conclusion of the process is self-consciousness and the recognition of the logic of the whole: causal and logical dependence of the individual finite mode on the infinite. So the outcome is similar to the

Hegelian scheme except that according to the Hegelian, Deleuze's individual remains as a 'bare individual', without personality and the rôle attributed to others in the production of self-consciousness is masked, the small subject being replaced by the big Subject or God.[29]

The principle of subjectivity

Deleuze's explicit position is that he is offering a materialist reading of Spinoza's *Ethics* and he defines his own ethical theory as a materialist ethic of the body. This explicit position is in discord with the actual implications and inferences of the doctrine. Manifestly, the Deleuzian account offers us a way to think about the integrity of individuals and to deduce systems of behaviour that would suit the individual nature. Throughout I have been arguing that there is discordance between manifest and latent content and I have suggested that Deleuze not only 'blots out the principle of subjectivity' but also empties all content from the thought of individuality. This is thus to accept Hegel's description of Spinoza's system as acomism, and to apply it to Deleuze.[30] It is not that either Spinoza or Hegel explicitly state that the world of finite things does not exist it is rather that the logic is unable to afford the claim any substance.

We can detect this occurring in three places. First, because of the logic of his argument, Deleuze is actually unable to account for the existence, necessary or otherwise, of finite modes: that is, for individuals of any type. Secondly, his argument relating to the mind–body unity is manifestly a double-aspect theory, or a non-reductive materialism but actually leads to an extreme form of materialism, closer to eliminativism. This I suggested was partly the result of an anaemic account of mental content and problems here spilled into his description of purposive behaviour, creating insurmountable difficulties for the ethical naturalism. From these arguments it is only possible to draw one conclusion; each is determined to behave in the way it does. Finally, ethical naturalism is, on the face of it, concerned with healthy bodies in good encounters, but is, in fact, an argument which leads us to eulogise individual disembodiment; where freedom is identified with acquiescence to, reflection or contemplation upon, a universal world order.

We have noted that there is a problem with mental content and that there is nothing about objects that can be relevant to the causal story, except in so far as they affect this body, here, now – although, given the problem of indexicals, even this is problematic. Prosaically, this means that there is nothing about other subjects which is, or should be, relevant to me, except, insofar as these others are useful to me, principally by creating greater or pleasurable affects within my system, rather than lesser or unpleasurable ones. There is no moral injunction to stop me behaving in any way that benefits me. The force of the argument is such that, in Hegelian terms, I am driven to annihilate the other or to bend the other to my use. The other does help me come to a recognition of the logic of the whole but only because the more good encounters I have the more I learn about structures and thence to ideas of attributes and finally to God. At the heart of *Expressionism* there is missing an interpersonal psychology and this creates a vacuum in the moral and political philosophy. The vacuum is filled by the inevitable conclusion that any one or thing should be used to increase this individual's joyful passions. Deleuze's rational egoism begins with the individual and justifies all actions in terms of that individual's constitution. This analysis leads to us to reject May's assertion that Deleuze is the most profound contemporary thinker of 'Otherness'.

There seems good reason to accept that Deleuze eliminates the principle of the 'small' subject, if by subject we mean something like an individual with personality, agency, embedded in human relationships. There is also good reason to accept that he introduces a 'big' subject, round the backdoor, so to speak. This is not simply a comment on the pantheism but an analysis of rationalist and idealist tendencies within *Expressionism*. These tendencies are most obvious in three places.

First, Deleuze argues that God must produce himself as he understands his own nature. Secondly, it is clearly present in his semantic parallelism and shown by the fact that this interpretation of the attributes leads him to posit a weakened identity thesis. All modes, we found, were first and foremost, descriptions, even modes of the attribute of Extension, all were within the attribute of Thought. This, we argued, takes us back to subjectivism. Indeed, we concluded, rather than proving that there are infinite attributes, Deleuze seems unable to convince us that there is more than one. Finally, I would suggest that his proof requires a number of assumed rational principles. The *Principle of Sufficient Reason* is one such principle but the parallelism itself presumes certain transattributive features: causality, logic, the entailment between the two, the concept of part/whole.[31] Deleuze can only argue that these principles are 'made known to us'. I have already begun to suggest general problems with this logic of affirmation. Here we can see how the presumption that a particular state of mind can correctly identify and intuit an object may lead the enquirer to detect a number of principles which support a metaphysical system. Even when that system, in fact, leads to rather unpalatable conclusions, the enquirer, who has intuited these principles, is induced to assent to those conclusions.

The question of mediation

In Hegel's *History of Philosophy* Yovel discerns nine criticisms of Spinoza's *Ethics*. The first is that substance, *qua* substance, is only pure being and simple identity excluding all negation. The second is that, therefore, the absolute must exclude all inner differences and particularisation. Following from this is the point that Spinoza cannot show the necessity of there being particular things at all: the finite aspect of the universe remains inexplicable and at best contingent. Deeper than this runs a fourth criticism. Spinoza cannot attribute reality to the finite modes. Although declared to be real, they must be considered to be the fruit of 'external reflection' of the imagination. Similarly, the attributes cannot count as self-specifications of substance but only as external and subjective projections of our minds. The sixth criticism concerns the one way causal relation posited between substance and finite modes, which cannot, in turn, condition substance. By splitting the monistic whole into two – Natura naturata and Natura naturans – Spinoza reintroduces into monistic philosophy a basic and irreducible dualism. Because the two sides of this whole are not, and according to Spinoza, cannot be, in a mutually effecting relationship, Spinoza is unable to explain the development of self-consciousness, to offer a substantive ethics or to give a convincing account of historical development. Finally, this results in the perception of the absolute as a thing without either spirit or subjectivity.

Now, in bringing this argument to a close, I would like to complete the comparison between Hegel and Deleuze. It should be clear that these criticisms of Spinoza are true of Deleuze and each can be traced back to the problematic relationship of Thought and Extension. I have already argued that the logic of the system is idealist; here, I wish to pursue this and to suggest that the parallelist thesis actually removes the category of experience from our critical taxonomy. And that this hampers any attempt to view the subject or beliefs in their context. Indeed, context becomes irrelevant to the matter of philosophical speculation. There are a number of steps leading to this position and our journey needs to begin with an initial statement concerning the relationship between ideas, beliefs and their objects.

Due to the isomorphic relationship, each mode, in every attribute, has a corresponding idea but every idea has as its content a physical modification. This latter point offers a fairly direct link between the thinking subject with the object of thought and the idea is, in some sense, a product of a relationship between two subjects. Two steps are quickly taken. First, entertaining the idea, the reflection on the idea and the production of an idea of an idea, is described as 'automatic'. Deleuze hereby removes not merely the will from the act of judgement but also the 'small' subject of sentient intentionality. Secondly, he compels us to think *beyond* the physical affect. This means that the only sense of embodiment, the only access, even indirectly, to other subjects is transcended through the second and third stages of knowledge. So, not only have we removed the thinking function from judgement but also we now remove the material. The third step is taken when Deleuze insists that the immediate apprehension of essences and their dependence on the infinite constitutes ethical maturity and peace of mind. The parallelism is under great pressure by now and Deleuze is forced to invoke a Fregeian or Platonic realm of ideas isomorphic with essences, which are nothing but 'parts' of power, existing independently from a perceiving individual subject. Aside from an apparent, somewhat meaningless, infinite regress, we can detect an aporia at the centre of *Expressionism*, indicated by the problem of indexicals. The stratospheric object of knowledge is so different from objects encountered in sense experience that few enquirers could possibly move from one to another. The enquirer could accept that an idea has as its content a mode of the attribute of Thought and then concentrate on the causal relationship between this and the infinite. Experience, either as private apprehension of states or the empirical notion of context, is finally removed as relevant data from the judgement of what is or should be. To put it otherwise, the two poles of subject and object are thoroughly emptied.

If we empty these poles what do we have left? The parallelism, combined with the description of the acquisition of ideas, guarantees no error and an identity between idea and its object. The idea is neither content for judgement nor entertained, it is just 'present'. The collapsing of the ontological with the epistemological parallelism itself depends upon an identity of an unspecifiable 'thing' which asserts its unity through the Absolute. What we have, therefore, is not a great move ruining representation, but an assertion of simple identity. All that is ruined is the subject's ability or inclination to critique the *relationship between* idea and its object. The parallelism assumes and glues identity, whereas dialectical thought would aim to dismantle the logical character of the movement between subject and object[32] 'unfolding the difference between the particular and the universal, dictated by the universal'.[33] Dialectically, one would instead take objects to be mediated by concepts. The materialist addition would be to insist that conceptual mediation is linked to social practice which mediate the ideas available to a culture and the objects thus mediated. In contrast to the system preferred by Deleuze and his sympathisers, dialectical thinking concerns itself with the assurance by which a metaphysical system claims identity. This is because there is a fundamental suspicion that such assurance merely mimics the assurance beloved of administrative systems in the social context within which the system is presented.

Given a fundamental disagreement as to the nature of the One, Deleuze and Hegel do share a metaphysical conviction that Substance is identical to the One, the universal or the Absolute. This rationalist metaphysics contains a hidden positivism, a restoration of the existing state of affairs. Hegel shares with Deleuze the fact that neither is negative enough. Their abstract categories inscribe principles of the social world into the philosophical systems and this, in the end, leads either to a philosophical quietism or to an affirmation of the way things are. Let me illustrate this with two examples. When Deleuze analysed the origin of the belief in a monistic or Christian God he wished to argue that the idea was an effect of a causal process but, due to his naturalised epistemology, he was unable to locate the causal chain anywhere except at an abstract level. He manages therefore to abstract and distort the actual mechanisms causing the individual to believe certain (false) things. Deleuze, thereby, distorts a distortion. The second example concerns his explanation for suffering. Suffering, Deleuze rightly notes, is a consequence of actions caused by objects external to the individual. He induces the individual to reflect upon the chain causing the affect and this is supposed to inaugurate a break from passions and freedom from bondage. On closer inspection we find that the individual is being asked to reflect on a mechanism and to accommodate its necessity. This recognition is supposed to lead the individual to a state of bliss, fully reconciled to his or her fate and to the infinite. The mechanism remains but the individual, to come to terms with it, is to alienate thought from passions and the intellect from emotions. There are two propositions operating at slightly higher levels of abstraction. First, there is the presumption that suffering is caused by actions of one individual on another. Secondly, there is the assertion that the enquiring individual should abstract from the event the causal process itself. So, Deleuze naturalises and distorts the actual conditions causing suffering and he hypostasises the cause and by doing this mystifies the actions which would be required to alter the causes of suffering.

Any assertion that a method can conceptualise the totality of being is likely to be a serious error of judgement. The belief in the power of thought to grasp the totality is without substance but what we tend to find is that substance returns in a disguise or illusory form. We have found evidence within *Expressionism* that the philosophical method, heralded as a radical break from the modern project, does little more than eternalise the conditions of the present. A break from idealism, from the systems of Hegel as well as Deleuze, occurs when we pass to the object's preponderance and thereby a material critique of the nature of the universal. The task of criticising ideology, Adorno maintains, is to judge the *subjective* and *objective* moments and their *dynamics*. This returns to thought its three moments, the thought or judgement, the intentional object and the materiality of the object, as well as returning to substance its content. It is also to deny the false objectivity of concept fetishism by reducing it to the social subject and to deny false subjectivity the, sometimes unveiled, claim that all being lies in the mind while showing its immanent hostility to the mind.[34]

Commenting on Deleuze's transcendental empiricism, Baugh advises us to examine the consequences of accepting such a system. The extent to which it is justified, he says, depends on the extent to which it facilitates critical and positive moral and political practice and whether those practices are themselves good.[35] Colebrook repeats this sentiment. I hope that I have shown that the content of thought cannot be justified by the consequences of the thought or system. This is partly because the consequences cannot be properly grasped without an analysis of the system and partly because judging the consequences themselves according to the criteria of the system leads to perpetual self-reproduction. Deleuze's moral and political philosophy actually concludes by blotting out the principle of critical subjectivity and affirms the individual as dependent upon an Absolute, while living a life which is nasty, brutish and short. The utilitarian ethic governing behaviour, the link between pleasure and truth, happily nestles with the principle of instrumentalism. Despite protestations to the contrary, the mode in *Expressionism* is the affirmation of the negated individual in reality. The attempt to reconcile this individual to the universal through contemplation of inevitability is the final abandonment of any political mandate. It is only the negativity within critical thought that can break down this self-assurance and self-containment.

Negative thinking is the driving force of dialectical thought and the combination of the two provides the most powerful tool for analysing the world in terms of its contradictions and internal inadequacy: for negating the negation.[36]

Thus we see that the philosophy of affirmation is the affirmation of a negated state, the ideological presentation of modern times.[37] We can perhaps surmise that the power, common to all individuals, from which Deleuze deduces Hobbesian laws of conflictual behaviour, or rational accommodation to the whole, is the mirror image of the universal medium common to all human beings, separating, alienating, inciting monadic conflict: the exchange principle. Modernity, certainly neither post-modernity nor post-fordism, was the condition for the production of *Expressionism* and is the conditions under which we receive it. We are obliged to reflect upon those conditions and to recognise that where there is a revenging tendency towards atomism within civil society, the individual often acts in line with, what is perceived as, the inevitable. The reification of this feeling of inevitability to being accords with a certain drama of authenticity. This symbiosis casts a spell which seems to offer an exit from the confines and limits of modernity, a promise that the suffering and tutelage can be explained and transformed immediately: into individualistic anarchy.[38] It is a promise with neither integrity nor heart:

> Spell and ideology are one and the same. The fatal part of ideology is that it dates back to biology. Self-preservation, the Spinozist *sese conservare*, is truly the law of nature for all living things. Its content is the tautology of identity: what ought to be is what is anyway; the will turns back upon the willing; as a mere means of itself it becomes an end. This turn is already a turn to the false consciousness.[39]

Idealism, posing as materialism, sustains thought's claims to be total, which, then, manages to sanction the actual force of the object world. Philosophical reflection can make sure that the non-conceptual element of the concept is maintained and can offer a sophisticated form of materialism that neither reifies the object as naïve realism nor subjugates it into a form of idealism – either objective or subjective. Insight into this constitutive character of the non-conceptual in the concept indicates the tension between subject and object and the recognition of the non-identical relationship at least affords a way to break from mystical romanticism, a metaphysical spell cast by those such as Deleuze.

Notes

Introduction

1. A. Sokal and J. Bricmont, *Intellectual Impostures: Postmodern Philosopher's Abuse of Science* (Profile Books: London, 1998).
2. J. Habermas, *The Philosophical Discourse of Modernity*, trans. F. Lawrence 1st pub. 1985 (Cambridge: Polity Press, 1987), p. 94.
3. A. Schrift, 'Between Church and State: Nietzche, Deleuze and the Genealogy of Psychoanalysis', *International Studies in Philosophy*, vol. 24 (1992) 41.
4. T. May, 'The system and its Fractures: Gilles Deleuze on Otherness', *Journal of the British Society for Phenomenology*, vol. 24, 1 (Jan 1993), 3.
5. J. Fleiger, 'Becoming-Woman: Deleuze, Schreber and Molecular Identification,' in I. Buchanan and C. Colebrook eds, *Deleuze and Feminist Theory* (Edinburgh: Edinburgh University Press, 2000) pp. 38–63.
6. J.M. Salankis, 'Idea and Destination,' in P. Patton ed. (1996) op. cit. pp. 57–80.
7. See J. Lechte, *Fifty Contemporary Thinkers: from Stucturalism to Postmodernity* (London and New York: Routledge, 1994).
8. Biography; see J. Miller, *The Passions of Michel Foucault*, (London: Flamingo, 1994).
9. L. Ferry, L. and A. Renaut, *French Philosophy of the Sixties: an Essay on Antihumanism*, trans. M. Schackenberg 1st pub. 1985 (University of Massachusetts Press: Amherst, 1990).
10. Compare and contrast Deleuze and Heidegger on Nietzsche. M. Heidegger, *Nietzsche* trans. D. Krell (London: Routledge and Kegan Paul, 1981) vol. 1 and (San Francisco: Harper Row, 1984), vol. 2.
11. J. Marks, *Gilles Deleuze: Vitalism and Multiplicity* (London and Virginia: Pluto Press, 1998), p. 56.
12. L. Ferry and A. Renaut (1990) op. cit., p. xvi.
13. R. Bernstein, *the New Constellation: The Ethical and Political Horizons of Modernity/Postmodernity* (Cambridge: Polity Press, 1991), p. 4.
14. R. Rorty, *Contingency, Irony and Solidarity* (New York and Cambridge: Cambridge University Press, 1989), pp. 79–80.
15. Letter to M. Cressole, quoted P. Douglass (1992) op. cit., p. 111.
16. For a discussion on Deleuze's attitude to systems, see T. Clark, 'Deleuze and Structuralism: Towards a Geometry of Sufficient Reason', in K.A. Pearson ed., *Deleuze and Philosophy: the Difference Engineer* (London and New York: Routledge, 1997), pp. 58–72 and R. Bogue, 'Gilles Deleuze: the Aesthetics of Force', *Journal of the British Society for Phenomenology*, vol. 24, 1 (Jan 1993), 56.
17. M. Hardt, *Gilles Deleuze: an Apprenticeship in Philosophy* (London: UCL Press, 1993), p. 57.
18. Ibid.
19. 'By singularity, we mean not only something that opposes the universal, but also something that can be extended close to another, so as to obtain a connection; it is singularity in the mathematical sense'. Cadava, Connor,

Nancy eds, *Who comes after the Subject?* (Routledge: New York, 1991), p. 94. See also *Difference and Repetition* and *The Fold*. For a discussion of his identification of the mathematical, material and metaphysical, see A. Badiou, 'The Fold: Leibniz and the Baroque', in C. Boundas and D. Olkowski (eds), *Gilles Deleuze and the Theatre of Philosophy* (New York and London: Routledge, 1994), p. 53.

20. 'The early stages of this "revolution in rigour" (led) to an examination of the concept of natural number'. D. Gillies, *Frege, Dedekind and Peano on the Foundations of Arithmetic* (The Netherlands: Van Gorcum, 1982), p. 9.
21. In the same year as Brentano took the Professorship at the University of Vienna, Frege returned to Jena from Gottingen where he had attended lectures given by Lotze. 1874 was also the year in which Lotze elaborated his 1843 *Logik*, a work described by Heidegger as the 'fundamental book of modern logic' due to its four principal themes: anti–psychologism, distinction between object of knowledge and its recognition, a reformulation of Platonic theory of Ideas and an account of concepts as functions. Meinong, Stumpf and Husserl all worked with and studied under Brentano and were all guided by the idea that the characteristic feature of a mental event is that it points towards an object. Meinong, concerned that Brentano had confused that which is before the mind – the object – with the apprehension of it – content – developed a theory of objects or objectives. It has been said that at each stage of his development Husserl tried to find new ways of combining Frege and Brentano.
22. 'It transpires that what he (Ryle) means by "the massive developments of our logical theory" is the progression from Russell's theory of descriptions to Wittgenstein's theories of meaning. These developments he characterises as "The Cambridge transformation of the Theory of Concepts" thus bypassing the slightly awkward fact that Wittgenstein was more Germanic than Anglo-Saxon. Wittgenstein, for all he wrote in German and felt like an alien in England was, it seems, a Cambridge man though and through, and not really a Continental at all'. Monk, 1996, p. 3 quoted in S. Glendenning, *Edinburgh Encyclopedia of Continental Philosophy* (Edinburgh: Edinburgh University Press, 1999), p. 9.
23. M. Dummett, *Origins of Analytical Philosophy* Cambridge, MA: Harvard University Press.
24. See C. Norris, 'Continental Philosophy of Science,' in S. Glendenning (1999) op. cit., pp. 402–15.
25. S. Mitchell, 'Post-structuralism, Empiricism and Interpretation', in S. Mitchell and M. Rosen eds, *The Need for Interpretation: Contemporary Conceptions of the Philosopher's Task* (London: Athlone Press, 1993), p. 55.
26. R. Jacoby, 'The Politics of Subjectivity', *New Left Review*, 79 (May 1973), 41.
27. S.R.L. Clark, 'Have Biologists wrapped up Philosophy?' *Inquiry*, 2000, 43, 148.

1 God

1. The one exception to this that he names is the 'tender-minded' or 'soft' Bergson', B. Russell, 'From Comte to Bergson in A. Urquart and A. Lewis eds, (1988) op. cit., vol. 9, p. 435.

2. P. Macherey, 'The Encounter with Spinoza', in P. Patton (ed.) (1996) op. cit., pp. 139–61.
3. 'Pour servir de commentaire à Sérénité,' in Questions III quoted in Ferry and Renault (1990) op. cit., p. 226.
4. L.P. Gerson, *God and Greek Philosophy* (London: Routledge, 1990), p. 144.
5. 'They liken philosophy to an animal, comparing logic to the bones and sinews, ethics to the flesh, and physics to the soul. Or again to an egg: logic is the outermost part, further in is the ethics, and the inmost part is the physics'. Diogenes Laertius, vii 40 quoted in W. Kneale and M. Kneale, *The Development of Logic* (Oxford: Clarendon Press, 1962), p. 139. Deleuze is fond of this particular metaphor.
6. J. Sellars, 'The Point of View of the Cosmos: Deleuze, Romanticism and Stoicism', *Pli: The Warwick Journal of Philosophy*, vol. 8, 1999, 1–24.
7. See for example 'The body without organs is the immanent substance in the most Spinozistic sense of the word; and the partial objects are like its ultimate attributes, which belong to it precisely insofar as they are really distinct and cannot on this account exclude or oppose one another'. G. Deleuze, and F. Guattari, *Anti-Oedipus: Capitalism and Schizophrenia*, trans. R. Hurley, M. Seem, H. Lane, 1st pub. 1972 (London: Athlone Press, 1984) p. 327 and *A Thousand Plateaus: Capitalism and Schizophrenia,* trans. B. Massumi, 1st pub. 1980 (London: Athlone Press, 1988), p. 153. See N. Land, Making it with Death: Remarks on Thanatos and Desiring-Production', in *Journal of British Society for Phenomenology*, vol. 24 (1993) no. 1, pp. 66–76.
8. Hardt describes this part of *Expressionism* in relation to Deleuze's work on Bergson. 'Deleuze uses the opening the *Ethics* as a rereading of Bergson: he presents the proofs of the existence of God and the singularity of substance as an extended meditation on the positive nature of difference and the real foundation of being'. M. Hardt, *Gilles Deleuze: an Apprenticeship in Philosophy* (London: University College London Press, 1993), p. 60.
9. K. Jaspers, *Spinoza* (London: Harvest, 1974), p. 10.
10. The other argument is that if there were several substances with the same attribute, they would have to be distinguished by their modes which is absurd as substance is prior in nature to its states.
11. See M. Hooker, 'The Deductive Character of Spinoza's Metaphysics', in R. Kennington ed., *The Philosophy of Baruch Spinoza* (Washington: Catholic University of America, 1980), p. 25.
12. See G. Deleuze, *Spinoza: Practical Philosophy*, trans. R. Hurley, 1st pub. 1970 (San Francisco: City Lights, 1988), p. 61.
13. A. Matheron, Essence, 'Existence and Power', in Ethics 1: The Foundations of Proposition 16, in Y. Yovel, ed., *God and Nature. Spinoza's Metaphysics* (Netherlands: E.J. Brill, 1991), p. 24.
14. See letter 9 to Simon de Vries in A. Wolf ed. *The Correspondence of Spinoza* (London: George Allen and Unwin, 1928).
15. 1p11d2 suggests that a cause or reason must be assigned to each and everything for why it exists or does not exist. 2p8s2 informs us that of every existing thing there is a certain cause on account of which it exists. Add to this 2df2 where we have the definition of essence as that which when given the thing is necessarily posited and we can see the viability of linking self-cause with self-explanatory through the concept of essence.

16. J. Bennett, *A Study of Spinoza's Ethics* (Cambridge: Cambridge University Press, 1984), p. 64.
17. W. Kessler, 'A Note on Spinoza's Concept of Attribute', in M. Mandelbaum, ed., *Spinoza: Essays in Interpretation* (Illinois: Open Court, 1975), p. 191–4.
18. Delahunty actually lists ten possible objections. See Delahunty (1985) op. cit., pp. 116–17.
19. 'The intellect only reproduces objectively the nature of the forms it apprehends' (65).
20. According to Braugh, Deleuze's transcendental empiricism takes as its starting point the assertion that there is a difference between real difference and conceptual difference: the being of the sensible. He refers us to *Difference and Repetition*, p. 80. B. Braugh, 'Transcendental Empiricism: Deleuze's Response to Hegel', *Man and World* (25) 1992, pp. 133–48.
21. R. Cross, *Duns Scotus* (New York and Oxford: Oxford University Press, 1999), p. 43.
22. For Scotus the argument would be that if God can be identified with the external world then composition would be possible because composition in the external world is possible. But we know, through revelation, the divine simplicity and uniqueness of God.
23. R. Bogue, *Deleuze and Guattari* (London and New York: Routledge, 1989), p. 67.
24. Ebert argues that Sextus defined a sign as an antecedent in a conditional of a certain type and tied this to the consequent of the conditional. As a consequence something can be a sign for one person and not another and the interpretation of some phenomenon as sign was written into the very notion of the sign. This might be one way that Deleuze expects to straddle the objectivist and subjectivist divide. T. Ebert, 'Stoic Theory of Signs in Sextus Empiricus', in J. Annas, ed., *Oxford Studies in Ancient Philosophy*, vol. 5 (Oxford: Clarendon Press, 1987), pp. 86–9.
25. Outlines of Pyrrhonism, 11. 104, quoted in Ebert, ibid., p. 87.
26. Quoted in Ebert, ibid., p. 105.
27. May reasons that Deleuze offers an interpretation of meaning that invokes the Stoic distinction between bodies and 'incorporeal entities to construct an interpretation of meaning as an intersection between the effects of words and effects of things'. I fail to see how the notion of *lekta* helps here as the content of an idea is its bodily modification and this is secured by the parallelism. The theory of affects is separate from this. See T. May, 'The System and its Fracture: Gilles Deleuze on Otherness', *Journal of the British Society for Phenomenology*, vol. 24, no. 1 (1993), 7.
28. Sextus, Adv. Math. Viii 11, 12 quoted in W. Kneale and M. Kneale (1962) op. cit., p. 140.
29. For an insight into how the thought of 'intentional inexistence' connects Aristotle's *Objektiv* which is an object of perception and Brentano's intentional object, see R. Sorabji, 'From Aristotle to Brentano', in J. Annas (ed.), *Oxford Studies in Ancient Philosophy: Aristotle and the Later Tradition* (Oxford: Clarendon Press, 1991), pp. 245–8.
30. Diogenes Vitae VII 64. quoted in B. Mates, *Stoic Logic* (Berkeley, Los Angeles: University of California Press, 1961), p. 17.
31. Ibid., p. 19ff.

32. A.A. Long, *Hellenistic Philosophy: Stoics, Epicureans, Sceptics* (London: Duckworth, 1986), p. 71.
33. In *What is Philosophy?*, Deleuze and Guattari discuss the different uses of concepts in science and philosophy. Picking up Frege's own concerns regarding the possibility of definition, they extrapolate this problem of reference and discuss the contributing role played by the concept as function. p. 135ff. Their discussion there does not affect the general point here of explication and designation. Indeed they are keenly aware of the different extensions we are concerned with. It is indeed instructive that Deleuze is forced to grapple with this problem to maintain the strength of his overall argument. See J. Marks (1998) op. cit., p. 22 for a discussion of the distinction between the concept/philosophy pair and function/science pair.
34. See F.E. Peters (1967), op. cit., p. 112.
35. S. Rosen, *The Question of Being: a Reversal of Heidegger* (New Haven and London: Yale University Press, 1993), p. 69.
36. J. Heaton, 'Language Games, Expression and Desire in the work of Deleuze', *Journal of the British Society for Phenomenology*, vol. 24, 1, 1993, 81.
37. See R. Delahunty (1985) op. cit., p. 122 for a discussion of this analogy and Donagan's apposite criticisms.
38. Ibid., p. 149.
39. C. Boundas, 'Deleuze, Serialisation and Subject-Formation', in C. Boundas and D. Olkowski eds, *Deleuze and the Theatre of Philosophy* (New York and London: Routledge, 1994), p. 105.
40. Some might prefer to try this through the philosophy of Meinong. According to Meinong, although mental acts are real they do not always intend real objects but the meaning of the word is always the object that is intended. Real objects are either those which exist or could exist. Other objects include certain complexes and relations. While the former exist and are presented passively to the mind, higher objects are divided into objects which exist and those which merely subsist or obtain. For example, before the mind might be a and b as simple objects and ideas would reflect the real being of these objects (a and b). The formation of a and b into a complex whole (aRb) involves a relation, which itself must be connected to an object R. We now have three entities a, b and R which seem to form a complex whole, a fourth entity, and each idea must intend a simple object (a, b and R). An 'objective' is a state of affairs, that is, 'the election took place without incident'. Not only did this idea raise the problem of the nature of these 'objectives' but also seemed to turn all objects into 'objectives', that is, 'judgment that x is the case'. Due to Meinong's theory of complete and incomplete objects of intention, we find that there is no convincing way to argue that if x (a, b, c, d) and if a, b, c, d, are 'properties', and so intend objects which have being, we can apprehend the whole or the singular. And as this was our original problem I consider such avenues to be not worth exploring. For a clear and helpful account of this, see R. Grossman, *Meinong* (London: Routledge and Kegan Paul, 1974).
41. G. Frege, 'On Sense and Reference', in P. Geach and M. Black eds, *Translations from the Philosophical Writings of Gottlob Frege* (Basil Blackwell: Oxford, 1952), p. 57.
42. C. Thiel, *Sense and Reference in Frege's Logic* (Dordrecht-Holland: D. Reidel, 1965), p. 127.

43. Letter to Husserl, 6 Dec 1906 (VII/4 XIX/6) in G. Frege, *Philosophical and Mathematical Correspondence*, G. Gabriel, H. Hermes, F. Kambartel, C. Thiel and A. Verart, eds, trans., H. Kaal (Basil Blackwell: Oxford, 1980), p. 70.
44. Theil characterises this as the contamination of the semantic role with ontological status.
45. H. Sluga, *Gottlob Frege* (London: Routledge and Kegan Paul, 1980), p. 145.
46. 'The method of analytic geometry supplies us with a means of intuitively representing the values of a function for different arguments. If we regard the argument as the numerical value of the abscissa and the corresponding value of the function as the numerical value of the ordinate of a point, we obtain a set of points that presents itself to intuition (in ordinary cases) as a curve. Any point on the curve corresponds to an argument together with the associated value of the function'. G. Frege, 'Function and Concept', trans. P. Geach, in B. Mcguinness, ed., *Collected Papers on Mathematics, Logic and Philosophy* (Oxford: Blackwell, 1984), p. 141.
47. '(T)hat the extension of a concept is constituted in being, not by individuals, but by the concept itself i.e., by what is said of an object and brought under a concept', p. 224. 'The extension of a concept does not consist of objects falling under the concept in the way, e.g., that a wood consists of trees; it attaches to the concept and to this alone. The concept thus takes logical precedence of its extensions', p. 228, G. Frege, Elucidation of points in Schröder's Lectures, trans. P. Geach, in B. Mcguinness, ed. (1984), op. cit.
48. For example $x(x - 4) = x2 - 4x$.
49. See G. Currie, *Frege: an Introduction to his Philosophy* (Brighton: Harverster Wheatsheaf, 1982), p. 86. See also, letter to Husserl, 24 May 1891.
50. See letter 8, from Simon de Vries and Spinoza's replies and letter 9 and 10, in A. Wolf, ed., (1928), op. cit.
51. R. Carnap, *The Logical Foundations of Probability* (Routledge and Kegan Paul: London, 1951), p. 3.
52. For a discussion of the relationship between objective and logical possibility, see J. Coombs, 'Created Entities in Seventeenth-Century Scotism', in *The Philosophical Quarterly*, vol. 43, 173 (1993) 447–59.
53. Letter to Husserl, 24 May 1891, in G. Gabriel *et al.* eds (1980) op. cit., p. 61.
54. P. McGrath, 'The Refutation of the Ontological Argument', *The Philosophical Quarterly*, vol. 40, No. 159 (1990).
55. R. Descartes, *Philosophical Writings*, trans. and ed. Elizabeth Anscombe (Middlesex: Nelsons University Paperbacks, 1970), p. 103.
56. '(W)hen we attend to the immense power of this being, we shall be unable to think of its existence as possible without also recognising that it can exist by its own power; and we shall infer from this that this being does really exist and has existed from eternity, since it is quite evident by the natural light that what can exist by its own power always exists. So we shall come to understand that necessary existence is contained in the idea of a supremely powerful being, not by any fiction of the intellect, but because it belongs to the true and immutable nature of such a being that it exists'. R. Descartes, 'First Set of Replies', in *The Philosophical Writings of Descartes*, vol. II trans. J. Cottingham, R. Stoothoff and D. Murdoch (London and New York: Cambridge University Press, 1984), p. 85.

57. The corollary states that God is not only the cause of all things beginning to exist but also that they continue to exist – God is the cause of being (*causa essendi*) of the things. The argument is that when we consider the essence of particular things we discover that the essence includes neither existence nor duration.
58. J. Coombs (1993) op. cit., p. 457.
59. A. Kenny, *Descartes: a Study of His Philosophy* (New York: Random House, 1968), p. 162.
60. M. Wilson, *Descartes* (London: Routledge and Kegan Paul, 1978), p. 175–6.
61. Stoics believed that in the course of its transformation the cosmic fire creates the universe, destroys it, and re-creates it again in eternal cycle. It is no wonder that those taken with Nietzsche's theory, including the thesis of the Eternal Recurrence, retrace his steps through to their Greek roots.
62. D. Hahm, *The Origins of Stoic Cosmobiology* (Ohio: Ohio State University Press, 1977), p. 137.
63. Ibid., p. 71.
64. *Pneuma* is actually the second of the Stoic's four categories: substance or matter (*hypokeimenon*), the active principle of change and qualification (*pneuma*), state or disposition and relative disposition.
65. L. Gerson, op. cit, p. 159.
66. G. Deleuze, *Nietzsche and Philosophy*, trans. H. Tomlinson 1st pub. 1962 (London: Athlone Press, 1983), p. 186.
67. R. Delahunty (1985), op. cit., p. 115 but also see p. 124.

2 From the Infinite to the Finite

1. K. Ansell Pearson, *Germinal Life: the Difference and Repetition of Deleuze* (London and New York: Routledge, 1999), p. 15
2. R. Cross (1999) op. cit., p. 37.
3. See J. Bennett, (1984) op. cit., p. 30 for a discussion of causal rationalism and M. Wilson, Spinoza's Causal Axiom (*Ethics* 1, Axiom 4) in Y. Yovel (1991) op. cit., p. 133ff for a response.
4. M. Hardt (1993) op. cit., p. 69.
5. For a good and informative account of this see A. Donagan, 'Substance, Attribute and Mode', in *Spinoza, Ethics* 1, in Y. Yovel ed. (1991) op. cit., p. 10ff.
6. Because there is more than one attribute, an attribute cannot be a substance. This relies on the suppressed premise that there is only one substance. This itself requires the argument that substance cannot be in a causal (conceptual or material) relation with anything else (otherwise it would not be infinite and because substance is unlimited and infinite this would result in a contradiction).
7. For a discussion of the problem of mediate infinite modes, see E. Giancotti, on the Problem of Infinite Modes' in Y. Yovel, ed. (1991) op. cit., 105ff.
8. Y. Yovel, 'The Infinite Mode and Natural Laws in Spinoza', in Y. Yovel ed. (1991), op. cit., p. 93.
9. 'Its individuality is a function of, and subsequent to, individuating causal processes not a function of the unity or simple particularity of a 'this' or an 'I': it is a matter of intersecting series, like a mathematical point'. B. Baugh (1992), op. cit., p. 140

10. This would indicate an externalist position, such that what is thought, said or experienced is essentially dependent on aspects of world external to mind.
11. 'God's power is his essence' (1p34). 'From the necessity of the divine nature there must follow infinitely many things in infinitely many modes' (1p16). 'Whatever we conceive to be in God's power, necessarily exists' (1p35). 'God is the efficient cause not only of the existence of things but also of their essence' (1p25). 'The striving by which each thing strives to perserve in its being is nothing but the actual essence of the thing' (3p7). 'The striving by which each thing strives to preserve in its being involves no finite time, but an indefinite time' (3p8). 'God or substance consisting of infinite attributes, each of which expresses eternal and infinite essence, necessarily exists' (1p11). 'The essence of man does not involve necessary existence ... man thinks' (2ax1,2).
12. F. Haserot, 'Spinoza and the Status of Universals', *Philosophical Review* vol. 59, 1950, 480.
13. A. Balz, *Idea and Essence in Hobbes and Spinoza* (New York: AMS Press, 1967), p. 30.
14. For a clear and usable account of the relationship between the Idea and differential calculus in the later work, see J.M. Salankis, 'Idea and Destination', in P. Patton, ed., *Deleuze: Critical Reader* (Oxford: Blackwell, 1996), p. 57ff.
15. P. Macherey (1996) op. cit., p. 151.
16. '(T)he pernicious consequences, to which such a theory gives rise in practice, are at once evident. And this mere mathematical view, which identifies with the Idea one of its special stages viz., quantity, is no other than the principle of Materialism. Witness the history of the scientific modes of thought, especially in France since the middle of last century. Matter, in the abstract, is just what, though of course there is a form in it, has that form only as an indifferent and external attribute' *Hegel's Logic*, trans. W. Wallace (Oxford: Clarendon Press, 1975), para 99.
17. It should be noted that the exponent itself may be considered a quantum constituted by individual units, i.e., 7 is constituted by seven units, if one is subtracted then proposition 7 + 5 + 2 becomes, say, 6 = 2 + 5 and is false.
18. For a discussion of amongst other things the continuous and discrete magnitudes, see J.E. McTaggart, 'Hegel's Treatment of the Categories of Quantity', *Mind: A Quarterly Review of Psychology and Philosophy*, vol. X111 (1904), p. 180ff.
19. It is hard to miss the philosophical relevance of the idea of continuum from Leibniz through Russell, from the mathematics and the exposition of the philosophy of Leibniz, to more contemporary philosophy of mathematics.
20. The implication is that we can consider an essence of a mode as a term in the series. Deleuze is thus taken not only by Bergson but also by the influence of Reimann.
21. This example would find echoes within Meinong's theory of perception.
22. 'The essences are neither logical possibilities nor geometric structures; they are parts of power, that is degrees of physical intensity'. SPP 65.
23. H.F. Hallett, *Creation, Emanation and Salvation: a Spinozistic Study* (The Hague: Martinus Nijhoff, 1962), p. 43.
24. Such a refutation would impact not only on Deleuze's vitalism but also have ramifications for his appropriation of the Leibnizian continuum in

The Fold: Leibniz and the Baroque, 1st edn Les Editions Minuit 1988, trans. T. Conley (London: Athlone Press, 1993).

25. P. Macherey, 'From Action to Production of Effects', in Y. Yovel, ed. (1991), p. 164. He argues that Spinoza's use of immanent causality indicates a reversal of Cartesian causality in favour of Aristotelian ideas of causality.
26. A. Taylor, 'Some Inconsistenices in Spinozism', in R. Kennington, ed. (1980), op. cit., p. 196.
27. J. Bernardete, 'Spinozist Anomalies', ibid., p. 61.
28. Recall these arguments: 'the more perfections something has the more power, God has infinite perfections, God has infinite power of existence, God is omnipotent' and 'the more reality or perfection that belongs to the nature of some thing, the more power it has, the more forces tend towards its existence, God is infinitely perfect, God has infinite power of existing therefore God exists'.
29. Descartes used the possibility of conceivability to prove mind–body distinction and Kant used it prove the *a priori* nature of space and time. In a similar vein, Deleuze conflates psychological with logical necessity.
30. This seems to be the basis for the argument that modes are conceptually dependent on their attributes (196).
31. Duration and, in the case of modes of extension, figure and place – seem to beg the question, what, exactly is meant by extension?
32. The only secondary argument I can find is a Scotist argument that a finite being has power from itself but is caused to exist. Indeed, Deleuze does draw the Scotist distinction between an essence and the existence of an essence and grounds this distinction on the fact that the essence is caused to exist by God (194) but he says this means we can say that 'existence of essence' and 'being caused to be' are synonymous. Recall too that essence for Deleuze means a *res physica* and not a logical possibility.
33. The conceptual distinction between attributes marks something actual, idea has as much reality as cause of idea, etc.
34. We have already covered two main problem areas. The first is the move from one attribute to infinity of attributes to the Absolute. This is supposed to give the rational support for the claim that there is one substance and through other metaphysical arguments that substance is omnipotent. The second are the general criticisms of the Argument from Power. A third problem area was opened on the section on the attributes and involves the reification of the copula. We can now see its full effect.

3 The Weak Identity Thesis

1. The description of the former as substance and the latter as finite or particular things would not acknowledge two problems. The first is the problematic claim that one follows from but is not identical to the other. The second relates to the role and description of the immediate infinite mode. The immediate infinite mode of the attribute of Thought is the infinite intellect and that of the attribute of Extension is motion and rest.
2. E. Kaufman, 'Towards a Feminist Philosophy of Mind', in I. Buchanan and C. Colebrook, eds, *Deleuze and Feminist Theory* (Edinburgh: Edinburgh University Press, 2000), p. 128.

3. Thus, against Mullarkey, I argue that it is the logic of the argument that leads to the cybernetic appropriation of Deleuze. See J. Mullarkey (1999), op. cit., 65ff.
4. After an analysis of the problem, he concludes that 'sadly, then, Spinoza has not cut the Gordian knot of the mind/body problem. His stroke was more swift than sure; and his aim was distracted by too many other ambitions. The most important proposition of the Ethics is not a rigorously demonstrated theorem; it is an article of faith, or rather it is a creed in miniature'. R. Delahunty, (1984), op. cit., p. 204.
5. We have already observed an ambiguity between the claim that the mediate mode can be identified with the 'relations that govern the determination of the modes as existing' and the claim that the mediate mode 'is constituted by the actual finite mode'. The latter would be more in tune with Spinoza's notion that the mediate mode is the series of finite modes.
6. Here the notation follows Bennett's suggestion that because Spinoza describes the idea as idea of its object (bodily modification) it makes sense to use the shorthand idea (x) for 'content' and I(x) for idea of (modification).
7. God can have an idea of every reality ((p1) thought is an attribute of God) and whatever God can do, God does, therefore God has an idea of every reality. Bennett suggests that we should understand the first premise as meaning that the nature of the universe does nor rule out there being a mental counterpart of everything. It is logically possible that there is a mental counterpart of everything. This requires the *enthymeme* 'whatever is logically possible is true'. See J. Bennett (1984), op. cit., p. 133.
8. M. Della Rocca, *Representation and the Mind–Body Problem in Spinoza* (New York and Oxford: Oxford University Press, 1996), p. 19.
9. 'Whatever follows from the infinite nature of God follows also from the idea of God in the same order and the same connection'. In the note he expands this as 'thinking substance and extended substance are one and the same substance which is now comprehended through this and now that attribute'.
10. In SPP, Deleuze names this identity of connection 'isomorphism'.
11. 'He produces them in the same order in each, *and so* there is a correspondence between modes of different attributes'. See also 2p3.
12. In SPP, he names this identity of connection 'isonomy'.
13. See 2p7c: 'Hence it follows that God's power of thinking is equal to his actual power of acting; that is whatever follows formally from the infinite nature of God, follows also invariably objectively from the idea of God in the same order and connection'.
14. M. Della Rocca, 'Causation and Identity in Spinoza', *History of Philosophy Quarterly*, vol. 8, no. 3 (July 1991), 273 for the argument that even if we were to concede the principle of numerical identity this would not entail an identity of causal chains.
15. See for example Spinoza's admittance that he had not been able to write anything about these things in proper order. Letter 83 to E.W. Von Tschirnhaus, in A. Wolf ed. (1928) op. cit.
16. 1p7, 1p8, 1p15 and proof. The fact that there is only one substance would militate against the suggestion that the parts could themselves be substances. Spinoza also claims that parts to be parts would have to be substances.

17. Curley argues that modes are the wrong logical type to be related in this predicative relation as they are definitely modes and not qualities or properties.
18. Bennett raises the same question with reference to Spinoza's account of extension when he asks 'if we start merely with the concepts of "region" and "impenetrability" we cannot answer the question "not penetrable *by what*?" He believes that we can develop a physical theory alongside a spatio-temporal metric.
19. Which it cannot be, due to the monism.
20. C. Huenemann, 'Predicative Interpretations of Spinoza's Divine Extension', *History of Philosophy Quarterly*, vol. 14, no. 1 (Jan 1997), 53ff.
21. See S. Hampshire, *Spinoza: an Introduction to His Philosophical Thought*, 1st edn, 1951 (Harmondsworth: Penguin, 1987), pp. 64–70
22. For example, L. Shipper, *Spinoza's Ethics: the View from Within* (New York: Peter Lang, 1993), p. 13 and Gleik's discussion of Smale, Lorenz and Poincaré and the complicated relationship between differential equations and the understanding of chaos and stability, see J. Gleick, *Chaos: Making a New Science* (London: Penguin, 1987).
23. J. Bennett, (1984), op. cit., p. 55.
24. One might also see this as Deleuze's attempt to explain the movement from attribute to immediate mode of the attribute.
25. C. Huenemann (1997) op. cit., p. 65.
26. 'X is part of Y *in the weak sense* just in case if Y were annihilated X would be annihilated (and, if we want only proper parts, X is not identical with Y)', ibid.
27. When a number of bodies, whether of the same or different size are constrained by other bodies to press upon one another; or if they move, whether with the same degree or different degrees of speed, so that they communicate their motions to each other in a fixed manner – we shall say that those bodies are united with one another and that they all together compose one body or individual, which is distinguished from other individuals'.
28. 'Descartes elects to individuate bodies on the basis of their motions as wholes ... but he is then left with the unfortunate consequence that a body which ceases to move is no longer individuated from the matter that surrounds it by individuating bodies not on the basis of their motions as wholes, but on the basis of the ratio of motion and rest among their parts, Spinoza avoids this unfortunate consequence', C. Huenemann (1997) op. cit., p. 70.
29. Deleuze refers us to Kant's notion of space and time as *a priori* intuitions, space being that of outer sense and time that of inner. This seems singularly unhelpful, apart from the arguments against the description of these as a priori intuitions, Kant's arguments are steps within his subjective idealism presuming, or leading to the deduction of, a transcendental subject (214).
30. There is an obvious problem here. If the body is subject to external determination then an inside to the body is implied. This, in turn, erases the distinction between the simple and complex body.
31. On this point, see letter from E.W. Von Tschirnhaus (65) and Spinoza's reply, letter 66 in A. Wolf, ed. (1928), op. cit..
32. The terms formal and objective being have routes through Descartes back to, yet departing from, Aristotle. A. Donagan (1988), op. cit., p. 36.
33. J. Bennett (1984) op. cit., p. 153.

34. 'The same attributes that are formally distinguished in God are objectively distinguished in the idea of God', p. 120.
35. This would be to follow in Spinoza's footsteps, 2p5: 'The formal being of ideas acknowledges God as its cause in so far as he is considered as a thinking thing and not as he is explained by some other attribute: that is, the ideas, not only attributes of God but also of particular things, do not acknowledge those things of which they are the ideas i.e. objects perceived as their efficient causes but God himself as far as he is a thinking thing'.
36. 'The ideas of particular things (i.e. modes) which do not exist must be comprehended in the infinite idea of God in the same way as the formal essences of particular things (modes) are contained in the attributes of God'; see also 1p8s2, 2p8c, 2p45s, 5p29s.
37. R.E. Aquila, 'Identity of Thought and Object in Spinoza', *Journal of the History of Philosophy*, vol. 16 (1978), 281.
38. Ibid., 279.
39. 'If it be true that every idea that participates in the power of thinking belongs formally to the attribute of Thought, then, conversely, every idea that belongs to the attribute of Thought is the object of an idea that participates in the power of Thinking'.
40. See F.E. Peters, *Greek Philosophical Terms: a Historical Lexicon* (New York and London: New York University Press, 1967), pp. 29, 199.
41. The content of the idea is irrelevant here.
42. In SPP the Identity of Being is named 'isology'.
43. R.J. Delahunty (1984) p. 197.

4 The Body and its Passions

1. Here I am following the example of Mason who uses the term 'realm' as way to avoid the problem of the distinction *in re* and in *de dicto*, which is our problem of weakened sense of real distinction. R. Mason, 'Spinoza on Modality', *The Philosophical Quarterly*, vol. 36, no. 144, July 1986, 311–42.
2. This work is commonly referred to as *The Emandation of the Intellect*. Emandation connotes correction or improvement. It was both early and unfinished, although some have claimed that it was his first published work. Deleuze's description of the structure is supported by Feldman. See B. Spinoza, *Ethics, Treatise on The Emandation of the Intellect and Selected Letters*, trans. S. Shirley, edited and introduced by S. Feldman (Indianapolis: Hackett Publishing Company, 1992).
3. K. Jaspers (1974) op cit., p. 9.
4. For the meaning of this term see C.B. Macpherson, *The Political Theory of Possessive Individualism: Hobbes to Locke*, 1st pub. 1962 (Oxford: Oxford University Press, 1983).
5. Gatens argues that Deleuze presents a 'cartography' of powers of the body rather than a natural biology. I argue that the latter is determined not merely by the former but also by the metaphysical argument accounting for (a) power (b) singularity. M. Gatens, 'Through a Spinozist Lens: Ethology, Difference, Power', in P. Patton, ed. (1996), op. cit. 162ff.

6. These seeds grew most notably into the account of psychopathology in Deleuze and Guattari's AO.
7. He calls the first level 'the physics of intensive force', the second level 'the physics of extensive quantity' and the third level 'the physics of force'.
8. Deleuze refers to this as the first modal triad.
9. This is the second modal triad. It is worth noting here that 'power' can be translated as *pouvoir* or *puissance*. Both have the same origin: the Latin verb 'posse' (to be capable of, to have the strength to). *Pouvoi*r is the infinitive of the verb and according to Littré's definition, 'merely denotes the action' while *puissance* (the participle) designates 'something lasting' and 'permanent'. One has the *puissance* to do something and one exercises the *pouvoir* to do it. An English equivalent might be 'potential' and 'act'. For the use of these terms in political philosophy, see discussion in D.D. Raphael, *Problems of Political Philosophy* (London: Macmillan, 1976), pp. 66–9.
10. It might be helpful to see much of this as a discussion between Deleuze and Aristotle of the Metaphysics: for example, bk 5: 3:15 on organic unity and bk 11: 1: 10 on forms and perishability. R. McKeon ed., *The Basic Works of Aristotle* (New York and London: Random House, 1968).
11. In 3p4d, Spinoza links necessary properties to the essence of a body.
12. This thesis is pursued by Wienpahl (1979), op. cit.
13. A separate criticism is that for the necessitarianism of the system to be retained Deleuze must justify how any changes can occur at all and especially occur without changing the identity of the modes – and this is to accept that the whole can remain constant while there are modal alterations.
14. Except a retrospective judgement; 'that body was destroyed, therefore its necessary properties or structure must have been compromised'.
15. Deleuze compares the relation of God–mode (nature–properties) to mode–alterations (nature–properties), 219.
16. Derivative 4p39d.
17. If we take arrangement of the body's extensive parts to be its nature then this would be quite consistent with Spinoza's claim that the definition of thing involves nothing and expresses nothing but the nature of the thing defined (1p8s2).
18. This could suggest a vitalist thesis but rather begs the question of materialism.
19. Deleuze's equivalent of Spinoza's remark that the proportion of motion and rest can be expressed as a fraction.
20. Thus avoiding modal problems associated with possible worlds.
21. An existing mode has for its part, an essence that is identical to a degree of power; as such it has an ability to be affected, 218.
22. Modes are part of divine power, singular parts, intensive quantities or irreducible degrees. 227.
23. It also fits neatly with Deleuze's explanatory rationalism. The question 'why this movement and this shape' is answered by appeal to the God as the *Principle of Sufficient Reason* and the necessity of the system therein deduced.
24. Bennett offers suicide as a counterexample.
25. Spinoza distinguishes between 'contrary' and 'different', i.e. a different body is one which does not share an attribute.

26. An ancillary criticism is that because the universe is unique, a single individual, there must be a deeper way in which all parts are compatible even if they appear to be in disagreement.
27. When explained by nature of affected body then affections are active and themselves actions. 219.
28. This is the same point made by Spinoza d2, 3p6 and 3p7.
29. Bennett clarifies appetite as the thesis that appetite for x is to be analysed in terms of intrinsic state that causes one to move towards x. J. Bennett (1984), op. cit., p. 222.
30. Hampshire attempts to answer this point through the principle that self-maintenance could be involved in concept of individual. 'This striving towards cohesion and the preservation of its own identity constitutes the essence of any particular thing... . Its character and individuality depends on its necessarily limited power of self-maintenance; it can be distinguished as a unitary thing with a recognisable constancy of character insoafar as, although a system of parts, it succeeds in maintaining its own characteristic coherence and balance of parts'. This is circular. S. Hampshire (1987), op. cit., p. 67.
31. 'The initial thought by means of which we become aware of something does not differ from the second thought by means of which we become aware that we are aware of it, any more than this second thought differs from the third thought by means of which we become aware that we are aware'. AT VII 599/16–20, quoted A. Donagan, (1988), op. cit., p. 39.
32. *Effectus cognitio a cognitione causae dependet, & eandem involvit*, 1ax4.
33. J. Bennett (1984), op. cit., p. 129.
34. It must be noted that this variation would mean that the causal axiom could no longer prop up the parallelism.
35. The three stages outlined by Deleuze are those presented by Spinoza: opinion and imagination, knowledge through common notions and reason and intuitive science. The same stages can be found in *Maimonides' Guide for the Perplexed*: imaginative knowledge (of particular, corporeal things), scientific or philosophical knowledge (of universal and incorporeal things), and prophetic knowledge (of incorporeal particulars).
36. J. Annas, *Hellenistic Philosophy of Mind* (Berkeley: University of California Press, 1992), p. 70.
37. For example, Chryssipus argued that the imprint could not be a copy of the external object and so developed the idea that perception could be analysed in terms of the reception of content and its articulation in linguistic form.
38. For an informative discussion of Deleuze and Bergson, see P. Douglas (1992), op. cit.
39. For instance he claims that we have ideas of external objects. This implies that the relationship is direct rather than indirect and that there is room for representational efficacy.
40. The term 'explicare' can mean to explain or unfold.
41. J. Bennett, (1984), op. cit., p. 157.
42. Spinoza encounters similar difficulties when he discusses the child affirming the presence of a winged horse. The move is made from 'imagining x as present' to 'regarding x as present'.
43. 2p24d.

44. Because alterations can be identified with properties we can see why Deleuze both wishes to draw an analogy between mode and its properties and God and the modes with one important proviso, 218.
45. An emotion is a qualified affect: 'the socio-linguistic fixing of the quality of experience. Emotion is qualified intensity, the conventional, consensual point of insertion of intensity into semantically and semiotically formed progressions, into narrativizable action-reaction circuits, into function and meaning'. B. Massumi, 'The Autonomy of Affect', P. Patton ed. (1996), op. cit., p. 220.
46. This is similar to Hume's notion of impressions of reflection and ideas of those impressions.
47. He also writes that an active affection asserts essence, 225.
48. cf. Leibniz.
49. There are then mechanical changes, changes in a mode, dynamic changes, alterations *vis* capacity to be affected and metaphysical changes in the essence itself, 225.
50. I believe that this ambiguity comes directly from Spinoza who claims that an affect is a state of the body and an idea of that affect, 3d3.
51. According to Bennett this would be a mistranslation as the terms are clearly meant to contrast pleasant and unpleasant states of mind (and body). White and Curley agree with Deleuze that *laetitia* should be translated as joy. Bennett considers this even further off track than his own attempt. He points to the German which defines the former as lust and the latter as unlust, p. 253.
52. This apparent equivocation was also noted by Moore against Mill where the former criticised the latter for confusing means and ends: 'a pleasant thought' with 'a thought of pleasure'. Here again, we see the problem of cognitive apprehension.
53. Again we can see the ambiguity at play: pleasure either is the increase in vitality or it causes the increase.
54. 'passive affections ... involve some degree, however low, of our power of action'.
55. 3p9s.
56. This is very close to Spinoza: 'which therefore is nothing else that the essence of man, from the nature of which all things which help in his preservation necessarily follow; and therefore man is determined for acting in this way', 3p9. This however raises problem of giving consistent sense to the concept of desire, 3p37d – desire is teleological; 3p56d – desire is so broad as to cover all affects; 3p57d – desire as active (explained by intrinsic nature).
57. 'For the joy is added to the desire', 240.
58. Deleuze confuses the issue by not clarifying the transattributive nature of the term feeling. 239.
59. See 3p33d, 3p48, 5p15d.
60. His reference to 3p37 merely confuses the matter because the proposition states only that the individual would wish to preserve the pleasurable state, which is quite different.
61. For Spinoza, memory is the recalling of the causal chain according to how the body was originally modified: 'each passes from the thought of one thing to the thought of another according as habit has arranged the images

of things in the body'. This shows a remarkable convergence with Hume and maybe explains one of Deleuze's connections between Spinoza and Hume, 2p17, 2p18.

62. Here Deleuze follows Spinoza's example by attempting to provide an internal mark of adequacy while escaping the problem of external reference.
63. This seems to be a departure from the *Ethics* where Spinoza implies that only where there is first of all an adequate idea will that adequacy be repeated. Deleuze thus avoids the Spinozistic difficulty in explaining how we 'know' the difference between the adequate and inadequate, truth and falsity, given that 'falsity has no form' and the assumption that in some sense falsehood must be self-disclosing.
64. Same point is made by Barker, 'Notes on the Second Part of Spinoza's Ethics', *Mind*, XLVII (1938), 418.
65. See letter 60 to Walter Von Tschirnhaus, in A. Wolf (1928), op. cit.
66. A common notion is an idea of that which is common to everything and which is equally in part as in the whole.
67. See D. Savan, 'Spinoza and Language', *The Philosophical Review*, 1965, p. 215.
68. A common notion is defined as a biological idea relating to the functions of an organism, 278.
69. He also favourably quotes Spinoza's belief that common notions internally *determine* the mind to understand the agreement of things, as well as their differences and oppositions, 276.
70. I pick up the anti-Cartesian and representational thrust of Deleuze's argument in Chapter 6.
71. 'Spinoza's nominalism places reality not merely in simple particulars but in individuals; and an individual may well be a global entity with certain features that characterise it overall, that is, are universally present in it. This non-generic universality does not reside in classes but belongs to (and helps to constitute) singular entities known as totalities. Spinoza, of course, was the philosopher of totality par excellence', in Y. Yovel (1991), op. cit., p. 84–5.
72. F. Haserot (1950), op. cit., p. 489.
73. J. Bennett (1984), op. cit., p. 182.
74. Delahunty looks at similar arguments in the *Ethics* and suggests that common notions may have to be taken to be *a priori*. R. Delahunty (1985), op. cit., p. 75.
75. Spinoza describes this as knowledge from 'vagrant experience' (*cognitionem ab experienta vaga*).
76. Opinion or imagination.
77. 'If we separate emotions or affects, from the thought of an external cause, and join them to other thoughts, then the love or hate, toward the external object is destroyed, as are the vacillations of mind arising from these affects', 5p2. It is interesting to note that Freud would describe this as a form of psychopathology.
78. The more we understand things as necessary, the less we feel the strength or intensity of passions rooted in imagination.
79. Spinoza makes the same point: 4d8, 4p24, 3p3.
80. For instance: 'passive affections are opposed to active ones because they are not explained by our power of action. Yet, involving the limitations of our

essence, they are in some sense involved in the lowest degree of that power', 246.

81. This also seems to contradict the assertion that thinking is automatic.
82. J. Bennett (1984), op. cit., p. 216.
83. For a discussion on the explanatory potential of goals see J. Bennett (1979), *Linguistic Behaviour,* 1st pub. 1976 (Cambridge: Cambridge University Press, 1979)
84. I believe this to be true even though he reasserts the role of formal and objective being and appeals to the two powers of God to justify the idea of distinctness and identity.
85. We continued by arguing that substance is fully conceived or explained through the attributes, that which is self-explanatory is self-caused, substance is self caused.
86. We continued this line of argument by saying that the attribute can be understood to be a designating term which can itself be converted into an object of semantic investigation. This then allowed us to say that substance is that which is designated through the complete set of descriptions.
87. This followed from the argument that God is self-caused and can and must bring about infinite things.
88. G. Deleuze, DR, p. 123.
89. If I (x) is a thought then x will be corresponding cerebral event and the idea will have as its content a brain state. We thus lose the sense of 'aboutness' or ideational referential component.
90. '(I)n proportion as a body is more capable than others of doing many things at once, or being acted on in many ways at once, so its mind is more capable than others of perceiving many things at once. And in proportion as the actions of a body depend more on itself alone ... so its mind is more capable of understanding distinctly', 2p13s.
91. See letter 65 and Spinoza's response, in A. Wolf ed. (1928), op. cit.
92. 2p13, 2p9, 2p19, 2p15.
93. 'What I mean by the concept of a person is the concept of a type of entity such that both predicates ascribing states of consciousness and predicates ascribing corporeal characteristics, a physical situation etc are equally applicable to a single individuals of that single type'. P.F. Strawson, *Individuals: an Essay in Descriptive Metaphysics,* 1st pub. 1959 (London: Methuen, 1969), p. 102.
94. R.J. Delahunty (1984), op. cit., p. 190.

5 The State of Nature

1. R. Bradotti, 'Discontinuous Becomings. Deleuze on the Becoming-Woman of Philosophy', *Journal of the British Society for Phenomenology,* 24, 1 (Jan 1993), 44ff.
2. G.W.F. Hegel, *Lectures on the History of Philosophy,* 1st pub. 1892–96, trans, E.S. Haldane and F.H. Simson (Lincoln and London: University of Nebraska Press, 1995), vol. 3 p. 287.
3. J. Bennett (1984), op. cit., p. 11.

4. This idea of God beyond representation reappears in contemporary negative theology where the term is more of a marker of Otherness. For example, see H. Armstrong, 'Negative Theology, Myth and Incarnation', in J. O'Meara, ed., *Neoplatonism and Christian Thought* (Norfolk: Suny, 1982), pp. 213–22. See also D. Cuppit, *After All: Religion without Alienation* (London: SCM Press, 1994).
5. On simplicity in Jewish, Christian and Islamic theology, see D. Burrell, *Knowing the Unknowable God* (Bloominton IN: Notre Dame, 1986).
6. J.P. Kenny, *Mystical Monotheism: a Study in Ancient Platonic Theology* (Hanover, NH: University Press of New England, 1991), p. 101.
7. I would suggest parallels here with Kant's resolution of the Third Antinomy in his *Critique of Pure Reason* where the transcendental self is described as free because it cannot be intuited and is therefore not subject to causal laws of determinism. I. Kant's *Critique of Pure Reason*, trans. Norman Kemp Smith (London: Macmillan, 1983), p. 409ff.
8. And joy may or may not be identified as this increase in activity.
9. This is reminiscent of the Plotinian conception of the relationship between matter/form and the principle of evil.
10. Combination of nominalism and the claim that where I (x) x, x only indirectly involves mode y but knowledge of x depends on knowledge of the causal sequence.
11. 'They indicate the state of our body primarily and the presence of the external body secondarily'. These indications form the basis of an entire order of conventional signs (language) which is already characterised by its equivocity, that is by its variability of the associative chains into which the indications enter'. SPP, 106 where reference is made to II p. 18s.
12. Sadness may simply be a decrease in activity through the system and an idea which has as its content the physical modification.
13. This is not identical to Hume's account because for Hume the problem was to explain the idea of cause and necessity given that our impressions are only of sequential events.
14. This echoes Nietzsche's position on guilt and punishment and contracts premised on (the belief in) stable identity, for example, F. Nietzsche, *Genealogy of Morals*, trans. and ed. W. Kaufmann, (Toronto: Random House, 1969), 1:13, p. 45.
15. This explanation is very similar to Kant's explanation for the errors in cosmological speculation found in I. Kant, *Critique of Pure Reason*, op cit., 'The Ideal of Pure Reason', p. 485 ff.
16. This is to repeat Spinoza's own claim that (good) and (bad) are nothing but modes of the imagination by which the imagination is variously affected'. 1appendix.
17. This echoes Aristotle's account of the practical syllogism. See Aristotle, *The Nichomachean Ethics*, trans. D. Ross (Oxford and New York: Oxford University Press, 1980), pp. 48–78. M. Nussbaum, *Aristotle's De Motu Animalium* (Princeton: Princeton University Press, 1978). A. Kenny, *Aristotle's Theory of the Will* (London: Duckworth, 1979), p. 111–32. D. Wiggins, 'Deliberation and Practical Reason', in R. Rorty, ed., *Essays on Aristotle's Ethics* (London and Berkeley: University of California Press, 1980), p. 221ff.

18. As Bennett rightly says, if universal ideas are to serve as the basis of our value judgements, some subset of them must do the work: a hydrocephalic baby is good (a good example of a hydrocephalic baby) and a healthy baby bad (a bad example of a hydrocephalic baby). J. Bennett (1984), op. cit., p. 291.
19. J. Bennett (1984), op. cit., p. 289.
20. 1appendix.
21. The Stoical influence on Expressionism would not help us to solve the problem of mental content because the imprint, in Stoical epistemology, is both a mental and a physical event but the mental event, has as its propositional content, the external object. See J. Annas, 'Stoic Epistemology', in S. Everson, ed., *Epistemology* (Cambridge: Cambridge University Press, 1990), p. 186.
22. Even if we were to argue that 'God' functions as an *entia rationis,* which we presume has independent content, we would still beg the question.
23. This ought to be contrasted with the accounts of Feuerbach and Marx. See L. Stepelevich, 'The Young Hegelians: From Feuerbach to Schmidt', in S. Glendinning (1999), op. cit., p. 345ff.
24. SPP, 107.
25. D. Savan (1965), op. cit., p. 223.
26. 4 preface at 208.
27. J. Bennett (1984), op. cit., p. 296.
28. Cicero commented that '(this principle) does not admit of doubt; for it is fixed in our very nature and is grasped so firmly by each man's senses that if anyone tries to speak against it he is not heard', quoted J. Barnes, *The Toils of Scepticism,* 1st pub. 1990 (Cambridge: Cambridge University Press, 1994), p. 135.
29. Although the composition of relations give rise to the capacity, Deleuze quotes Leibniz approvingly and implies that we need to invert this causal law and hold that 'the mechanical laws presuppose an inner nature in the bodies they govern' (229).
30. See G.H.R Parkinson, 'On the Power and Freedom of Man', in M. Mandelbaum and E. Freeman eds, (1975), op. cit., pp. 27–31.
31. For a clear discussion on the open question argument posed by Moore to Mill, see W.D. Hudson, *Modern Moral Philosophy*, 1st pub. 1970 (London: Macmillan – now Palgrave Macmillan, 1983), pp. 69–84.
32. 'We can only speak of the becoming-Übermensch of human beings, of the process of accumulating strength and exerting mastery outside the limits of external impositions. Nietzsche called this process of becoming-Übermensch 'life enhancement'. A. Schrift, 'Between Church and State: Nietzsche, Deleuze and the Genealogy of Psychoanalysis', *International Studies in Philosophy*, XXIV, 2 (1992), 45.
33. 'An ethological evaluation will individuate according to principles of composability, sets of fast or slow combinations, the range of affects and degrees of affectability'. M. Gatens (1996) op. cit., p. 167.
34. Imitation of affects concerns how people respond to the emotions of others; see J. Bennett (1984), op. cit., p. 280.
35. 'A joyful chain may always, furthermore, be interrupted by destruction or even simply by the sadness of the loved object itself'. However, by dint of argument, if that occurred the first body would be compelled to destroy the loved object', 244.

36. 'For man in principle agrees in nature with man; man is absolutely or truly useful to man'.
37. Spinoza argued that those who commit suicide are weak spirited, conquered by external causes repugnant to their natures.
38. A. Armstrong, 'Some Reflections on Deleuze's Spinoza: Composition and Agency', in K. Ansell Pearson, ed., *Deleuze and Philosophy: the Difference Engineer* (London and New York: Routledge, 1997), p. 45.
39. J.J. Rousseau, *The Social Contract*, trans. M. Cranston (London: Penguin, 1968), 1:3 p. 52.
40. This is a move similar to that made by Weber in his discussion of legitimacy. See A. Giddens, *Studies in Social and Political Theory* (London, Hutchinson, 1979), p. 92.
41. TTP, xvi 23, quoted E. Curley, 'Kissinger, Spinoza and Genghis Khan', in D. Garrett, ed., *The Cambridge Companion to Spinoza* (Cambridge: Cambridge University Press, 1996), p. 325.
42. T. Hobbes, *Leviathan*, C.B. MacPherson ed., 1st pub. 1968 (London: Penguin, 1984), 1:11, p. 161–2.
43. See also Spinoza, TTP iv, 18–25.
44. Deleuze's equivocation concerning the role of reason is similar to Hobbes' account where there are two kinds of striving for power: an irrational striving, which is natural appetite of the individual and the rational striving of those who would be content with a moderate power but find they must strive for more to protect what they have.
45. For a clear account of the problem of the hypothetical contract, see C. Pateman, *The Problem of Political Obligation: a Critique of Liberal Theory*, 1st pub. 1979 (Cambridge, Polity Press, 1985).
46. I say categorical because only this would be consistent with Deleuze's necessitarianism.
47. E. Curley (1996), op. cit., p. 320.
48. Ibid., p. 321 for Curley's argument.
49. Deleuze quotes TP xvi and P ii, iv.
50. M. Gatens (1996) op. cit., p. 164.
51. The right to judgement is abandoned but the power of knowing, thinking or feeling remains inalienable, i.e. through the parallelism modes of body and modes of mind are necessarily isomorphic, the reproduction of the form of idea I (I (x)) x is automatic and participates in attribute of Thought.
52. See *Ethics*, 4p28, 4p36: 'The human mind has ideas from which it perceives itself, its own body and external bodies as actually existing. And so it has adequate knowledge of God's eternal and infinite essence of God. From this we see that God's infinite essence and his eternity are known to all', 2p47d and s.
53. SPP, 21–2.
54. Preface 4.
55. We are reminded of Sartre's footnote concerning the possibility of radical conversion and authentic being as well as Kant's assertion that the act of synthesis is a mystery occurring deep in the soul. J.P. Sartre, *Being and Nothingness: an Essay on Phenomenological Ontology*, trans. H. Barnes 1st pub. Gallimard, 1943 (London: Methuen, 1972), p. 412. I. Kant, CPR, A73.
56. 'A person's interest in health ... would in fact be one of his interests, even if he mistakenly believed the contrary, and even if he wanted ill health and decay

instead of good health and vitality. In regard to this particular interest, at least, there may be a correspondence between interest and want, but the existence of the former is not dependent upon, nor derivative from, the existence of the latter'. J. Feinberg, *Harm to Others* (New York; Oxford University Press, 1984), p. 42; quoted in S. Lukes, *Individualism* (Oxford: Basil Blackwell, 1973), p. 6.

57. M. Frede, 'Stoics and Skeptics on Clear and Distinct Impressions', in M. Burnyeat, ed., *The Skeptical Tradition* (Berkeley: University of California Press, 1983), p. 69.
58. L. Dumont, quoted in S. Lukes (1973), op. cit., p. 74.

6 The Blessed State of Reason

1. D. Garratt, 'Spinoza's Ethical Theory', in D. Garret ed. (1996), op. cit., p. 269.
2. 5p3.
3. 2p40s2: modes as 'participating in' their attributes. See also 5p 4.
4. 3p58 has it that the mind experiences pleasure insofar as it conceives adequate ideas: 'pleasure from the fact that man contemplates himself and his power of activity' – *acquiescentia in se ipso*.
5. This is taken from the 'Treatise on the Emendation of the Intellect', in *Ethics, Treatise on The Emandation of the Intellect and Selected Letters*, trans. S, Shirley; S. Feldman, ed. (Indianapolis and Cambridge: Hackett Publishing Company, 1992), p. 233.
6. 'The more we understand singular things, the more we understand God', 5p24.
7. J. Bennett (1984), op. cit., p. 364.
8. 2p40s2.
9. M. Wilson, Spinoza's Theory of Knowledge, in D. Garret, ed. (1996), op. cit., p. 120.
10. 'To what extent are ideas of the second and third kinds the same ideas? Are they differentiated only by their function or use? The problem is a complex one. The most universal common notions do definitely coincide with ideas of attributes. As common notions they are grasped in the general function they exercise in relation to existing modes. As ideas of the third kind, they are considered in their objective essence, and insofar as they objectively contain modal essences', n. 34, p. 398, Exp.
11. 5p32d.
12. M. Greene, Spinoza: a Collection of Essays (New York: Garden City, 1973), p. 122.
13. That said, there are certain similarities with Kant's faculties of imagination, understanding and reason.
14. Y. Yovel, *Spinoza and Other Heretics* (Princeton, NJ: Princeton University Press, 1989), p. 156.
15. If I assert one proposition, claiming to know it by intuition, you can assert another, claiming to know that by intuition. And where do we go from there? It would seem that 'here ends the argument and begins the fight'': J. Hospers, *An Introduction to Philosophical Analysis*, 1st pub. 1953 (London: Routledge and Kegan Paul, 1973), p. 137.
16. This would be a rejection of Spinoza's causal thesis such that in order to have an adequate idea (x) one must have knowledge of the causal sequence

of modifications or perfect causal knowledge. Instead, from 2p45, 'singular things (p. 15) cannot be conceived without God; but because ... they have God for a cause, insofar as he is considered under the attribute of which the things themselves are modes, the ideas of them (by 1ax4) must necessarily involve the concept of their attribute, that is the eternal and infinite essence of God'. The implication of 1ax4 then is that for knowledge, one must have a grasp of causal relations, the attributes, their conceptual distinctness, the infinite modes and (therefore) of God.

17. This description of faculties and stages of knowledge properly worked out in his work on Kant's critical philosophy. See R. Meerbote, 'Deleuze on the Systematic Unity of Critical Philosophy', *Kant Studies* (1986), vol. 77, 347–52.
18. We must remember that the idea can never actually represent the external object as the ideational content is (of) the physical modification itself. At best there is an indirect representational facility and even that is obscure.
19. There are unmistakable parallels between this assertion and Hegel's explanation for the first step and second stages in the Self–Other relationship. These ideas from the *Phenomenology of Spirit* were repeated by Sartre in *Being and Nothingness* and used to explain the pre-reflective drive against contingency.
20. J. Bennett (1984), op. cit., p. 366.
21. We ought to ask here whether t is the case that as God intuits himself does that mean that God too experiences an affect.
22. For discussions on the distinction between ethics premised on care and compassion and Rights-based morality, see M.J. Larrabee, ed., *An Ethics of Care: Feminist and Interdisciplinary Perspectives* (London and New York: Routledge, 1993). See also G. Howie, 'Gender Roles', in R. Chadwick, ed., *Encyclopedia of Applied Ethics*, vol. 2 (1998), 373–4.
23. R. Harland, *Superstructuralism, the Philosophy of Structuralism and post-Structuralism* (London and New York: Methuen, 1987), p. 154.
24. See, for example, B. Croce *Aesthetic*, trans. D. Ainslie (London: 1922). R. G. Collingwood, *The Principles of Art* (Oxford: Oxford University Press, 1938), esp. pp. 130–5.
25. Wollheim clarifies this connection and claims that 'language is regarded as expressive if and only if it displays certain characteristics that in the first instance pertain to behaviour'. R. Wollheim, *On Art and the Mind: Essays and Lectures* (London: Allen Lane, 1973), p 85. This distinction reflected an eighteenth-century division between expressing and asserting: a distinction that Deleuze does not maintain.
26. J. Hospers (1973), op. cit., p. 138.
27. See letter 8, Simon de Vries and Spinoza's reply, letters 9 and 10, in A. Wolf, ed. (1928), op. cit.
28. See letter 60, in A. Wolf ed. (1928), op. cit. and 1df6: 'By God I understand a being absolutely infinite, that is, a substance consisting of an infinite attributes, of which each one expresses an eternal and infinite essence', 1df6. '(B)ut if something is absolutely infinite, whatever expresses essence and involves no negation pertains to its essence', 1df6E.
29. D. Raidner, 'Spinoza's Theory of Ideas', *The Philosophical Review*, LXXX (1971), 343.
30. See A. Gerwith, 'Clearness and Distinctness in Descartes', *Philosophy*, XVIII (1943), 17–36.

31. For a discussion of the inner object theory of perception in relation to philosophical problems concerning representation see R. Rorty, *Philosophy and the Mirror of Nature* (Oxford: Basil Blackwell, 1980), esp. pp. 131–213.
32. C.D. Broad, *Kant*, ed. C. Lewy (Cambridge: Cambridge University Press, 1978), p. 14.
33. I take it this is Walker's position. R.C.S. Walker, *Kant* (London: Routledge and Kegan Paul, 1982).
34. 'If I say, for instance, 'All bodies are extended', this is an analytic judgement. For I do not require to go beyond the concept which I connect with 'body' in order to find extension as bound up with it. To meet with this predicate I have merely to analyse the concept, that is, to become conscious to myself of the manifold which I always think in that concept. The judgement is therefore analytic. But when I say, 'All bodies are heavy' the predicate is something quite different from anything that I think in the mere concept of body in general; and the addition of such a predicate therefore yields a synthetic judgement. Judgements of experience, as such, are one and all synthetic', I. Kant, CPR:B11, 12.
35. See T.E. Wilkerson, *Kant's 'Critique of Pure Reason': a Commentary for Students* (Oxford: Clarendon Press, 1976), pp. 203–5. The problem with trying to reframe Kant's argument in these terms is that it relies on us being able to say, 'I can conceive of this in no other way'. For example, arguments concerning the nature of time and space depend on us assenting to the proposition that it is *inconceivable* that objects can be thought outside space, that idea of spatial relations precede idea of space as a whole. The ambiguity over the role and function of 'conceivability' concerns the very point of the relationship between psychology and logic, between that which is 'merely' synthetic and that which is 'necessary' in a stronger sense.
36. These assumptions are: (a) that the ultimate data of sense experience are simple, isolated atomic units; (b) that the it is the mind which actively brings these together according to specifiable rules and principles; (c) that the mind cannot know the whole unless it has built up the whole from simple elements. See C.D. Broad (1978), op. cit., p. 15 and R. Stern, *Hegel, Kant and the Structure of the Object* (London: Routledge, 1990).
37. It is not at all clear how these 'ideas of reasons' figure under the parallelism.
38. Deleuze writes that for instance we could begin with the circle with equal radii and form a fiction of its cause, e.g. a straight line revolving around one of its end points.
39. This is where Deleuze moves from the thesis that 'completeness' entails full knowledge of the complete causal chain of material events. Instead, he takes from 2p45 '(S)ingular things cannot be conceived without God – on the contrary, because they have God for a cause insofar as he is considered under the attribute of which the things are modes, their ideas must involve the concept of their attribute that is must involve an eternal and infinite essence of God'.
40. 'This causal or genetic character of a real definition applies not only to things that are produced (such as a circle, the movement of a line of which one end remains fixed) but to God himself (God as constituted by an infinity of attributes). Indeed, God is amenable to a genetic definition in that he is the cause of himself, in the full sense of the word cause, and his attributes are true formal causes', SPP: 61.

41. A. Schrift (1992), op. cit., p. 43.
42. Bruce Braugh (1992), op. cit., p. 141.
43. It could be argued that Leibniz constructed a system of absolute simples and aimed to connect what exists individually to an appropriate logic. The expression of exteriority might be said to be the translation of interiority in which spatially distributed characteristics come together in an immaterial unextended centre. According to a logic of inclusion, all that can be predicated of a subject is contained within that subject. Thus all predicated statements are simply statements of identity. This is supposed to give good reason to accept the *Principle of Sufficient Reason.* The problem of extenionless but material points was discussed by Hume and by Kant.
44. R. Delahunty (1985), op. cit., p. 12.
45. Ibid., p. 19.
46. 'x has a natural belief just in case (i) it is the fact that p which causes it to seem to x that p and (ii) it is the fact that it seems to x that p which causes x to believe that p. Follows trivially that all such beliefs are true. If something is caused by the fact that p then it is a fact that p'. J. Barnes (1990), op. cit., p. 137.
47. S. Benhabib, *Situating the Self: Gender, Community and Postmodernism in Contemporary Ethics* (Cambridge: Polity Press, 1992), p. 156.
48. For a full discussion of the fraternal contract in political theory, see C. Pateman, *The Sexual Contract* (Cambridge: Polity Press, 1988).
49. Let us recall that the first level of knowledge is vague and of sense experience. Compare and contrast this with the thesis that the position of the subject is relevant to claims to know. See G. Howie, 'Feminist Philosophies', in O. Leaman, ed., *The Future of Philosophy* (London: Routledge, 1998), pp. 109–15.
50. N. Shukin, 'Deleuze and Feminisms: Involuntary Regulations and Affective Inhibitors', in I. Buchanan and C. Colebrook, eds (2000), op. cit., p. 146.
51. Compare Bradotti's argument that the time is 'not yet' with Adorno's assertion in *Negative Dialectics* that the time for difference has not yet arrived due to social principles of equivalence.
52. This is for two reasons: (a) problem with indexicals; (b) the description of essences is supported by identity of indiscernibles without which simply repetitions of the same. See R. Bradotti (1993), op. cit., p. 48.
53. I. Buchanan and C. Colebrook (2000), op. cit., p. 2.
54. For an investigation into the claim that he can, see E. Grosz, 'A Thousand Tiny Sexes', in C. Boundas and D. Olkowski eds. (1994), op. cit., p. 194.
55. See G. Deleuze: DR190.
56. A. MacIntyre, *After Virtue: a Study in Moral Theory*, 1st pub. 1981 (London: Duckworth, 1985), p. 73.
57. F.W. Hegel (1995), op. cit., p. 288.
58. S. Falundi, *Backlash: the Undeclared War Against Women* (Vintage, 1992).
59. N. Shukin, op. cit., pp. 148, 150.
60. See V. Descombes 'Apropos of the 'Critique of the Subject' and of the Critique of this Critique' in E. Cadava, P. Connor and J. Nancy eds, *Who Comes After the Subject?* (London and New York: Routledge, 1991), p. 120ff.

Conclusion

1. G. Deleuze: DR, preface.
2. D. Olkowski, *Gilles Deleuze and the Ruin of Representation* (Berkeley and London: University of California Press, 1998), p. 2.
3. Just as he simplifies the answer by collapsing reasons with causes thereby assuring propositional content without relying of standard representational theories of truth.
4. For a discussion of the incorporeal event as singularity and infinitive, see C. Boundas, 'Deleuze: Serialisation and Subject-Formation', in C. Boundas and D. Olkowski, eds (1994), op. cit., p. 105.
5. This would imply a form of nominalism which is not a new philosophical position. For a discussion of problems associated with nominalism, see J. Loux, *Metaphysics: a Contemporary Introduction* (London and New York: Routledge, 1998).
6. For example, see Haraway's 'Cyborg Manifesto' for a discussion relating to the relationship between natural ontology and various assumptions concerning political allegiance. D. Haraway, 'A Cyborg Manifesto: Science, Technology and Socialist-Feminism in the Late Twentieth Century', in A. Herrmann and A. Stewart, eds, *Theorising Feminism: Parallel Trends in the Humanities and Social Sciences* (San Francisco and Oxford: Westview Press, 1994), pp. 425ff.
7. In metaphysics, the term 'identity' indicates the supposition of a 'something' that remains the same throughout alteration or simply, continuity through time and space. Epistemologically, the term denotes the supposition of a 'something' as a subject of judgement and may indicate the further belief that the salient features of that something can be identified and form the basis for cognitive discrimination.
8. K. Marx, *Economic and Philosophical Manuscripts of 1844* (London: Lawrence and Wishart, 1977), p. 131.
9. Toole is here quoting Jameson's comments on Adorno. D. Toole, 'Of Lingering Eyes and Talking Things: Adorno and Deleuze on Philosophy since Auschwitz', *Philosophy Today*, vol. 37 (1993), 228.
10. For a discussion on identity and non-identity thinking, see S. Jarvis, *Adorno: a Critical Introduction* (Cambridge: Polity Press, 1998), p. 167.
11. G. Deleuze, NP, p. 157.
12. A. Spethanson, 'Interview with Cornel West', in A. Ross, ed., *Universal Abandon?: the Politics of Postmodernism* (Edinburgh, Edinburgh University Press, 1989).
13. Y. Yovel (1989), op. cit., p. 29.
14. F.W. Hegel (1988), op. cit., p. 257.
15. C. Colebrook, 'Introduction', C. Colebrook and I. Buchanan, eds (2000), op. cit., pp. 6–8.
16. C. Malabou, 'Who's Afraid of Hegelian Wolves?', in P. Patton, ed. (1996), op. cit., p. 114ff.
17. G. Deleuze: SPP, 97.
18. R. Grossman, *The Existence of the World: an Introduction to Ontology* (London: Routledge, 1992), p. 124.
19. Ibid., p, 132,

20. I. Kant, CPR, B600.
21. F.W. Hegel, Logic, trans. W. Wallace (Oxford: Clarendon Press, 1975), p. 135–6.
22. For a discussion of existence as a predicate see J. Bennett, *Kant's Dialectic* (Cambridge; Cambridge University Press, 1974), pp. 62–5, 228–34.
23. On diachronic and synchronic linguistic relations, see F. de Saussure, *Course in General Linguistics*, trans. W. Baskin, C. Bally and A. Sechehaye, eds (New York and London: McGraw Hill, 1959).
24. The point that negation is a second order activity the judgement that (not (it is dark)) finds its corollary in Deleuze's assertion that forces are first positive and these positive forces are used to negate reactive forces.
25. 1p8s1.
26. This argument is premised on the conclusion of a previous argument that God is omnipotent and that his power is actual.
27. Let us note here not only are attributes distinct in a weakened sense but that this immediately leads to a problem of subjectivitsm.
28. C. Boundas, 'Foreclosure of the Other: From Sartre to Deleuze', *Journal of the British Society for Phenomenology*, vol. 24, 1 (Jan 1993), 38.
29. By virtue of the parallelism the idea has as its content a bodily modification and this maps onto an actual bodily modification which is caused by an external body. Because self-consciousness is reduced to the idea of an idea one could suggest that there is an indirect relationship between self-consciousness and the external body. However, not only is there no way to figure this external object or to consider it, but also the proper cause, according to Deleuze, is attribute and substance.
30. For a discussion of Hegel's critique of Spinoza's acosmism, see G. Parkinson, 'Hegel, Pantheism and Spinoza', *Journal of the History of Ideas*, vol. 38 (1977), p. 449ff.
31. J. Bennett (1984), op. cit., pp. 45–50.
32. This would be to take the subject as both idea and thinking function.
33. T. Adorno, *Negative Dialectics*, 1st pub. 1966, trans. E.B. Ashton (London: Routledge and Kegan Paul, 1973), p. 6.
34. Ibid., p. 198.
35. B. Braugh (1992), op. cit., p. 144.
36. See H. Marcuse, *Reason and Revolution: Hegel and the Rise of Social Theory*, 1st pub. 1941 (New York: Beacon Press, 1960), preface.
37. The description of a state as negated might be said to presume an original definition of human nature. Alternatively, because we keep in mind the fact that words and concepts are borrowed from previous generations, we should hesitate to give positive content to any such notion. Instead, negation here functions to indicate both a limit and an analysis of that limit. See H. Marcuse, The Concept of Essence', in *Negations: Essays in Critical Theory*, trans. J. Shapiro (London: Free Association Books, 1988). T. Adorno (1973), op. cit., pp. 211–300.
38. See, for example, T. May, *The Political Philosophy of Poststructuralist Anarchism* (Pennsylvania: Pennsylvania State University Press, 1994).
39. T. Adorno (1973), op. cit., p. 349.

Works Cited and Abbreviations

Deleuze

Nietzsche and Philosophy, trans. H. Tomlinson 1st pub. 1962 (London: Athlone Press, 1983) (NP).
Expressionism in Philosophy: Spinoza, trans. M. Joughin 1st pub. 1968 (New York: Zone Books, 1992) (Exp).
Difference and Repetition, trans. P. Patton, 1st pub. 1968 (London: Athlone Press, 1994) (DR).
Spinoza: Practical Philosophy, trans. R. Hurley 1st pub. 1970 (San Francisco: City Lights, 1988). (SPP).
The Fold: Leibniz and the Baroque, trans. T. Conley 1st pub. 1988 (London: Athlone Press, 1993).
Negotiations, trans. M. Joughin, 1st pub. 1990 (New York: Columbia University Press, 1995).
Deleuze, G. and Guattari F., *Anti-Oedipus: Capitalism and Schizophrenia*, trans. R. Hurley, M. Seem H. Lane 1st pub. 1972 (London: Athlone Press, 1984).
Deleuze, G. and Guattari, F., *A Thousand Plateaus: Capitalism and Schizophrenia* trans. B. Massumi 1st pub. 1980 (London: Athlone Press, 1988).

Commentaries: Deleuze

Bogue, R., *Deleuze and Guattari* (London and New York: Routledge, 1989) p. 67.
Bogue, R., 'Gilles Deleuze: the Aesthetics of Force', *Journal of the British Society for Phenomenology*, vol. 24, 1 (Jan 1993).
Boundas, C., 'Foreclosure of the Other: From Sartre to Deleuze', *Journal of the British Society for Phenomenology*, vol. 24, 1 (Jan 1993).
Boundas, C. and Olkowski, D., *Gilles Deleuze and the Theatre of Philosophy* (New York and London: Routledge, 1994).
Bradotti, R., 'Discontinuous Becomings. Deleuze on the Becoming-Woman of Philosophy', *Journal of the British Society for Phenomenology* 24, 1 (Jan 1993).
Braugh, B., 'Transcendental Empiricism: Deleuze's Response to Hegel', *Man and World* (25) 1992.
Buchanan, I. ed., *A Deleuzian Century* (Durham and London: Duke University Press, 1999).
Buchanan, I. and Colebrook C. eds, *Deleuze and Feminist Theory* (Edinburgh: Edinburgh University Press, 2000).
Hardt, M., *Gilles Deleuze: an Apprenticeship in Philosophy* (London: UCL Press, 1993).
Heaton, J., 'Language Games, Expression and Desire in the work of Deleuze', *Journal of the British Society for Phenomenology*, vol. 24, 1, 1993.
Land, N., 'Making it with Death: Remarks on Thanatos and Desiring-Production', *Journal of British Society for Phenomenology*, vol. 24 (1993).

Marks, J., *Gilles Deleuze: Vitalism and Multiplicity* (London and Virginia: Pluto Press, 1998).
May, T., 'The System and its Fractures: Gilles Deleuze on Otherness', *Journal of the British Society for Phenomenology*, vol. 24, 1 (Jan 1993).
Meerbote, M., 'Deleuze on the Systematic Unity of Critical Philosophy', *Kant Studies* (1986), vol. 77.
Olkowski, D., *Gilles Deleuze and the Ruin of Representation* (Berkeley and London: University of California Press, 1998).
Patton P. ed., *Deleuze: Critical Reader* (Oxford: Blackwell, 1996).
Pearson, K.A. ed., *Deleuze and Philosophy: the Difference Engineer* (London and New York: Routledge, 1997).
Pearson, K.A., *Germinal Life: the Difference and Repetition of Deleuze* (London and New York: Routledge, 1999).
Schrift, A., 'Between Church and State: Nietzsche, Deleuze and the Genealogy of Psychoanalysis', *International Studies in Philosophy*, vol. 24 (1992).
Sellars, J., 'The Point of View of the Cosmos: Deleuze, Romanticism and Stoicism', *Pli: The Warwick Journal of Philosophy*, vol. 8, 1999.
Toole, D., 'Of Lingering Eyes and Talking Things: Adorno and Deleuze on Philosophy since Auschwitz', *Philosophy Today*, vol. 37 (1993).

Spinoza

Spinoza, B., *Ethics*, trans. E. Curley (Harmondsworth: Penguin, 1996).
Spinoza, B., *Ethics, Treatise on The Emandation of the Intellect and Selected Letters*, trans. S. Shirley. S. Feldman ed. (Indianapolis and Cambridge: Hackett Publishing Company, 1992).

Commentaries: Spinoza

Aquila, R.E., 'Identity of Thought and Object in Spinoza', *Journal of the History of Philosophy*, vol. 16 (1978).
Balz, A.G., *Idea and Essence in Hobbes and Spinoza* (New York: AMS Press, 1967).
Barker H., 'Notes on the Second Part of Spinoza's Ethics', *Mind*, XLVII (1938), 418.
Bennett, J., *A Study of Spinoza's Ethics* (Cambridge: Cambridge University Press, 1984).
Delahunty, R.J., *Spinoza* (London: Routledge and Kegan Paul, 1985).
Della Rocca, M., 'Causation and Identity in Spinoza', *History of Philosophy Quarterly* vol. 8 no. 3 (July 1991).
Della Rocca, M., *Representation and the Mind-Body Problem in Spinoza* (New York and Oxford: Oxford University Press, 1996).
Garrett, D. ed., *The Cambridge Companion to Spinoza* (Cambridge: Cambridge University Press, 1996).
Hallett, H.F., *Creation, Emanation and Salvation: a Spinozistic Study* (The Hague: Martinus Nijhoff, 1962).
Hampshire, S., *Spinoza: an Introduction to His Philosophical Thought*, 1st edn. 1951 (Harmondsworth: Penguin, 1987).
Haserot, F., Spinoza and the Status of Universals, *Philosophical Review* vol. 59, 1950.

Jaspers, K., *Spinoza* (London: Harvest, 1974).
Huenemann, C., 'Predicative Interpretations of Spinoza's Divine Extension', *History of Philosophy Quarterly*, vol. 14, no. 1 (Jan 1997).
Kennington R. ed., *The Philosophy of Baruch Spinoza* (Washington: Catholic University of America, 1980).
Mandelbaum M. ed., *Spinoza: Essays in Interpretation* (Illinois: Open Court, 1975).
Mason, R., 'Spinoza on Modality', *The Philosophical Quarterly* vol. 36 no. 144 (July 1986).
Negri, A., *The Savage Anomaly: the Power of Spinoza's Metaphysics and Politics*, 1st pub. 1981, trans. M. Hardt (Minneaplois, Oxford: University of Minnesota Press, 1991).
Parkinson, G., 'Hegel, Pantheism and Spinoza', *Journal of the History of Ideas*, vol. 38 (1977).
Raidner, D., 'Spinoza's Theory of Ideas', *The Philosophical Review*, LXXX (1971).
Savan, D., 'Spinoza and Language', *The Philosophical Review*, 1965 p. 215.
Shipper, L., *Spinoza's Ethics: the View from Within* (New York: Peter Lang, 1993).
Wolf, A. trans. and ed. *The Correspondence of Spinoza* (London: George Allen and Unwin, 1928).
Yovel, Y., *Spinoza and Other Heretics* (Princeton (NJ): Princeton University Press, 1989).

Primary sources and commentaries: ancient philosophy

Annas, J. ed., *Oxford Studies in Ancient Philosophy*, vol. 5 (Oxford: Clarendon Press; 1987).
Annas, J., *Hellenistic Philosophy of Mind* (Berkeley: University of California Press, 1992).
Aristotle, *The Nichomachean Ethics*, trans. D. Ross (Oxford and New York: Oxford University Press, 1980).
Barnes, J., *The Toils of Scepticism*, 1st pub. 1990 (Cambridge: Cambridge University Press, 1994).
Burnyeat, M., ed., *The Skeptical Tradition* (Berkeley: University of California, 1983).
Coombs, J., 'Created Entities in Seventeenth-Century Scotism', *The Philosophical Quarterly* vol. 43, 173 (1993).
Everson, S. ed., *Epistemology* (Cambridge: Cambridge University Press, 1990).
Gerson, L.P., *God and Greek Philosophy* (London: Routledge, 1990).
Hahm, D., *The Origins of Stoic Cosmobiology* (Ohio State University Press, Ohio, 1977).
Kenny, A., *Aristotle's Theory of the Will* (London: Duckworth, 1979).
Kenny, J.P., *Mystical Monotheism: a Study in Ancient Platonic Theology* (Hanover (NH): University Press of New England, 1991).
Kneale, W. and Kneale, M., *The Development of Logic* (Oxford: Clarendon Press, 1962).
Long, A.A., *Hellenistic Philosophy: Stoics, Epicureans, Sceptics* (London: Duckworth, 1986).
McKeon, R. ed., *The Basic Works of Aristotle* (New York and London: Random House, 1968).

Nussbaum, M., *Aristotle's De Motu Animalium* (Princeton: Princeton University Press, 1978).
Peters, F.E., *Greek Philosophical Terms: a Historical Lexicon*, (New York: New York University Press, 1967).
Rorty, A. ed., *Essays on Aristotle's Ethics* (London and Berkeley: University of California Press, 1980).

General

Adorno, T., *Negative Dialectics*, 1st pub. 1966 trans. E.B. Ashton (London: Routledge and Kegan Paul, 1973).
Benhabib, S., *Situating the Self: Gender, Community and Postmodernism in Contemporary Ethics* (Cambridge: Polity Press, 1992).
Bennett, J., *Kant's Dialectic* (Cambridge; Cambridge University Press, 1974).
Bennett, J., *Linguistic Behaviour*, 1st pub. 1976 (Cambridge: Cambridge University Press, 1979).
Bernstein, R., *The New Constellation: the Ethical and Political Horizons of Modernity/Postmodernity* (Cambridge: Polity Press, 1991).
Broad, C.D., *Kant*, ed. C. Lewy (Cambridge: Cambridge University Press, 1978).
Burrell, D., *Knowing the Unknowable God* (Bloomington, IN: Notre Dame, 1986).
Cadava, Connor, Nancy eds, *Who comes after the Subject?* (New York: Routledge, 1991).
Carnap, R., *The Logical Foundations of Probability* (London: Routledge and Kegan Paul, 1951).
Chadwick, R. ed., *Encyclopedia of Applied Ethics*, vol. 2 (1998).
Clark, S.R.L., 'Have Biologists wrapped up Philosophy?' *Inquiry*, 43, 148.
Cross, R., *Duns Scotus* (New York, Oxford: Oxford University Press, 1999).
Currie, G., *Frege: an Introduction to his Philosophy* (Brighton: Harvester Wheatsheaf, 1982).
Descartes, R., *Philosophical Writings* trans. and ed. Elizabeth Anscombe (Middlesex: Nelsons University Paperbacks, 1970) p. 103.
Descartes, R., First Set of Replies, in *The Philosophical Writings of Descartes*, vol. II trans. J. Cottingham, R. Stoothoff and D. Murdoch (London and New York: Cambridge University Press, 1984).
Dummett, M., *Origins of Analytical Philosophy* (London: Duckworth, 1993).
Falundi, S., *Backlash: the Undeclared War Against Women* (London: Vintage, 1992).
Feinberg, J., *Harm to Others* (New York: Oxford University Press, 1984).
Ferry, L. and Renaut, A., *French Philosophy of the Sixties: an Essay on Antihumanism*, trans. M. Schackenberg 1st pub. 1985 (Amherst: University of Massachusetts Press, 1990).
Frege, G., *Philosophical and Mathematical Correspondence*, ed., G. Gabriel, H. Hermes, F. Kambartel, C. Thiel and A. Verart, trans. H. Kaal (Oxford: Basil Blackwell, 1980).
Geach, P. and Black, M. eds, *Translations from the Philosophical Writings of Gottlob Frege* (Oxford: Basil Blackwell, 1952).
Gerwith, A., 'Clearness and Distinctness in Descartes', *Philosophy*, XVIII (1943).
Giddens, A., *Studies in Social and Political Theory* (London: Hutchinson, 1979).

Gillies, D., *Frege, Dedekind and Peano on the Foundations of Arithmetic* (The Netherlands: Van Gorcum, 1982).

Gleick, J., *Chaos: Making a New Science* (London: Penguin, 1987).

Glendenning S., *Edinburgh Encyclopedia of Continental Philosophy* (Edinburgh: Edinburgh University Press, 1999).

Grossman, R., *The Existence of the World: an Introduction to Ontology* (London: Routledge, 1992).

Habermas, J., *The Philosophical Discourse of Modernity*, trans. F. Lawrence 1st pub. 1985 (Cambridge: Polity Press, 1987).

Harland, R., *Superstructuralism. The Philosophy of Structuralism and Post-Structuralism* (London and New York: Methuen, 1987).

Hegel, G.W.F., *Lectures on the History of Philosophy*, 1st pub. 1892–96, trans. E.S. Haldane and F.H. Simson (Lincoln and London: University of Nebraska Press, 1995) vol. 3.

Hegel's Logic trans. W. Wallace (Oxford: Clarendon Press, 1975).

Herrmann A. and Stewart, A. eds, *Theorising Feminism: Parallel Trends in the Humanities and Social Sciences* (San Francisco and Oxford: Westview Press, 1994).

Hobbes, T., *Leviathan*, C.B. MacPherson ed., 1st pub. 1968 (London: Penguin, 1984).

Hospers, J., *An Introduction to Philosophical Analysis*, 1st pub. 1953 (London: Routledge and Kegan Paul, 1973).

Hudson W.D., *Modern Moral Philosophy*, 1st pub. 1970 (London: Macmillan – now Palgrave Macmillan, 1983).

Jacoby, R., 'The Politics of Subjectivity', *New Left Review*, 79 (May 1973), 41.

Jarvis, S., *Adorno: a Critical Introduction* (Cambridge: Polity Press, 1998).

Kant, I., *Critique of Pure Reason*, trans. Norman Kemp Smith (London: Macmillan – now Palgrave Macmillan, 1983).

Kenny, A., *Descartes: a Study of His Philosophy* (New York: Random House, 1968).

Larrabee, M.J. ed., *An Ethics of Care: Feminist and Interdisciplinary Perspectives* (London and New York: Routledge, 1993).

Leaman, O. ed., *The Future of Philosophy* (London: Routledge, 1998).

Lechte, J., *Fifty Contemporary Thinkers: from Structuralism to Postmodernity* (London and New York: Routledge, 1994).

Loux, J., *Metaphysics: a Contemporary Introduction* (London and New York: Routledge, 1998).

Lukes, S., *Individualism* (Oxford: Basil Blackwell, 1973).

McGrath, P., 'The Refutation of the Ontological Argument', *The Philosophical Quarterly*, vol. 40 (April 1990), 159.

McGuinness, B. ed., *Collected Papers on Mathematics, Logic and Philosophy* (Oxford: Blackwell, 1984).

McTaggart, J.E., 'Hegel's Treatment of the Categories of Quantity', *Mind: A Quarterly Review of Psychology and Philosophy*, vol. X111 (1904).

MacIntyre, A., *After Virtue: a Study in Moral Theory*, 1st pub. 1981 (London: Duckworth, 1985).

Macpherson, C.B. *The Political Theory of Possessive Individualism: Hobbes to Locke*, 1st pub. 1962 (Oxford: Oxford University Press, 1983).

Marcuse, H., *Reason and Revolution: Hegel and the Rise of Social Theory*, 1st pub. 1941 (New York: Beacon Press, 1960).

Marcuse, H., *Negations: Essays in Critical Theory,* trans. J. Shapiro 1st pub. 1968 (London: Free Association Books, 1988).
May, T., *The Political Philosophy of Poststructuralist Anarchism* (Pennsylvania: Pennsylvania State University Press, 1994).
Marx, K., *Economic and Philosophical Manuscripts of 1844* (London: Lawrence and Wishart, 1977).
Mitchell, S. and Rosen, M. eds, *The Need for Interpretation: Contemporary Conceptions of the Philosopher's Task* (London: Athlone Press, 1993).
Nietzsche, F., *Genealogy of Morals,* trans. and ed. W. Kaufmann (Toronto: Random House, 1969).
Pateman, C., *The Problem of Political Obligation: a Critique of Liberal Theory,* 1st pub. 1979. (Cambridge: Polity Press, 1985).
Pateman, C., *The Sexual Contract* (Cambridge: Polity Press, 1988).
Rorty, R., *Philosophy and the Mirror of Nature* (Oxford: Basil Blackwell, 1980).
Rorty, R., *Contingency, Irony and Solidarity* (New York and Cambridge: Cambridge University Press, 1989).
Rosen, S., *The Question of Being: a Reversal of Heidegger* (New Haven and London: Yale University Press, 1993).
Ross, A. ed., *Universal Abandon?: The Politics of Postmodernism* (Edinburgh: Edinburgh University Press, 1989).
Rousseau, J.J., *The Social Contract,* trans. M. Cranston (London: Penguin, 1968).
Sartre, J.P., *Being and Nothingness: An Essay on Phenomenological Ontology,* trans. H. Barnes 1st pub. Gallimard 1943 (London: Methuen, 1972).
de Saussure, F., *Course in General Linguistics,* trans. W. Baskin, C. Bally and A. Sechehaye, eds. (New York and London: McGraw Hill, 1959).
Sluga, H., *Gottlob Frege* (London: Routledge and Kegan Paul, 1980).
Sokal, A. and Bricmont, J., *Intellectual Impostures: Postmodern Philosopher's Abuse of Science* (London: Profile Books, 1998).
Stern, R., *Hegel, Kant and the Structure of the Object* (London: Routledge, 1990).
Strawson, P.F., *Individuals: an Essay in Descriptive Metaphysics,* 1st pub. 1959 (London: Methuen, 1969).
Thiel, C., *Sense and Reference in Frege's Logic* (Dordrecht-Holland: D. Reidel, 1965).
Walker, R.C.S., *Kant* (London: Routledge and Kegan Paul, 1982).
Wilkerson, T.E., *Kant's 'Critique of Pure Reason': a Commentary for Students* (Oxford: Clarendon Press, 1976).
Wilson, M. *Descartes* (London: Routledge and Kegan Paul, 1978).
Wollheim, R., *On Art and the Mind: Essays and Lectures* (London: Allen Lane, 1973).

Index